PENGUIN BOOKS

INDONESIA OUT OF EXILE

Max Lane has been engaged with Indonesia for over fifty years. In the 1970s, he translated W.S. Rendra's play *The Struggle of the Naga Tribe*, which was performed in English in Australia and Malaysia. He spent time with Rendra's group, Bengkel Teater. In the 1980s, he worked in the Australian Embassy in Jakarta when he started translating Pramoedya Ananta Toer's *This Earth of Mankind* and its three sequels, together now known as the *Buru Quartet*. He was withdrawn from the Embassy by the Australian government for translating these banned books. He later translated Pramoedya's novel, *Arok Dedes* and historical work, *The Chinese in Indonesia*. Upon returning to Australia, he helped found the *Inside Indonesia* magazine and became its first editor. In the 1990s, he actively supported the democracy movements in Indonesia and East Timor and as a journalist wrote hundreds of articles about Indonesia. He has written several books on Indonesia, including *Unfinished Nation: Indonesia Before and After Suharto, Catastrophe in Indonesia, An Introduction to the Politics of the Indonesian Union Movement and Indonesia* and *Not, Poems and Otherwise: Anecdotes Scattered*. Some have been published in Indonesian alongside other original writings. He has lectured at the University of Sydney and Victoria University and at universities in Indonesia, Southeast Asia, Europe, and the United States. He has been a research fellow at Murdoch University, the National University of Singapore, and the Institute of Southeast Asian Studies—Yusof Ishak Institute, also in Singapore. He is married to Indonesian playwright and theatre producer, Faiza Mardzoeki.

Advance Praise for *Indonesia Out of Exile*

'If you want to start to understand modern Indonesia, you should read this book. It has a gripping story, fascinating detail, compelling analysis and is at the same time very accessible and a good read. Max Lane uses his great knowledge of Pramoedya Ananta Toer, and his writings, and his collaborators, to explain how and why Indonesia is as it is today, and how it might become what Pramoedya hoped.'
—David Reeve, Honorary Professor of Indonesian Studies,
University of New South Wales, Australia

'In telling the story of how Pramoedya Ananta Toer, Hasyim Rachman and Joesoef Ishak recaptured the original Indonesia, Max Lane reveals a hidden, complex yet critical part of Indonesia's unfinished revolution.'
—Dr Riwanto Tirtosudarmo, writer and
senior researcher on Indonesian society,
Indonesian Institute of Sciences until 2017

'Max Lane has written a fascinating book about the creation and impact of one of the world's greatest literary works. If you are already familiar with the *Buru Quartet*, *Indonesia Out of Exile* will deepen your understanding of it. And if you aren't, here is a compelling and provocative introduction to these brilliant novels, written by the man who translated them into English and did more than anyone else to get for them the attention they so richly deserve in the anglophone world and beyond.'
—Will Schwalbe, New York Times bestselling author
of *The End of Your Life Book Club*

'I met Pramoedya Ananta Toer, thanks to Max Lane, whose meticulous translation of the books of Indonesia's greatest novelist introduced the English speaking world to a man whose literature stood like a beacon during the long darkness of General Suharto's dictatorship. *Indonesia Out of Exile* is Max Lane's landmark new work in which he places

Pramaoedya at the heart of a struggle that can teach and inspire all of us today.'

—John Pilger, journalist and filmmaker

'*Indonesia Out of Exile* shows how a book can play an important role in forming people's outlook and consciousness, even that of a nation. Even today demonstrators at protest actions wear Tshirts quoting Pramoedya Ananta Toer's books or featuring characters from his novels. On Buru Island prison camp, his stories helped raise the morale of the political prisoners. Many of the young activists who organised in the struggle to overthrow the New Order dictatorship were inspired by Pramoedya's novels. Max Lane's own book brings alive this exciting story of the impact of Pramoedya Ananta Toer's books on Indonesia.'

—Linda Christanty, Indonesian writer and journalist

Indonesia Out of Exile
How Pramoedya's
Buru Quartet Killed a
Dictatorship

Max Lane

PENGUIN BOOKS

An imprint of Penguin Random House

PENGUIN BOOKS

USA | Canada | UK | Ireland | Australia
New Zealand | India | South Africa | China | Southeast Asia

Penguin Books is part of the Penguin Random House group of companies
whose addresses can be found at global.penguinrandomhouse.com

Published by Penguin Random House SEA Pte Ltd
9, Changi South Street 3, Level 08-01,
Singapore 486361

First published in Penguin Books by Penguin Random House SEA 2022

Copyright © Max Lane 2022

ISBN 9789814914178

Typeset in Garamond by MAP Systems, Bangalore, India

www.penguin.sg

This book is dedicated to everybody who struggled to make Hasta Mitra the vanguard it was during the 1980s, especially Joesoef Isak, Hasjim Rachman and Pramoedya Ananta Toer.

It is also dedicated to Mary, who so admired these men and their works, and was waiting to read this book, but now cannot.

Contents

Preface

This book tells the story of the writing, publication and impact of the books written by Pramoedya Ananta Toer during his time at the Buru Island prison camp and published by Hasjim Rachman, Joesoef Isak and Pramocdya soon after they were released from more than ten years in prison. The story of these men's struggle cannot be separated from the story of Indonesia. This means that from time to time, we stray from the storytelling to short essay-type reflections on the course of Indonesian history. Perhaps these will tantalize more than explain, but fuller explanations may require writing another book or, more likely, books. In the meantime, the reader should take advantage of the Internet and seek out more information on historical incidents and figures that are only briefly mentioned here.

Hopefully what you will read will answer some questions, even if it adds to your list of unanswered questions about the world's fifth largest country.

List of Main Players in the Story

Indonesia

A community of people that evolved into a nation, beginning at the start of the twentieth century. Originally comprising around 60 million people, by 2020, there were 260 million, predicted to be 400 million by 2050. This new nation's borders and common economic life were initially formed under Dutch colonialism, especially during the period between 1900–1945. Its national language, Indonesian, and the new Indonesian culture was brought into being and spread during the same period, as the political and cultural movement for Independence grew. Youth from (almost) all the different ethnic groups committed to one country and one language.[1] This continued after the winning of Independence, as millions of people debated and struggled for their visions for their new country. From the start, the new culture—embodied in its literature, songs, arts, political speeches and in its mass organizations—was characterized by a vigorous struggle for the future. It was a country created by a revolution of the youth. It still will be.

This community, however, underwent a traumatic change, starting in 1965, when all the struggle over different visions for the future was suppressed, in favour of just one vision: that of General Suharto and his military and other supporters. A million people were killed and tens of thousands jailed, some for up to fourteen years—all without trial.[2] Among those were some of the other characters in this story.

Pramoedya Ananta Toer (1925–2006)

Pramoedya, originally Javanese but later becoming very much an Indonesian, was a novelist and writer since his youth. He was part of the '45 Generation'—those who fought the Dutch during the war for independence between 1945–49.[3] He was captured by the Dutch and imprisoned for months. After Independence, he was one of Indonesia's most prolific writers. He became increasingly critical of the country's stagnation and corruption and in the later 1950s, threw himself into a study of history to identify the origins of Indonesia's inability to progress. He was arrested in 1965, aged forty, along with tens of thousands of others, when a wing of the Indonesian Army, under the control of General Suharto, seized power, and crushed the 20 million-strong mass movement for socialism. Pramoedya was imprisoned, without trial, for fourteen years, most of which he spent in Buru Island prison camp. During that time, he wrote six novels, one play and many essays. These were published after he was released from prison in 1979. They were all quickly banned.[4]

Joesoef Isak (1928–2009)

Isak was a very young journalist of the 45 Generation. He later emerged as a leading journalist, and leader of the journalist union in Indonesia during the 1950s and 1960s. He was the Secretary-General of the Asian–African Journalists Association and travelled across Asia and Africa, meeting many of the leaders of the Third World in the 1960s. Later, he spent ten years in prison in Jakarta after 1965, being one among the tens of thousands of supporters of Sukarno and socialism. He played a role in advising the U.S. Carter administration on the question of the release of those still in prison, including on Buru Island. After Pramoedya was released, he joined him and another comrade-in-arms, Hasjim Rachman, to form the Hasta Mitra publishing company, that defied Suharto and published all of Pramoedya's prison writings, including the series of novels that began with *This Earth of Mankind*.

Hasjim Rachman (1925–1999)

Hasjim, a North Sumatran, was a journalist and the publisher of Jakarta's biggest circulation daily newspaper before 1965, the *Eastern Star*. He was also prominent in the journalist's union. Pramoedya had a weekly cultural column in the *Eastern Star*. Hasjim, who had smuggled guns from Malaya to Sumatra during the war against the Dutch, was a part of the 45 Generation, as was Pramoedya. A charismatic businessman with a debonair style, he also ended up on Buru Island and in the same hut for the most defiant prisoners, along with Pramoedya. It was during their time together on Buru that Pramoedya and he agreed that they would publish Pramoedya's prison writings when they were released.

Narrator: Max Lane

Max Lane has translated five of Pramoedya's Buru Island works: *This Earth of Mankind, Child of All Nations, Footsteps* and *House of Glass*, as well as *Arok Dedes* (as *Arok of Java*). The first four are published by Penguin Random House and have been in print since the 1980s. He also translated Pramoedya's 1960's book *The Chinese in Indonesia*. He was inspired by the politics and spirit of Hasta Mitra and Pramoedya's books, having many conversations with all three main players.

NOTE: Throughout this book, I use the Indonesian titles of the four books in the This Earth of Mankind series, namely *Bumi Manusia, Anak Semua Bangsa, Jejak Langkah* and *Rumah Kaca*, when it is being *emphasized* that I am referring to Indonesian language editions.

PART I

Chapter 1

Introduction

One moment at which I could start this story might be my first meeting with Pramoedya Ananta Toer, in 1980, a year or so after he was released from the Buru Island prison camp. Or, perhaps, I could start with my first meeting with his publishers and fellow former political prisoners, Joesoef Isak and Hasjim Rachman, whom I also met in 1980. It was at the meeting with Joesoef and Hasjim that I offered to translate Pramoedya's book, *Bumi Manusia*. The translation was published by Penguin Books in Australia a few years later, as *This Earth of Mankind*.[1] Or maybe, it should start in 1965 with the actual arrests of all three men? But no, I will start this story today, or rather with something that happened in September 2019. Yes, I am telling a history, but it is not a history of something finished and over, it is a history of an unfinished nation, Indonesia, and the books and men who have sparked the revival of its process of completion, who brought it back from its exile of itself.

So, September 2019.

---

[1] Throughout this book, when I am referring to the Indonesian language edition of any of Pramoedya's books, such as *Bumi Manusia*, I will use the Indonesian title. I will use English language book titles to refer to the English language editions.

The grey painted timber bench was uncomfortable. The heavy dark coffee was bitter and delicious. My back was turned away from the table from behind which the coffee had been served. Indonesian street stalls are simple affairs. A bench to sit on. A wooden table with a plastic tablecloth serving as a counter. A gas burner to boil water for coffee and tea. Not much else. I was sitting so I could watch the students— thousands and thousands of them.[5] University students. Mainly first- and second-year students, I thought. They marched the kilometre or so to a crossroads where everybody rallied. I too had come directly from the Gajah Mada University campus myself, but by car, and was now watching the proceedings from a street-side stall where people were gathering. As I had walked from the Social Sciences building to the car park, I had seen students pouring out of buildings everywhere, heading for the demonstration. Lecturers too. They gathered at the main entrance to the university, ready to march to the rally location.

Gajah Mada is the biggest campus in the university town of Jogjakarta in Central Java. In fact, it was probably the biggest campus in Indonesia, with more than 30,000 students. There were several other universities in the city of 3 million people. There were students from all over Indonesia studying here, from all the scores of ethnic groups, not just locals. It was a Jogja demo, they would call it, but it was also national.

Thousands and thousands, I thought, more than anybody had expected. A glance at my mobile phone and I could see that the same thing was happening in many other towns across Indonesia. The young were angry and seething with an irreverence for those they saw as idiot politicians running the country, recently elected or re-elected to the parliament. There were many things that angered the students, and these issues were wrapped up and on display in the unanimous consensus among the members of parliament when they passed five new laws, giving the State more power than ever, including over people's personal and sex lives. At the same time, the parliament and president were weakening the powers of the Corruption Eradication Commission (KPK), which had been arresting one corrupt official after another, over the last ten years. Hundreds of them, maybe even thousands, had been arrested. At least seventy members of parliament had been arrested. Under the new law, the processes now needed before the KPK could tap the phones of a politician, bureaucrat or businessman, or raid their office or arrest them, would be more complicated and take more time.[6]

'Need to clean out your toilet, call the Parliament', shouted a handwritten poster. There were many placards and posters that portrayed members of parliament as the shovellers of rubbish. These students had no respect for the politicians as persons, nor for their authority. The mood was of anger but it manifested in an often humorous irreverence. Two young women wearing the Islamic hijab over their heads, but lightly and joyfully, held up their own poster: 'The only thing standing erect in Indonesia,' it read, 'was not justice but only some men's dicks'. One of the laws also gave local authorities the power to raid people's homes to investigate if they were having sex outside marriage, an act that was being criminalized. 'Our genitalia are no business of the state,' shouted other posters, carried by both male and female students.

The thousands streamed in from several directions. There were also contingents of high school students, mainly from the vocational technical schools.

A group passed me by, carrying placards talking about West Papua: 'end the violence in Papua, democracy now!' They were both Papuan and non-Papuan students. They marched with vigour.

I sipped my coffee and checked my handphone again. Photos from Jakarta protests on Facebook; nearby Solo, too. Almost everywhere . . . Kalimantan, Sulawesi.

What amazed me was how quickly the demonstration had been organized. Messages went out on social media late Sunday afternoon and now, on Monday morning, there were these thousands. I was to teach a class that morning and the evening before, I had been contacted to ask if the class could be held earlier as all the students wanted to attend the rally. I asked one of the organizers later, and he said they had not expected this kind of turnout at all. 'A thousand, maybe, not 20,000, especially so quickly.'

The anger was spontaneous; it was real; it was the voice of a new generation fed up with endemic corruption and political and cultural backwardness. It was also unorganized. Organized contingents were rare. These were thousands of unorganized individuals, all angry and fed up, but not yet channelled into a unified political force.

And they were mostly very young. Young. But we could already see that coming during the year before and can see that it will develop even further.

'Very young,' I thought again, 'A new generation.'

Then he stopped just in front of me. He was young. A high school student, I thought. He stopped and his T-shirt caught my eye. The back of the T-shirt was empty, plain white. But on the front was the picture of a man. I recognized the picture straight away. It was a well-known portrait—I suppose genuine—of a Javanese journalist from the beginning of the twentieth century, named Tirto Adhi Soerjo. He had a typical early-twentieth-century black Malay Islamic cap on his head. He also wore a very prominent moustache. The picture was well-known. I wondered if the young man wearing the T-shirt knew who Tirto was? Of course he did, I immediately reminded myself. Tirto had been made famous through the novels of Pramoedya Ananta Toer, especially the novel *Bumi Manusia*, published in the early 1980s and still being read and discussed in 2019.

Original cover of *Bumi Manusia* with the words 'Karya Pulau Buru' meaning 'A Work From Buru Island' on the top.

Indeed, only a few months earlier, more than a million Indonesians had gone to the movies to see a (somewhat politically abridged) cinema adaptation. Indonesia's thousands of little book kiosks selling secondhand and pirated editions, as well as the official editions, all carried *Bumi Manusia*, as well as other titles by Pramoedya.

The main character in the novel, a young Javanese high school student called Minke, was inspired by Tirto—or at least lived the author Pramoedya's idea of what Tirto's teenage life might have been like—or perhaps the way Pramoedya imagined how Tirto, who was also a writer, might have fictionalized his teenage years. Wonderfully complicated in a simple way.

Pramoedya wrote *Bumi Manusia* in a prison camp in Eastern Indonesia under the Suharto dictatorship between 1965–1998. Many prisoners died there. He was there for more than ten years, with 13,000 other prisoners. But that is another story told later in this book.

Here in 2019, another high school student, whatever his name was, stood with his friends, proudly wearing this T-Shirt with Tirto's picture decorating it—the young adult Tirto, the journalist, not the high school student as imagined in Pramoedya's book.

As the crowd grew, the boy in question was jostled closer to me—he and his three friends. He was close enough for me to say something.

'Good morning—the demo is big, yes?'

'Yes, pak, very big. Where are you from, bapak?'

'Australia,' I replied. And then I asked: 'You're a fan of Tirto?'

'Ya, Minke.'

'You've read *Bumi Manusia*?'

'I've read all four,' he replied, holding up his thumb in strong approval. *Bumi Manusia* was the first novel in a series of four, all inspired by the life—and especially the times—of Tirto. They told the story of the very beginning, the very, very beginning, the conception, of the process that created Indonesia. This was deeply connected to the evolution of a modern resistance to Dutch colonialism and its humiliations. This resistance was waged by a new kind of human being, later to be known as the 'Indonesian'. Together, *This Earth of Mankind, Child of All Nations, Footsteps* and *House of Glass*, as they are titled in the published English translations, are Pramoedya's and Indonesia's greatest literary works.

'All four! Fantastic!' I replied, 'Me too.'

'You have read them all?'

'Yep.' I didn't tell him then that I had translated them all into English. But I did tell him I had known Pramoedya. Pram, as he is called, died in 2006.

'You knew him?'

'Ya, I knew him.'

All three of his friends, including two boys and a girl, turned to face me. The crowd of protesters made it difficult to talk. Some of the students were chanting slogans against the parliament. Others were shouting instructions over megaphones.

'Please, sit down,' I said. 'What's your name?'

'Iqbal,' he said.

'So you know about Tirto?'

'Yes, *Sang Pemula*,[7] the pioneer. I use his picture as my emblem on Facebook also,' he grinned, 'and Instagram.'

'You support the uni students?' I inquired.

'Yes!' the four of them replied in unison. 'The parliament is shit. Our whole class answered the question in our civics exam the same way. "What is the function of parliament?" "To sleep and take bribes!"'

They all laughed; loudly too.

'The whole class?'

'Yep, all of us.'

I went back to the topic of Tirto and Pram.

'I once went with Pram, and his two comrades from Hasta Mitra . . .'

'Hasta Mitra, ya, know about them', one of them interrupted.

'I went with Pram, and Joesoef and Hasjim to visit Tirto's grave. We were the first to visit it in a long time. Poor Tirto, his grave abandoned like that, not at all maintained.'

'Where was it?'

'In Bogor.' Bogor is a mountain town just outside Jakarta. 'I wrote an article about it back then, in 1993. Would you like to read it?'

'Is it in Indonesian?' Iqbal asked.

'Yep, it was published in an activist magazine, *Progres*.[8] I can email it to you if you like?'

'Yes, thank you,' smiled Iqbal. 'I never heard of *Progres*.'

'Activists published it but it was banned after a year or two, in 1992.'

'Suharto times.'

'What is your email?' I asked. Iqbal scribbled it on a piece of paper, legibly enough.

They moved away as the demonstration started off on a march. Someone came around with a bucket to collect rubbish—they wanted to leave the street clean after the demo. 'DPR! DPR!' they shouted, mentioning the parliament was now a synonym of rubbish.

The demonstrations were, of course, widely reported in the media, and even more widely reported on Instagram, Twitter and Facebook. Some, like in Jogja, went off smoothly. Others were dispersed with water cannons and tear gas, especially in Jakarta, where the political elite still remembered vividly May 1998, when the students occupied the parliamentary grounds and Suharto fell from power.[9] Hundreds of students were detained and not a few injured. But President Joko Widodo ignored the students' call to not weaken the Corruption Eradication Commission, despite the demonstrations having wide community support. That was September 2019 and so since then, the time-bomb for a social explosion against corruption and elite self-interest is still slowly ticking.

That evening, I emailed Iqbal what I had written back in 1992, when I was twenty-seven years younger. It was written immediately after visiting Tirto's gravesite. Here it is, below, and I haven't changed it.

I have not visited many cemeteries. I am not able to make many comparisons. Even so, I feel I can say that the cemetery in Blender, Bogor, West Java is an appropriate location as a place of final rest on this earth. It was cool under the many frangipani trees shading the hundreds at rest here. There was no chance for the sun to even peep through the canopy to bake the earth and dry up the atmosphere. Cool, quiet, peaceful.

But like so many places in Indonesia, even this cemetery was busy with human activity. The call to prayer echoed across the cemetery from a nearby mosque reminding the faithful of their duties on earth. The local villagers also used the cemetery for their household activities, for example, hanging out their laundry on the cemetery fence.

There were many children playing there. There were people selling flowers that would be placed on loved ones' graves. There were the workers looking after the cleanliness of the cemetery, whose duty it was to fight off the ever-forward-creeping grass and weeds. (Indeed, here and there, weeds had conquered some graves, making them their little fiefdom).

There were five of us there that day: Pramoedya Ananta Toer, the publisher Hasjim Rachman, the editor of Pram's books, Joesoef Isak, and the documentary filmmaker, Gil Scrine, and I.

'Where is the grave of Tirto Adhi Soerjo?', asked Joesoef addressing one of the crowd of children that was following us, their curiosity aroused by the presence of two foreigners.

Hasjim Rachman and I bought five little packets of fresh flowers that we would scatter over the grave. 'Ya, where is his grave, the grave of this famous person?' Hasjim also asked the children.

'Djokomono Tirto Adhi Soerjo?' added Joesoef.

Pramoedya Ananta Toer was silently observing the goings-on, gathering a sense of the atmosphere and keeping tabs on how our efforts were progressing.

'This way, pak' spoke a child. So our whole group obediently followed behind the little guide, we in turn followed by a growing entourage of other children. On the way, we met an old man, a gardener at the cemetery. He had retired from this job, but had decided to continue to work because there were not enough people hired to do it.

'They are looking for the grave of Djokomono Tirto Adhi Soerjo?', asked a teenage boy who had joined the now even larger entourage of children. 'If I am not mistaken, it is over there', spoke the gardener pointing towards the edge of the cemetery.

Our entourage swelled as we headed in that direction. Hasjim and Joesoef grew more confident as they started to remember their visit here from a few years earlier. At that time, they were researching for Pramoedya's non-fictional biography of Adhi Soerjo, entitled *The Pioneer*. Pramoedya, my friend Gil and I walked along quietly, only occasionally whispering to each other—it was a cemetery after all.

'Here, pak, here.' We had arrived, it seemed.

We walked passed a grassy patch, not very well-maintained. There was a fenced-off area with seven graves inside. The grass and weeds had taken over. Without being given any orders, the horde of children started to tear out all the weeds, inside and outside the area of the seven graves. Some also started to sweep the area, including the graves themselves.

So this was the resting place of The Pioneer, Sang Pemula, 'Minke'. This family gravesite was quite presentable, tiled, although not with expensive tiles. The graves were in a row, with the exception of two, which were next to each other but slightly separated. The oldest grave was that of The Pioneer, 'Minke'.

Djokomono Tirto Adhi Soerjo died in 1918 and was buried in Jakarta, and only later in 1971, disinterred and moved to Bogor to be with his family.

'Which is Minke's grave?' Joesoef, Pramoedya and Hasjim examined each of the seven headstones. They seemed to know the family tree of the family buried here. Indonesians seem to know these things. And there it was:

R.M. DJOKOMONO TIRTO ADHI SOERJO
PIONEER OF INDEPENDENCE
PIONEER OF THE INDONESIAN PRESS
DJAKARTA
PASSED AWAY 1918—DJAKARTA
RE-INTERRED 30-12-1973—BOGOR

I was moved in that moment. It's true, yes, my friends say I am a bit sentimental. However, I knew the man buried there quite well as a result of Pram's creativity. I had translated the four volumes Pram had written in the Buru Island prison camp, which were novels telling a story inspired by the life and times of Raden Mass Tirto Adhi Soerjo—the character Minke. I realized, of course, that Pramoedya had taken some poetic licence and that they are novels and not histories. But still, the real Tirto Adhi Soerjo does come alive for the reader. There is also the book, *The Pioneer*, edited by Pramoedya, which contained some original writings by Tirto, short stories, that also help understand the man resting here. *The Pioneer* was published by Hasta Mitra, founded by the three men paying their respects now at this gravesite.

Did I really know him all that well, the boy Minke and the man, T.A.S.? Hmm, well, I certainly felt I knew him, and as a friend. And this was where he was resting now.

'Bung Pram, why has his name faded on the headstone?'

Pramoedya looked closely and compared with the other headstones. 'Yes, why?'

The writing on the other headstones was clear and easy to read, painted in black. The paint had faded on Tirto's headstone, with some of the letters having disappeared altogether. If the letters had not been etched into the stone, his name would be altogether illegible.

'Pak, can you find some charcoal?' Hasjim asked for help from the throng that had gathered to watch us. Somebody headed off to find some charcoal to write with.

'Does somebody have a ballpoint?' Pramoedya asked. I gave him my pen, which happened to be a black ink pen, very suitable for rehabilitating the disappeared letters.

Pramoedya squatted and began tracing in the letters. One by one the letters reappeared spelling out the name of The Pioneer. Pramoedya's countenance was tense with concentration; his lips pulled tight as he focused.

The four of us stood watching. Hasjim turned to examine the audience that had gathered. There were maybe 15–20 people now, mostly children, but a few adults, including the two gardeners who looked after the cemetery.

'You are honoured to be able to look after and guard the gravesite of such a great man as this, a great man in Indonesian history. Tirto Adhi Soerjo. Don't forget that name. Yes, he has been forgotten by history, by the Indonesian nation. But we three have not forgotten. Look, there are foreigners too who have come here to pay their respects.' Thus Hasjim opened his speech.

Pram was still carefully finishing his work. The vanished name was indeed long, and the ballpoint was not the most suitable tool for the task. Joesoef and I chatted with the gardener. Gil took photos. Hasjim was still addressing his audience.

'This is new', said Joesoef pointing to the headstone, 'Pioneer of Independence. When we were here last that was not there . . . It just said a 'pioneer of the press'. We had suggested such a change to one of his descendants, an army General. It seems they have added that.' That General, a great grandson of Tirto's, now also rested here.

The charcoal was handed to us, but it turned out that the ballpoint had been up to the job.

'Here, Max', Hasjim called out to me, inviting me to scatter some flowers over the grave. I drew close and scattered the handful of petals over it.

Was I just performing? I thought. Was thus just a photo opportunity? No, the answer came swiftly. I was proud to have known the man buried here and proud, too, to be here with people as dedicated as Pram, Joesoef and Hasjim.

What an amazing person Tirto Adhi Soerjo was. He could sense that a nation would be formed by history even before the nation itself could become aware of this trajectory. And he just didn't sit by and watch, this Tirto, the pioneer. He worked and struggled to turn his vision into reality. He was a founder of the Islamiyah Traders Union, and the first native of the Indies to publish a newspaper with a future perspective for his people.

I knew that if we looked at things objectively, it wasn't always a healthy attitude to be so proud of one's country's past. One could become lost in the past and become blind to the present and future. And the achievements too of those that have gone before us are not our achievements. But as I scattered those lovely petals over his grave, I could not stop myself from thinking that if I was an Indonesian, I would be proud that my country had had a pioneer such as Tirto.

Hasjim and Joesoef took turns in scattering the flowers, and then Gil took over. Hasjim had some of the talents of a lay preacher so he then recited a Moslem prayer in Arabic. We bowed our heads; nobody spoke a word.

Pram completed inking in the full name: R.M. Djokomono Tirto Adhi Soerjo. Hasjim took his turn at inking in the epitaph.

'We have a new audience', Pram joked to Gil who was taking photographs. Pram pointed to a small herd of goats that was feeding on the grass nearby. We smiled at the scene.

Pram scattered some petals. He was silent. What was he thinking?

It was time to leave. There was no point in drawing out this moment, no matter how moving. Pram and Hasjim reminded the caretakers to look after the grave of this very important man. We turned and started to make our way to the cemetery entrance but all of us glanced back at least once, drawn to Minke's resting place for another moment. The little gang of teenagers and children still watched our every move as we left.

'This man has been forgotten by history and by his own nation and people,' Hasjim complained to them one more time.

'Read the headstone. Died in 1918. Sukarno was still a boy at that time. Just imagine: this man was already fighting for freedom when Sukarno was still just a boy. This man is just as great a person as Sukarno, maybe even greater.'

They followed us to the entrance, both the children and the few adults, listening to Hasjim. Hasjim's exuberance startled them. He was a handsome, imposing man and when he was excited, it was a serious matter.

Hasjim lagged behind. 'Who here is in high school?' A boy—they were all boys—put up his hand.

'So then ask your teacher who Tirto Adhi Soerjo was. And ask him why nothing about Tirto is taught to the students at school. And tell your teacher that this great man is buried here in Bogor.'

Hasjim finally exited the cemetery. Even as he hurried to catch up with us, he still needed to stop and turn and repeat what he had been saying. He wanted to make sure he left behind a message they would not forget: that here in Blender Cemetery, Bogor, there laid in eternal rest a great Indonesian, a pioneer in the struggle for freedom and of the press.

A few days later, I received a message from Pramoedya. 'What Hasjim told them all at the cemetery—somebody should write about Tirto. National Press Day just passed, and we were the only ones who visited his grave.'

1992 was twenty-seven years after Pramoedya, Hasjim and Joesoef had been arrested, thirteen years after they had been released from prison and ten years after they had started publishing Pramoedya's books. And six years before Suharto was to fall. And twenty-seven years also before Iqbal, the high school student, read *Bumi Manusia* and joined the 2019 demonstrations against a corrupt elite—wearing, of course, his Tirto Adhi Soerjo T-shirt. I forgot to ask him whether he had also seen the movie that year.

So there are more stories to tell.

**Pramoedya, 1993.
Taken at the time of the
interviews quoted in this
book. Photo by Gil Scrine.**

Joesoef Isak

**Hasjim Rachman at a party for Max Lane when sent home by
Australian Ambassador, 1981.**

Chapter 2

Three Men and Indonesia

Countries change. Of course, they do. History *is* change—a story of changing societies. Nothing special about that. What of a case, however, where a country sends itself into exile? Where it vanishes, for fourteen years, and is replaced by something completely different, almost an alien being? But it sneaks back from exile and then finds itself confronting its alien self—a powerful totalitarian alien self? What happens then? It has two selves, opposing each other, one dominating, one only grudgingly allowed back from exile, and still suppressed. It is suppressed, but still no less a self.

After 1 October 1965, Indonesia was sent into exile. This exile took the form of a counter-revolution, which killed a million people, imprisoned tens of thousands, smashed organizations that had 20 million members and banned ideas with millions of adherents. The victims of the counter-revolutionary terror comprised at least half of the adult population. They went into exile. They were no longer considered Indonesians. They and their 'selves' were portrayed as alien devils. The men were 'communists' in its special new Indonesian satanic meaning, and the women were '*kuntilanak*': whoring witches come up from hell. They could all be killed and tortured with no hesitation or remorse. Even today, almost fifty years after the event, some of the killers still celebrate the 'glory' of what they did. Some, as shown in Joshua Oppenheimer's 2014 film, *The Act of Killing*, celebrate the murder they committed with insane fantasy.

The term 'counter-revolution' is the most apt to describe what happened. At the most mundane end of the spectrum of individual experience, there was arrest, imprisonment, torture, rape and sexual abuse for women, and exile to Buru Island concentration camp or to some tiny cell in a Jakarta prison or elsewhere. Such was the fate for fourteen years, of Pramoedya Ananta Toer, the author of *Bumi Manusia* and its three sequels and several other works written in the camp. It was the fate, too, of newspaper publisher, Hasjim Rachman, who, after fourteen years in exile, defied military dictatorship to publish Pramoedya's works. Joesoef Isak, who joined Hasjim and Pramoedya in establishing the publishing company, Hasta Mitra, in 1980, was in a Jakarta prison cell for more than ten years. At the more horrific end of the experience was torture and then death, by bullet, disembowelling or beheading. The dead can't tell us of the horror they experienced, but those who survived, can and have. In this book, later, we will hear from Pramoedya, Hasjim and Joesoef on how they were taken from their homes and families. but also how later, with books as their weapons, they defied power and brought Indonesia back from exile.

This story can be—and I hope will be—told vividly as a story of individual experience. That will never be enough, though, as it is also the story of a community: of the Indonesian nation. The counter-revolution, by sending Indonesia into exile, also brought to a halt the revolution that had begun at the turn of the twentieth century and which, in 1965, was still creating Indonesia: it was a national revolution. Those of us living in the 'West' have already forgotten that the national communities we live in today did not always exist and were themselves either created by great revolutions or were in some way by-products of such revolutions. The bourgeois revolutions against feudalism, which established capitalism, accompanied by the scientific revolution and then the Enlightenment, created the new community, the nation.

In Indonesia, this process was undertaken by the anti-colonial revolution. The anti-colonial revolutionaries also wanted to remove all the remnants of colonialism that had been preserved or had survived colonial rule. They were divided over whether capitalism too needed to go. The 1965 counter-revolution suppressed the anti-colonial revolution with its anti-feudal and anti-capitalist impulses. The 1965 savage and violent suppression of these revolutionary impulses did not resolve the struggle within the Indonesian nation about whether the abolition of feudalism and capitalism was needed. Rather, the suppression meant the burial of the contradictions before there was actual political resolution; where one vision had been able to win over the hearts and minds of a majority, or a significant and strategic component of the national revolution's proponents. In 1978, the exiles returned, wielding not the sword but the pen, and the contradiction rose again from its burial site. By 2020, generations had passed, and the struggle to resolve the contradiction simply could not resume, but is now being reborn: conception, development in the womb, birth, and then growth in the world.

But where should this story start? With the national epic of the suppression of revolution? Or with three men in their homes in October 1965?

Pramoedya Ananta Toer, Joesoef Isak and Hasjim Rachman were the three men who, almost immediately after their release from prison, ignored the decree banning them from working in 'vital sectors' of the economy, which included publishing. Brazenly and in complete defiance of the dictatorship, the words 'A Work from Buru Island Prison Camp' were emblazoned across the cover of the first book they published, Pramoedya's *Bumi Manusia—This Earth of Mankind*. They relaunched Indonesia back into circulation among Indonesians.

* * *

In October 1965, it was the radio that conveyed the sense of nation on a daily basis: the source of the news about life from one end of the country to another. Pramoedya Ananta Toer, writer, lecturer and columnist and polemicist for the cultural pages of the bestselling daily newspaper, *Bintang Timur* (*Eastern Star*), living in Jakarta, also listened to the radio on Friday morning 1 October. He was a young forty-year-old in 1965, but already very rich in experience of Indonesia: the anti-Dutch struggle, survival under the Japanese occupation, the armed struggle, prison under the Dutch, and a literary witness to the first years of independent national life.

He was at home, most of the day. He had no lectures that day at Universitas Respublika, he told me in a long interview in 1993 in Jakarta. 'Colonel Untung announced over the radio that he had detained some generals. The soldiers who had helped with the arrests were to be promoted; and those in the higher ranks demoted. What kind of coup was that, I thought?' Pram told me later. Colonel Untung was the commander of the Presidential Security Guard. For tens of millions of Indonesians, it was a mystery, this midnight detention of seven generals and an army captain. There had been shots fired. A child—the young daughter of a general—had been killed. That general, wounded, had escaped.

1 October

Colonel Untung and his men were subdued by late afternoon by other army units. A new face emerged: Lt General Suharto. The bodies of the detained generals were found at the bottom of a well. They had been shot dead. Communists were blamed. Arrests began. Party leaders and members and supporters, and everybody on the Left who had campaigned for Sukarno's Indonesian Socialism, were the priority targets. President Sukarno lost his organized support base overnight. He was helpless, unarmed and so were his 20 million supporters, inside and outside the Indonesian Communist Party (PKI).

Pramoedya was one such supporter. He was bound to be a target.

'Several of my friends visited the house to advise me to run away. I asked them, "why should I run away?" "Because," they answered, "even though you are an important figure, it will not protect you from the army." There did happen to be a military man who lived across the street from my house. He would pace up and down out front, mumbling loudly about how the army had its own politics and didn't care about President Sukarno. A few times, I flicked some of my lit cigarette butts at him and he yelled back at me.'

Sukarno had tens of millions of enthusiastic supporters. The political parties that supported him were the country's largest. More than half the country's adults—25 million or so—were active in one or other of the organizations that supported him. The biggest was the PKI, but the Indonesian National Party (PNI), which purged itself of moneyed elite elements in 1965, was also growing. President Sukarno was the tribune of the Indonesian Left, but had no party of his own. And the Left had no guns. The most important of those opposed to him, and with Sukarno's *Socialism ala Indonesia*, were army officers led by the most money-minded of them all: General Suharto. Even before he came to power after 1965, he had his army unit set up its own bank. And, of course, they did have guns. In fact, Suharto's Army Strategic Command had the most guns and could move the fastest.[10]

One after another, Pram's friends came to his house. 'Leave now', they told him. 'Hide in my village', said another. 'The army will play cat and mouse with you', another warned. 'They are coming to get you soon', said another visitor, a young writer, who helped himself to whatever he wanted from the food cupboard. Pramoedya told them that he would not leave his home. But his wife, Maemunah, and five children were evacuated, which was a wise decision. Maemunah, like all the wives of detained men, had over decade of having to hold their families together—struggles that also need to be written about.

13 October

Pram's brother, Koesilah Toer, and Pram were alone at home. A 100-watt light bulb, an extravagance in Jakarta in 1965, shone over the front door, lighting up the street outside. Pram had bought the light after the warnings and the reports of arrests and killings started circulating. Something might indeed happen. And it did. Men, some masked, arrived pacing back and forth in front of the house. All the neighbours' houses were closed up, Pram told me.

11 p.m. One rock was thrown and it hit Pram in the leg. He bled. Then more and more stones came flying in. The door and the ceiling were hit and damaged. Pram armed himself with a samurai sword and a broomstick. Then there were the sounds of automatic gunfire and shouts of 'the army is here!'.

'I opened the gate to our compound and invited the officer to enter. A friend who had visited me had said that the army was using this tactic, sending a group of young men to attack, and then the military would come to the rescue. I let them in. They searched the house. "We will take you somewhere safe," said the officer. "Bring whatever you need. Don't go against the people, sir," he said strangely. I gathered my typewriter and the manuscript I was working on, a collection of Sukarno's short stories. I told my brother not to run: "they are taking us somewhere safe," I said. Hah!' spat Pramoedya during the interview.

Escorted to a waiting small truck, Pram and Koesilah were taunted from all sides by the gang outside. They carried spears, daggers and even cleavers. There was murder in their hearts. In the truck, they had nooses tied around their necks. As Pram pleaded that his books and papers in the house be kept safe, a machine gun smashed into his face. He had turned quickly, and it broke his cheek bone.

'We were not taken to a "safe place", but to the Strategic Army Command headquarters.' These were Suharto's headquarters. Pram arrived with two injuries, leg and face, at a building crowded with prisoners. 'The screaming and howling of people being tortured never stopped,' he remembered. He sat there waiting with typewriter and papers in his lap. His brother was let go.

Such was the very beginning of his exile. And so it was beginning in hundreds of thousands other locations. It was a few years still, before Pramoedya and 14,000 others were shipped to a new prison camp, which the prisoners had to mainly build themselves, on Buru Island in Eastern Indonesia.

There were only thirteen days between the subduing of the midnight conspiracy that detained the seven generals and Pramoedya's arrest. The conspiracy was defeated by 1 October and Pramoedya was 'arrested'—kidnapped—on 13 October. The conspiracy was a botched job from a to z. Its execution in the field seemed to have been masterminded by a man known as Syam, the head of a Special Bureau responsible directly to the D.N. Aidit, the chairperson of the PKI.

The idea for the detention of the generals seemed to have come from Aidit himself, although one never knows the inner life of secret conspiracies. There are also theories that Aidit was not involved at all, and that it was a provocation organized by military intelligence operatives close to Suharto.[11] Nor do we yet know what other factors may have led to these decisions, such as any detailed information of an impending coup against elements in the army, against the government. The plan being implemented by the conspirators was to detain the generals, who were suspected to be plotting a coup against Sukarno, and present them to the President, whom, it was hoped, would dismiss them, and replace them with generals less hostile to the party, to Socialism ala Indonesia and the revolution.

Nothing went right. They couldn't find Sukarno that night. The conspiracy was delayed while the generals were detained near an Air Force base on the edge of Jakarta. The delay gave time for Suharto, who probably knew in advance what was happening, to make countermoves. The conspiracy started to unravel. Somebody gave orders for the detained generals and another officer to be executed. Their bodies were thrown down a well. When Sukarno was eventually found, brought to the Air Base and told of the murders, he angrily ordered Colonel Untung to stop what he was doing. The conspiracy, called the 'September 30 Movement' (G30S), had failed. Desperate, its organizers tried to salvage their doomed positions by issuing a decree decommissioning Sukarno's cabinet. By the afternoon of 1 October, the conspiracy to replace the Army command disintegrated and the formation of a Revolutionary Council was announced, which was never established. It was a hopeless attempt at a last-minute coup through nothing more than a radio broadcast. Untung's forces were quickly rounded up.[12]

It was easy for the army to present a case stating that the PKI was involved because of the role of the Special Bureau and made worse by an editorial in the party paper, *Harian Rakyat*, dated 2 October, supporting the G30S—which name Suharto quickly transformed into G30S/PKI. Sukarno could be implicated by Suharto because he was at the Air Base, where Aidit, Untung and other conspirators had also gathered. Those who had not been captured in operations in the field during the day, like Untung, had fled from Jakarta. Sukarno was flown to Bogor, where there was a presidential residence. Aidit was captured and shot, without process, a few days later. Untung was later tried and executed. Sukarno was placed under de facto house arrest, denied access to the media and in 1967, formally deposed.

Pramoedya was in jail by 13 October. But he had not been a part of the conspiracy. He had had no inkling of its planning. When he was released from prison camp fourteen years later, he was given an official letter—as were thousands of others who had been imprisoned at that time—stating that there was no evidence that he had been involved in the conspiracy.

What then were Pramoedya's crimes? And those of Hasjim Rachman and Joesoef Isak and the tens of thousands jailed for between one and twenty years? Not to mention the millions murdered.

* * *

Revolutions, being fundamentally creative processes, always pose the most existential questions. A revolution does indeed destroy an old order, but it does so in order to create a new one. And thus, the question: what shall we create? The greater the effort—that is, the greater the cost in energies and, indeed, in lives—in destroying the old, the more emotion and psychical energy there is invested in the struggle to create the new. But it cannot simply be a struggle to create the new. It is always also a struggle over *what kind* of new to create. Yes, it is an existential question—it is a question about everything, not just some things. Creation of the totally new is felt as an almost God-like process: the true being of the new is at stake. Men and women become 'busy revolutionizing themselves and creating something that did not exist before'.[13] And while creation does have this fundamental existential character, almost divine, it is still humankind, mortals, that do the creating.

As soon as the prospect of an independent Indonesia entered the vision of the agents of change in the 1920s, this emotion-invested existential question was posed: after Independence, what kind of Indonesia? From as early as the 1920s, this question divided the human beings that were to become the members of a new community, 'something that did not exist before', the nation. Partly, this division was due to the strength of traditions; from the old aristocracy having a greater grip on some minds more than others; and partly due to the simpler motivation of those who were already enjoying status and privilege, seeking a nation where they could continue to do so, or of those who envied the status and privilege of those that were enjoying such things, whether colonial or local.

The first great mass organization in the Netherlands East Indies, now known as Indonesia, that confronted colonialism was the Sarekat Islam,[14] with perhaps more than 1 million members spread across most of the archipelago. It was a broad tent organization, encompassing people from Left to Right, including some of Indonesia's first communists. As soon as its leading activists began to think seriously about an Indonesian future, the Sarekat split. It split over whether an independent Indonesia should be capitalist or socialist. Out of the split, emerged a bigger Communist Party of Indonesia, which survived as a major organization until it was suppressed by the Dutch colonial power after a rebellion in 1927. This existential question of whether Indonesia should be capitalist or socialist, born in the decade after the Russian Revolution—a question posed in so many colonies where national struggles were emerging—has been the axis of contradiction and struggle within the national revolution since the 1920s, until 1965.

Anybody familiar with the energies and passion unleashed by revolution—though perhaps too few people today are familiar with the revolutions that gave birth to the communities in which they now live—will know that they can move 'heaven and earth'. And also, that such great change can generate panic and a primordial fear among those threatened by the new. It is no small thing: this struggle over the content of the new, when revolutionary energy is unleashed.

And Pramoedya's crime? And the crime of a million others? A million! He—they all—were part of those energies that saw an Indonesian future that was not capitalist, but socialist. Indonesia after independence, however, inherited the capitalist social and economic structures of colonialism, with its attendant poverty and injustices. In Pramoedya's eyes, independence may have been won but the revolution itself was unfinished.

'. . . [Before 1965] people were dissatisfied with the results of the revolution. The question was: is the revolution over, or not? Sukarno said the revolution was not over, and I agreed, there were revolutionary promises that had not been turned into reality. The second reason, at that time, Indonesia was being bullied by the capitalist countries. There were attempts on Bung Karno's life.'

Pram took sides. He was a writer, so he wrote, he polemicized. He campaigned for an end to literary and artistic activity that was oblivious to the challenge of the unfinished revolution, that essentially assumed that the revolution was over. He wrote a series of articles with the theme 'What must be destroyed, and what must be built', which was a rephrasing of Sukarno's 'To destroy and to build'. The intent of the article, he told me, 'was to draw a line in the sand: those people who wrote just to play around, they should stop what they were doing, the country was in a critical state. We were targeted by capitalist countries who wanted to take over our market.'

He took sides, along with 20 million others. The Army, and other forces, spurred on by Washington, London and Canberra,[15] were on the other side. The failed midnight conspiracy of 30 September 1965 provided the army and its allies with the pretext for mass murder and, after that, giving the 'new' the content they wished, without hindrance or encumbrance from any forces from within the nation. Thus, they created the Indonesia of today. For Pram in 1993, 'The horse had already bolted. What we were worried would happen has already happened. Indonesia has become a playground for capitalists.'

* * *

Pramoedya took sides, actively, as the two sides came sharper into conflict. His weapon was the pen and the vehicle of struggle was the daily newspaper, *Bintang Timur*. Pramoedya edited the newspaper's weekly cultural section, *Lentera*, in which he also wrote a column. Probably the PKI's *Harian Rakyat* had a bigger circulation, but that also included copies that were available free of charge. At that time, all newspapers were obliged to affiliate to a political party, which were the main agencies for articulating visions for Indonesia's future. *Bintang Timur* was affiliated to the Partai Indonesia (Partindo), a small party that was the most enthusiastic supporter of Sukarno's Socialism ala

Indonesia ideology, and of his radical, nationalist anti-imperialism. Hasjim himself explained that a part of the paper's effectiveness was that it was read by people from all three of the major political streams supporting Sukarno: the communists, nationalists and Moslems, unlike *Harian Rakyat*, that was read primarily by people supporting the PKI.

The central figure publishing *Bintang Timur* was Hasjim Rachman. The reader will remember that he was also arrested in 1965 and detained without trial until 1977, including ten years on Buru Island where Pramoedya was also imprisoned. Hasjim and Pramoedya spent several years in the same prison hut on Buru Island, the hut for the most 'stubborn' prisoners.

Hasjim Rachman was also taken from his home in 1965, but not like Pram in the back of a truck, but in his own Mercedes. As owner-publisher of *Bintang Timur*, he had been able to buy an old Mercedes. He also had a position in the Indonesian Flight Industry Strategic Command, which had been tasked in 1965 with negotiating an agreement with the Dutch Fokker company to build planes in Indonesia, an agreement that was signed in August 1965.

Hasjim was arrested some days after Pramoedya. He had been sleeping in a friend's house, just in case there might be a raid at his. Then, seeing that there seemed to be no interest in his house, he went back home. A few days later, at breakfast time, his house was surrounded by about twenty armed policemen. His wife, Tetty Chairani, and seven children were also there and the youngest told him, 'Daddy, the police are here'. 'It's okay,' Hasjim said to his son, 'let them come in'. So one of them came up to Hasjim and said, 'Sir, I have a warrant to arrest you'. 'Do you have the warrant with you?' 'Yes,' he said, and he gave the warrant letter to Hasjim, to read it. Hasjim told me about what happened next.

'They were going to take me in the truck they came by, but I said, "Why do I have to go in the truck? I can go in my car." And they said, "Eh, sure, go ahead." Some of them went with me in my car, with my driver. That year, 1965, I was driving a Mercedes,' he chuckled. 'So that was how I was taken to police headquarters. I was sitting in the back and suddenly it dawned on me that this could get a bit tricky, they might confiscate my car. So once we got to the police headquarter, I told my driver to go straight back home.'

After some interrogation, Hasjim was taken to the District Military Command. The officer-in-charge lived across the road from him and knew Hasjim as a neighbour, but at that moment, Hasjim told me, his neighbour didn't want to have anything to do with this extra prisoner. From that place of detention, he was taken to Central Headquarters. The scene was the same as that witnessed by Pramoedya:

> I saw many things that I wished I had not seen. They were beating up people who had just come into the cell, more beatings, torture. I was surprised, and disappointed: I had defended this Republic, and there was the red and white flag there, but here I was, crouching under the same flag, on the uncovered floor. How had it come to this?
>
> Until one day, something very remarkable happened. There was a woman there with us, a famous woman from Sulawesi, a member of the parliament, a member of Gerwani (Indonesian Women's Movement), and a fighter in the independence war. … this woman was very famous, all the Republic fighters knew her. When she saw a young man getting beaten by a soldier, she got up and screamed at the soldier, "Why are you torturing this helpless young man? What did he do wrong? You're a coward!" That was the first time I saw a soldier stop torturing someone because a woman scolded him. The people of Sulawesi owed a lot to this woman.

Hasjim was referring to Salawati Daud, renowned as a fierce fighter for Independence in the war against the Dutch, who as a member of Gerwani was imprisoned in Java after 1965.

And so Hasjim's exile began. Only a few weeks before, Hasjim had been in Paris and Amsterdam, negotiating with Fokker. And now he was crouching on the floor, watching people being tortured. With him in France and the Netherlands, had been Joesoef Isak, who also had been appointed to work in the Indonesian Flight Industry Strategic Command. Joesoef knew Hasjim because they were both active in the Indonesian Journalists Association (PWI), but Joesoef did not get to know Pramoedya until 1979. Joesoef was detained also, but not sent to Buru Island. His home for ten years was a cell in Jakarta's Salemba Prison. One of his favourite non-prison stories was how he enjoyed his time sitting at Leidseplein in Amsterdam in 1965, then a centre for the gathering Dutch literati and intelligentsia and sipping on a cognac. His Salemba cell stories were different.

In Amsterdam, Joesoef Isak and Pramoedya Ananta Toer with A.M. Hanafi, former Indonesian Ambassador to Cuba in 1965, and then a political exile in France.

In 1965, Joesoef was active as a central figure in the Indonesian Journalists' Association (PWI). He had been elected to the executive back in 1959, when he had been editor of *Merdeka* newspaper, an old and established newspaper, owned by politically centrist nationalist businessman publisher, B.M. Diah. 1959, just nine years after the Dutch finally left Indonesia, was a turning point in Indonesian politics. Joesoef's story of what happened to him between 1959 and his arrests between 1965 and 1968 tells us some important things about Indonesia.

Readers of the stories I am telling in this book, and the analysis I am attempting, need to clearly grasp the time periods involved, what happened in each one and how long they lasted. Now, in 2020, because so much has changed—because a whole country went into exile for so long—what took place not so long ago, seems as if, perhaps, it never even happened.

Between 1949 and 1959, Indonesia had three Constitutions. First, there was the brief emergency revolutionary Constitution declared in August 1945. And then a Constitution of the United States of Indonesia, proclaimed on 27 December 1949. It was the United States of Indonesia that finally signed an agreement for the Transfer of Sovereignty from the Netherlands to Indonesia. On 17 August 1950, the federal United States of Indonesia became the Republic of Indonesia, again with a Provisional Constitution. At the time of the first parliamentary elections in 1955, a Constituent Assembly was elected to draft another Constitution. In 1959, citing the assembly's inability to come to agreement, Sukarno disbanded the Assembly and re-instituted the original 1945 Constitution. The re-institution of this Constitution was, however, part of deeper political change. Between 1945 and 1959, President Sukarno was one among equals, without a political party, and under a Constitution that gave the President only minimal powers. The prime minister and his cabinet were the more substantial repositories of power. Bringing back the 1945 Constitution did not make the president all-powerful, but it gave him much greater power than before.

Joesoef explained:

> This was an important moment in the political history of our Republic. Sukarno was back on the grand stage—by that I meant that he got another chance to turn his political vision into a reality. And the media became very important for him, and for the other parties as well. All the political parties were trying to curry favour with the newspapers. They were most interested in the centrist papers, as they were seen as more objective, not favouring either side. They all had their own papers as well, the Left, the Muslims, the Catholics, the Protestants—all of them had their own papers. Sukarno himself was a progressive nationalist; he was the most progressive out of all the nationalists. He appointed my former boss, B.M. Diah, to be the Indonesian ambassador to Czechoslovakia. Before Diah left, Sukarno asked him who was going to replace him as chief editor of *Merdeka*. Diah told him he was going to appoint me. Apparently, Sukarno then told him: "Your paper still has to be progressive, progressive-revolutionary. If it doesn't stay that way, I'll summon you back."

And Joesoef was convinced about the general direction in which Sukarno wanted to take the country. Joesoef became strongly involved in the politics of Asian–African solidarity. He travelled to Africa and around Asia, and to South America, including Cuba, as part of his role as secretary-general of the Asian–African Journalists' Association and vice president of the International Organization of Journalists. At the centre of both the PWI—active within Indonesia and internationally—Joesoef was in the thick of things.

> A lot of social and political forces were competing for power before 1965. The major powers were the political parties, and one of the biggest was the PKI (Indonesian Communist Party). The other forces were the military, especially the army. The third force is Islam. Then there were the nationalists, Sukarno's people. These four groups were fighting each other. There was a term that we used then, "jor-joran", or making lots of noise to appear to be among the most progressive parties to implement Sukarno's political ideas. But most of them were fighting against the PKI, their common enemy. In those years, before 1965, PKI was the leading party, much bigger than the others. They offered great programmes that were welcomed by the people. The Indonesian people felt the PKI were fighting to protect them. Things were very tense in the two to three years before 1965, as these forces jostled for attention and power. The forces against the PKI organized themselves under what they called "Cultural Manifesto", Manikebu. Amongst the journalists, there was the BPS, the Body in Support of Sukarnoism. These two institutions, two movements, were just the beginning, a prologue. There were others before Manikebu and BPS, but they really got themselves organized with those two. That was the prologue to what was going to happen in September.

The 'jor-joran' ended abruptly on 1 October. So did the activities of the PWI, or at least, the PWI that Joesoef and Hasjim had led. Journalists were quickly purged, arrested. Pramoedya himself witnessed journalists from the state news agency, Antara, being brought in to army headquarters, their legs all bloody. They had been forced to crawl around the concrete yard in the Military Police compound.

Joesoef became a man tossed around by the new currents and eddies that were set into motion after 1 October. Joesoef, unlike Pramoedya and Hasjim, was not so quickly arrested and jailed. Perhaps protected by his international standing in two major journalists' associations, his detention was delayed and more disorganized. Perhaps, the Army, too, was unsure of where he stood politically. When he had been elected to head the PWI in 1959, he had been supported by both Left and Right. He was then editor of a major centre-of-the-road daily newspaper, which he left only in 1962, after trying to take it in a more Left-wing direction. He was never known as a card-carrying PKI member, let alone as a party leader.

He was picked up and detained in one safehouse or another. Interrogated. What did he know about G30S? Like almost everybody, he knew nothing. That is the nature of a secret conspiracy. As a journalist, he had heard rumours of a Council of Generals planning a coup and a Council of Colonels opposed to their generals. But nothing else. He would be detained for a month or two months, and then released; and then detained by another army unit who hadn't realized he had already been interrogated. He went in and out of these places for almost three years; these places of interrogations and torture.

'Men were taken at midnight, Max,' he told me more than once. 'We were jammed into rooms like sardines and we would hear the footsteps approaching. We would remind each other that no matter how bad the pain might be, we would not die and that we should hold out and not give names. The worse treated were those whipped with the spiked skeleton of an eel,' he said. 'We had ointments ready for when they returned from the cell.'

Joesoef was lucky, and clever. He, like Hasjim, had the gift of the gab and could talk his way through interrogations. Pramoedya's blunt, less accommodating style, was what got him the rifle butt in his face.

It was almost three years after G30S, in 1968, that Joesoef's exile finally began in Salemba Prison, Jakarta. He was there for ten years.

* * *

Perhaps, or at least I hope, the reader wants to know how they survived their imprisonment over the coming decade. And, of course, the reader will probably also already know that Pramoedya's *This Earth of Mankind* and its three sequels were written in a prison camp and that the story had been related from mouth to mouth first, before even Pramoedya was allowed an old typewriter and some paper. The story of the strength of character of the little, fourteen-year-old village girl, Sanikem, sold by her father to a great hulk of a Dutchman, a sugar plantation manager, at the turn of the century, became an inspiration for the many of the prisoners on Buru Island when camp conditions and abuse by prison guards was at its worst. And Joesoef and Hasjim have no less interesting stories to relate.

Pramoedya. Joesoef. Hasjim. Yes, these three play three main roles in the epic I wish to relate, the epic of the return from exile of Indonesia to Indonesia, embodied in the publication of *This Earth Of Mankind* and its sequels (and prequels). And so, there is another character, or another self, or another presence, at least, in this story: Indonesia. Before we resume the stories of the exile of Pramoedya, Joesoef and Hasjim, we must struggle with something perhaps more complex: Indonesia's revolution and counter-revolution as a whole. Yes, I don't think we can avoid this.

Chapter 3

Indonesia

So. Indonesia. Yes, I can describe how it is an archipelago of hundreds of islands, hundreds of linguistic groups, with some areas dominated by Islamic or Hindu or Christian or animist belief systems. I could explain the several historical periods in which different political ideologies have contested: communism, socialism, nationalism—right-wing and left-wing—and political Islamism. Then there is its geopolitical situation: an elongated archipelago separating the Pacific from the Indian Ocean, through which all shipping between the two oceans must pass.

Today, it is a country of 260 million people—the fourth largest population in the world—which is likely to grow to more than 400 million by 2050, with at least half of its people living in a chain of under-industrialized sprawling mega cities. The economy, like most Third World countries, suffers the colonial legacy of severe under-industrialization with no more than 5 million of its 160 million workers employed in large or otherwise high-productivity enterprises. Its per capita GDP is around US$4,000 compared to the United States' US$70,000. Its median wealth per adult is around US$2,000 compared to around US$69,000 in the USA.

With such a huge, diverse and problematic economy and society, there will be a million angles from which to begin a discussion of Indonesia.

I choose to start from a most fundamental fact of history: even just 100 years ago, neither Indonesia nor Indonesians existed—not in concrete reality nor even as a notion. The word 'Indonesia' only began to circulate widely in the country in the 1920s. It had been used earlier only by a tiny few European sociologists. It is true that it was at the turn of the twentieth century, between 1890 and 1910, that the processes began that eventually led to the creation of that being, or that new community, a nation, that was later called Indonesia. It is this early period of conception—a period before the growth of the embryo even began— that is the topic of Pramoedya's greatest work, the tetralogy that began with *This Earth of Mankind*. Pramoedya began his novel with the lines:

> People called me: Minke.
>
> My own name . . . For the time being I need not tell.
>
> In the beginning, I wrote these short notes during a period of mourning: she had left me, who could tell if for a while only or forever? (At the time I didn't know how things would turn out.) That eternally harassing, tantalizing future! Mystery! We shall all eventually arrive there—willing or unwilling, with all our body and soul. And too often it proves to be a great despot. And so, in the end, I arrived too. Whether it be a kind or cruel god, is, of course, its own affair: humanity too often claps with just one hand.

The opening introduces the narrator of *This Earth of Mankind* and its two sequels, *Child of All Nations* and *Footsteps* (the final volume has a different narrator). He was called Minke, or 'Monkey' when pronounced with a hateful Dutch colonial accent. These several lines, however, could just as well be an introduction to 'Indonesia' before it knew it would come into existence. Indonesians-to-be were called 'monkeys'; they could not yet tell their own name for it had not yet been found; and it was true also that a totally new future where men 'revolutionized themselves and created something that did not exist on the earth before', was to eventuate, with the new Indonesians, both willing and unwilling in this process; and it did indeed absorb body and soul. There would be revolution, mental and physical, despotic and cruel, and kind too, in the liberation from colonialism.

Towards the end of *Footsteps*, when Minke is no longer the uncertain high school student but has become an experienced and tested political leader and writer, known by the initials T.A.S., he tells some of his comrades in struggle: 'So, my brothers, our nation is not just that of the Javanese, but includes many other peoples, bound together by the things I have explained to you.'

Earlier, he had told them that 'Indies nationalism'—although he says he didn't use those kinds of terms—would stretch beyond Java to wherever people spoke Malay, where Islam had built a strength of brotherhood, and where a culture was emerging based on the values of independent endeavour, in contrast to dependence on feudal rulers. 'It is much greater than that which people have described as the Indisch nation or the Indies nation. As for its name, I do not have one yet. Perhaps we will need a new name.'

T.A.S. was among the very few at this time, around 1910 or so, who could sense in what direction the developments were leading. And even he, whom Pramoedya described in a non-fiction work as 'The Pioneer',[16] could only sense it tentatively, 'tantazilingly'. The Minke and T.A.S. characters were, as in *Footsteps* and *House of Glass*, mostly inspired by and based on the life of Tirto Adhi Soerjo, a man who helped found the first mass based anti-colonial organization in Indonesia, the Sarekat Dagang Islam, as well as the first Malay-language newspaper with a clear political outlook trying to give a voice to the views 'of the governed' (as its tagline read) against the government. A part of Pramoedya's motivation in wanting to write about this pioneer was that Tirto had been removed from history by Dutch colonial scholarship.

Why did Pramoedya use initials—only T.A.S. and not the full name? In the original manuscript typed in the prison camp, he did use the full name. But a problem arose. In the novel—sorry for the spoiler if you haven't read *Footsteps* yet—T.A.S. was unable to have children. However, in fact, T.A.S. did have children. I remember well, a moment when Pram, Joesoef and Hasjim were discussing this question, with me listening in: the Jakarta Military Command General, Norman Sasono, was a descendant of T.A.S.'s. So the decision was that Hasta Mitra Publishers should not tempt fate and provoke a court case from angry descendants.

But why was it necessary for the novel's T.A.S. to have no children, from any of his wives or liaisons, when in fact he did have children? Was it because this first discovery of what the future might bring was aborted? T.A.S.'s project failed. Even that of his adopted ideological children, or those that looked up to him and then tried to go beyond him, failed. Tirto disappeared from history. The next immediate generation of revolutionaries, some of whom start to appear in *Footsteps* and *House of Glass* as characters, go on to form the Indonesian Communist Party in the 1920s. But it launches a rebellion, which is easily suppressed and it too disappears for a quarter of a century, and then only reappears as something different. Tirto was a pioneer who has no *direct* political descendants.

The fact of Indonesia's non-existence 100 years ago is not unique to the world. All those communities we know today as nations once did not exist. There was a time in the eighteenth century, when most people living in the now United States were not Americans. Even in the nineteenth century, that may have been the case for many people in Australia. In some cases, the transformation to nationhood process had smooth continuity with a different sort of community of an earlier period, but with a similar name. This fact of being a new creation is not important because it makes Indonesia unique—it doesn't. It is important, though, because it highlights for us that a process of creation has taken place, that some things have been revolutionized as things that did not exist before and were newly created. And all processes, have their beginnings and even the preparations for those beginnings, as well as further stages of development in their lives, including finally, maturation, and then, decay and death. It is being alive to this reality of process, of change, that enables any observer of a society, whether from within or without, to grasp what is happening, including how cause relates to effect, and how cause and effect serve to define that reality.

Pram's *This Earth of Mankind* tetralogy novels are brilliant and gripping examples of that ability. The meaning of the story of their writing, publication and circulation, and of the roles of the three men who published them must also be understood as a very significant moment, a very powerful and extended moment, in that process.

Pramoedya, Joesoef and Hasjim were a part of the Angkatan 45, the 45 generation: people who experienced and participated in the political and armed struggle between 1945 and 1949, which ended with the overthrowing of Dutch colonialism. And they were all a part of the radical Sukarnoist 60's wave of political energy that swelled from between 1959 until it was smashed in 1965. That made them people who were a part of the initial revolutionary surge but who did not think that the defeat of the Dutch in 1949 nor the expulsion of Dutch private businesses in 1956-58 marked the end of the revolution. They were Sukarnoists in the sense they agreed with Sukarno that structures of injustice still existed even after the Dutch were ousted: 'The Peoples' Awareness demands that every unjust situation or relationship be torn down and changed . . . changed fast and in a revolutionary way.' The Angkatan 45 were divided between those whose conviction was that the revolution was not finished and those, such as Sukarno's Vice President Mohammed Hatta, who argued that the revolution should be ended.[17]

Pram was a writer and he worked as a writer and propagandist for the Republican forces once the revolutionary war started in August 1945. He was captured by the Dutch and spent months in a Dutch prison. He wrote several stories and novels set during the period of the revolutionary war. He was not initially a Sukarnoist in the sense described above. His writings between 1945 and 1960 are still descriptive humanist works, not yet challenged by the need to understand causes of the situations he was describing and thus also not yet moved by the question of solutions. His descriptions, though, did become more and more angrily vivid and stylistically inventive.[18] He sought to understand the causes by deepening his study of history, immersing himself in the documents and writings of the turn of the twentieth century. It was during this period, as 1965 neared, that his writings on history increased. He wrote a detailed history of the pioneer of women's rights in Indonesia, Kartini,[19] who also wrote at the turn of the century, and who appears as a figure of inspiration for Minke/T.A.S. as he matured. He wrote a series of essays that later became a book on the history of the Chinese in Indonesia. And he wrote so many essays on the early nationalist struggles in the pages of *Bintang Timur*.

All three men's experience of the 1945–49 climax of the anti-colonial revolution comprised a central journalistic component. Hasjim Rachman, who had some engineering and technical training, worked for a Republican radio station in Bandung, after writing for the papers for a while. The rather adventurous nature of this debonair man from North Sumatra took an appropriately adventurous turn at the time and he left his radio work. He told me:

> I went to Singapore on government funding . . . on the way to learn to fly. I wanted to be a fighter pilot and the government was going to send me to India, eventually. So I got a scholarship from the Indonesian government, that was in 1946. I was going to India, but when we got to Singapore, me and my friends, we were asked to help the new Republic of Indonesia government fight the Dutch. I got an order—because I was from Sumatra, I was born on the north coast of Sumatra, in Tanjung Balai, Asahan—to smuggle weapons to North Sumatra, to Tanjung Balai. I had heard that battles had broken out in Surabaya, Bandung, Jakarta, everywhere. I could not escape this task. So I took it on: smuggling these weapons to an area that was under the Republic's control. Later on, I found out that it had all been worked out, I got the guns from Chinese communists based in Malaysia, but I didn't know this at that time. The guns were bought from them. My job was to pick them up from the jungle. I didn't make the payment. I went into the jungle in Malaysia . . . to pick up the guns, and took them to Sumatra, safely.

Minke or T.A.S. in Pram's novels, was explaining that the yet-to-be-named community would somehow be constituted of those who spoke Malay, the language of T.A.S's own newspaper *Medan Priyayi*, even at the turn of the twentieth century. Joesoef Isak didn't learn to speak any serious Malay until after 1942, until after Japan invaded and occupied the Netherlands East Indies. He had been brought up in a Dutch-speaking family, a Sumatran family living in Batavia, but a part of the colonial elite. Apart from Dutch, English was the other language he became familiar with. His father, who worked for an English telegram company, brought English language books home, which the very young Joeosef was expected to read. He was educated in Dutch-language schools. He did know how to speak enough Malay to buy snacks at the local market or from passing street peddlers—but that was it.

The Imperial Japanese Army occupied the Dutch East Indies; the Japanese adopted the name for the country being used among the nationalist movement: Indonesia. The Japanese interned all the Dutch colonial population they could find but released many Indonesians who had been political prisoners of the Dutch, including Sukarno and Hatta, as long as they offered no active resistance to the occupation. Both Sukarno and Hatta agreed to work with the Japanese, who promised independence for Indonesia. There were other nationalist figures, such as Tan Malaka, who stayed away from working with the Japanese.

Sukarno was allowed to tour Indonesia and speak to the people. He used these opportunities to rouse nationalist sentiments for Independence, without the Japanese picking up too much on this emphasis. Not many Japanese spoke Indonesian, and many of those who did, were sympathetic rather than hostile.[20]

It was Sukarno who taught Joesoef Indonesian. This was not in a classroom—except insofar as a town square filled with tens of thousands of Indonesians listening to Sukarno can also be seen as a classroom, and perhaps it should be seen that way.

'Max,' he told me this story many times, 'it was so frustrating. There were thousands of people cheering in response to what Bung Karno was saying. The people; fellow Indonesians. But I had no idea at all what was going on.'

Joesoef started reading Sukarno, and other nationalists. Mastering Indonesian was a necessary part of being part of the process, of the revolution. When a nation is being created, it is the 'tantalizing future' that makes a new common language necessary. A common future can only be grasped if all parts of the newly forming community can discuss, debate and fight over the future in a common language. Joesoef read the nationalists' new publications, including *Berita Indonesia*, a newspaper allowed by the Japanese but doing its best to subvert the official imperial message. Joesoef's uncle was an owner of *Berita Indonesia*. Many young people, who later formed the first generation of Indonesia's journalists, worked there. Joesoef also read even more widely in Dutch and English. Many of the houses of Dutch personnel interned by the Japanese became vacant and some had excellent libraries. Joesoef and his cousin were billeted in such a one for a while.

All three were men of the keyboard and the words typed out, stencilled, or printed and circulated by them, and by thousands of others; their writing enabled the sharing of a description of what was happening. Individual experience and thought became a mass experience. Of course, differences in experience, flowing from cultural backgrounds and social classes, also meant differences in how the underlying common experience of being part of the creation of a new nation was interpreted. Even as the Angkatan 45 struggled to rid themselves of Dutch colonialism, ideas about what should happen after the Dutch were expelled, was the basis of divisions. Bitter, serious armed clashes took place between Islamic and nationalist republicans, as well as between communists and anti-communists. Thousands died. The worst clash was in the town of Madiun on Java in 1948.

Some of these have been deep and long-lasting, felt even until today.

Most textbooks on Indonesian history, both outside and inside the country, divide modern Indonesian history into the following periods: 1945–49 national revolution; 1949–1959 parliamentary democracy; 1959–65 guided democracy and 1965–1998 the New Order. On the surface, there is a validity to this division, but it does not capture the essence of the *process* that was underway. It is static. The terms are too superficially descriptive.

The period between 1949, when the Dutch military forces and bureaucracy went home, and 1965, did see two different forms of government in place. There was a government between 1949 and 1959, which—though not initially formed through elections— assumed that free elections would take place. And they did: for the national parliament and a Constituent Assembly in 1955, and for local parliaments and executives in 1957. During these ten years, parliament and the cabinet were the dominant institutions. After July 1959 when President Sukarno disbanded the Constituent Assembly and decreed that the original 1945 Constitution would be re-activated, the institution of presidency became central. Quickly also, the strength of political parties and ideologies would no longer be measured through elections but by the ability to organize mass mobilizations in support of the president.

So it is understandable that textbook writers would latch on to such a periodization: parliamentary democracy followed by guided democracy. Using this as a framework for understanding the process that was happening and which led to the catastrophe of 1965 is, however, inadequate.

There was only one period between 1949 and 1965, not two. It was a single period of deep contestation, and as Pramoedya's opening paragraphs to *This Earth of Mankind* hinted, it was a contestation over the future carried out with body and soul—aware that it could see the rule of a cruel god, as well as, perhaps, a kind one. Minke-T.A.S. in Pramoedya's novel found that a cruel god reigned in that early pre-Indonesia. Pramoedya, Joesoef and Hasjim, and millions of others, found the same thing in 1965. Between 1949 and 1965, a struggle, passionate and ruthless, was wrought over Indonesia's future. If we ask what defined Indonesia during those (brief) sixteen years, it was indeed this contestation.

Indonesia and its future were the whole point of existence: 'Merdeka atau Mati!' ('Freedom or Death') was the slogan that was painted everywhere in 1945. And death was the price paid by many at least 100,000 Indonesians in those years between 1945–49. The 'essence' of Indonesia then was this fundamental contradiction: it was a community united by its members' passions to achieve almost diametrically opposed futures. The official national slogan was (and is) 'Bhinekka Tunggal Ika', a Sanskrit-based phrase meaning 'Unity in Diversity'. The slogan or motto was invented in response to Indonesia's ethno-cultural diversity across the archipelago. The real unity at that time was based on the deep and passionate commitment to the new Indonesia; the real diversity was the passionate polarization on the question of the future.

When Vice President Muhammad Hatta argued that the revolution must be dammed up, he was arguing for the damming up of what made, what was making Indonesia. After his release from the Buru Island prison camp, Pramoedya was asked when he would write something about the history of the New Order. He said he couldn't because he had writer's block and that was because the current era had not yet reached its synthesis. He wrote:

> The era of Sukarno and the Trisakti doctrine was nothing but a sort of thesis. The New Order, an antithesis. Therefore, for me, it is something that in fact cannot be written about yet, a process that cannot yet be written as literature, because the national process does not yet constitute a totality, because it is in fact still heading for its synthesis.

Although perhaps Pramoedya's explanation of why he had writer's block is more of an excuse than a satisfactory reason, it is also a manifestation of how, for him, Indonesia was itself a process, and an unfinished process at that.

If the era of Sukarno was a thesis, then Pramoedya, Joesoef and Hasjim were agents of that thesis, along with 20 million other people. Thinking of the period before 1965 as 'thesis' and the Suharto period as 'anti-thesis' focuses on the aspect of a contradiction—an unresolved contradiction in Pramoedya's view—dominated by the two different periods of time. A contradiction exists, however, whichever side of the contradiction may dominate at any one moment, and continues to exist until it is resolved and a new phenomenon, embodying new contradictions, emerges. Before 1965, not only were the agents of Pramoedya's thesis active in society but also those who were the agents of the anti-thesis. One of the aspects of Indonesian political history that has created enormous confusion, and allowed various malevolent interpretations of that history, is that while the agents of Pramoedya's thesis were *dominant* in political life among society, they were not in control of the State itself. They were not in power. While Sukarno, their most popular articulator, was President of Indonesia, the other large organized forces supporting the Sukarnoist revolution, the PKI and the growing Left wing of the country's second biggest party, the populist PNI, were not in power. Sukarno was almost alone inside the State, with the key leaders of its armed wing against him, the bulk of the bureaucracy unfriendly and a huge cabinet created out of messy compromises, but which excluded the PKI and, apart from token representatives, the Left wing of the PNI.

From 1945, from the 1920s even, this antagonism had been unfolding. Between 1959–65, it sharpened. Pramoedya, Joesoef and Hasjim were among the many at the forefront of struggle on one side of this antagonism: those who stood for Sukarno's Socialism ala Indonesia. But what did that mean?

The answer to this question cannot be found by simply looking at the policies of the government, not even its progressive policies: free education, nationalization of most foreign companies, increased taxation on foreign oil firms, free health services, and solidarity with the Third World in foreign policy. There was also legislation passed to redistribute land from large landholders to the landless; although, the implementation of this policy was largely, though not totally, blocked in the countryside by the resistance of landlords with army and police support. The direction of these policies, pushed by Sukarno and supported by the Left parties in the society, indicated their general progressiveness. However, neither the economy nor the society was characterized by the smooth and effective implementation of such a direction.

There was political, social and economic chaos. By 1965, inflation was running at 600 per cent. In 1962, it was already 174 per cent. The economic chaos had several causes. Colonialism had left Indonesia with zero industry, almost no manufacturing, no twentieth-century-level public transport system, and no education system for the mass of population. Four years of Japanese occupation, while expanding basic literacy in the Indonesian language, only further ravaged the economy. That was followed by four years of armed struggle with the Dutch. In 1949, all Dutch enterprises were handed back to the Dutch, but between 1956–57 these were nationalized, and they then fell into the hands of army personnel, who proceeded to corrupt and bankrupt them.

Indonesia's most valuable export in the 1950s and very early 1960s, was rubber. In 1962, synthetic rubber was invented and rubber prices fell by around 40 per cent. The already underdeveloped and unindustrialized Indonesian economy was hit hard. Everything went into a tailspin. The emerging or embryonic progressive character of the Sukarnoist direction for Indonesia is easily lost in the mess, although there was absolutely no sign of a decline in his popularity during this period of a worsening economy.

Pramoedya, who strongly supported Sukarno and remained an admirer all his life, has said that Sukarno was a true manifestation of the 'national subject'. This is a big assertion and its meaning can only be understood if it is remembered that the nation-in-creation process was based on contradiction and that its birth, entry into the world and growth to maturity, requires a resolution of that contradiction. In Pramoedya's words, it requires a synthesis. For the millions who did continue to support Sukarno's ideas, including Pram, Joesoef and Hasjim, all of whom were in the thick of it, Socialism ala Indonesia was the prospective synthesis. Their support for Sukarno and his ideas did not flow from satisfaction with the immediate social and economic situation, but because those ideas summed up the synthesis they wished for: a condition that would give concrete and specific reality to the Trisakti: sovereignty in politics, standing on one's own feet in economics and real character in culture. This was a synthesis reflecting the deep desire for a nation of a people newly self-created out of the resistance to colonialism. Was it real? Was the struggle being pursued, being led properly and founded on a strong basis? Well, on the one hand, more than half the population had been won over to provide active support to this struggle, and, on the other, it collapsed under attack, unable to defend itself. Almost all of its central political leaders were killed or disappeared into prisons. They were not able to defend themselves.

Pramoedya and Hasjim went to Buru Island prison camp. Joesoef lived ten years in a cell in Jakarta. So were 20,000 others exiled, who had survived the killings. They could not escape imprisonment, exiled from the new Indonesia about to be created—especially those on Buru Island. But they had helped to create Indonesia in the first place. They did not surrender and so Indonesia survived, even while in exile from itself.

Chapter 4

Prelude to Exile

It must have been surreal during those first days, although none of the three men I interviewed and had other frequent discussions with, ever used that or a similar word to describe them. On the morning of 30 September 1965, President Sukarno was the overwhelmingly popular leader of the country with tens of millions of enthusiastic supporters. More than half the population had joined political parties or mass organizations that supported Sukarno and Socialism ala Indonesia. While there was opposition to Sukarno, and it had incurred some restrictions, his popularity was massive and genuine. His ideas dominated. His speeches were listened to by everybody, reported in all the newspapers and followed by the people. Rallies and marches by organizations that supported him were huge, filling the sports stadiums in the cities and the main streets in small towns. Sukarno had already been declared the Extension of the Voice of the People (Penyambung Lidah Rakyat). Even his opponents felt the need to use the revolutionary vocabulary he had created.

So, there was no sense in any aspect of the public atmosphere that Sukarno was under threat of being deposed. For the three men themselves: Hasjim's newspaper *Bintang Timur* was number one in street sales. Pramoedya's column was widely read by friends and foes. Joesoef was preparing for another international trip representing revolutionary Indonesia. It looked like a '*Sosialisme ala Indonesia*' government based on a coalition of Sukarnoists, the PKI and a purged more revolutionary PNI, was on the verge of winning power. Sukarno headed the Supreme Command for Retooling the Instruments of the Revolution (KOTRAR), which gave him the power to dismiss and replace most public officials. 'Max', Joesoef told me, 'we were just waiting for the order to go and drag out from their offices all the corrupt officials, the Kabir (capitalist bureaucrats) and throw them into the canals.' It seemed that victory was within reach, and it would come soon.

By the morning of the next day, it had all disappeared. Within a few days, Pramoedya was in the back of a pick-up being taken to a 'safe place'. Hasjim was being driven to prison in his Mercedes. Joesoef was living in limbo, waiting for his next detention. The mass killings and arrests had started. Sukarno was on the defensive. His ability to speak to the masses—the radio—was now in the hands of somebody else, General Suharto. Sukarno made many important speeches over the next several weeks but most of them were never heard, except by small audiences in the palace.[21] He was gone as a force. Hasjim's newspaper stopped publishing. Pramoedya's typewriter was seized from his hands. Joesoef was soon unilaterally replaced as a leader of the Indonesian Journalists' Union.

They did not explain their arrests as surreal. Of course, I talked to them through the eighties and nineties, and after that. They were looking back when they talked to me. There is another explanation for why there were surprised but not shocked. All the many ex-prisoners from 1965 that I have talked to, say that they were surprised and didn't understand what happened between the evening of 30 September and the morning of 1 October. They were puzzled and confused when they heard the radio announcements of 30 September Movement during the brief period they had control of the national radio station. In an atmosphere where victory seemed just around the corner, a strange mutiny in the armed forces seemed counter-intuitive to most of them. The President was with the Left; mass support was tremendous. Why the need for a 'coup'? So while there was surprise that evening, there was no sense of surrealism or unreality—no shock—at least among those most involved in politics.

The mass support for Sukarno was palpable. The Right-wing and anti-communists were almost hysterical with fear at the size of Sukarno's support. The open opposition was small and seemed isolated. It was isolated from the mass of people—though not from a big section of the army officer corps. The officer corps was also divided into pro- and anti-Sukarno factions. The PKI had a programme of winning over officers to align with their cause. Sukarno's personal following was also great, especially in the Air Force and Navy.

The bulk of the army top generals were, however, either anti-Sukarno or both anti-Sukarno and anti-PKI. Sukarno urged the poor millions to organize and mobilize, to protest the capitalist bureaucrats and foreign embassies of neo-colonial countries, to have *semangat* (great enthusiasm) for struggle. He urged them to volunteer for people's militia service and started the process of seeking weapons to arm a national people's militia as a fourth wing of the armed forces. The army generals wanted order, no mobilizations, better relations with the United States and Britain, and certainly no national popular militia.

If you were a journalist like Hasjim and Jocsoef, or a newspaper columnist like Pramoedya, or if you had links with the broad pro-Sukarno organizations and knew their leaders, as all three did, you would have heard about the army opposition and its moves. Your friends in different regions reported back how the army had banned this or that Left newspaper or activity. When peasants had occupied farmlands that landowners were refusing to re-distribute in accordance with new land reform laws, everybody could see that it was elements in the army and police that attacked the peasants. Pramoedya himself, as early as 1960, had been escorted to prison by an army officer, where he stayed for one year without trial, for writing articles defending the Chinese community against racist policies.

And yes, you heard the persistent rumours of a Council of Generals plotting against Sukarno. Tunnelling away under the rising mass support for Sosialisme ala Indonesia was a hardening opposition of armed elements (the army generals) who were talking to all anti-Sukarnoists in Indonesia and abroad. The army had worked with a group of anti-Left writers who issued a cultural manifesto meant to push back the growing hegemony of the ideas of people like Pramoedya, and of the mass cultural organizations associated with the Left parties. It had done the same with a group of journalists who had taken the name of the Body of Supporters of Sukarnoism. The army had started the process of sponsoring and forming rival trade unions to those under the sway of the Left.[22]

Sukarno had enormous popularity on the one hand, with people like Joesoef waiting for the order to act, but there was also a hardened armed opposition lurking in the shadows and popping out into the open occasionally, through its few civilian partners. The hostility ran deep in those circles. So, in the days after 30 September, there was surprise among the Left, but not a sense of unreality. Although, as we shall see from on the early prison experiences of Pramoedya and Hasjim, it took some people time to grasp the significance of the new reality. It was a reality of exile while Indonesia had its Suharto makeover.

From arrest to exile required a journey. It was a journey from one state of existence to another. For Pramoedya Ananta Toer and Hasjim Rachman, it also meant a physical journey by train, ship and on their own two legs. Even for Joesoef Isak whose exile was in Jakarta, there was a journey. The journey between states of existence was not simply matter of going from being free to imprisoned, from being at liberty to move around to being confined to a specific physical space. The journey into exile was a journey of saying goodbye to one Indonesia and arriving in a new 'Indonesia'.

For perhaps a million people, this was not a journey from one Indonesia to another but rather one that ended in death. Systematic killings, coordinated by the army, and with the cooperation of Rightist civilian militia, took place during the last months of 1965, throughout 1966, and into 1967 and 1968.[23] Perhaps the 20,000 people who survived in prison for the next fourteen years, were a small minority of the counter-revolution's victims. For the three men in this story, and hundreds of thousands of others, this journey was still one of terrible physical immediacy.

Prelude to Exile, But Not Really a Prelude: Jakarta 1965–68

The sound of 'screams and groans' marked and marred the first twenty-four hours of the journey for Pramoedya and Hasjim. They came later for Joesoef but were no less present.

Arrested on different days, both from home but under different pretexts, both Hasjim and Pramoedya transited through Jakarta's Central Military Command Centre. Pramoedya was taken there straight from his house. Told he was going somewhere safe, Pramoedya thought only to take with him his typewriter and an unfinished manuscript. 'I thought I would be able to work,' he told me. Pram's younger brother started to escape out the back but, still thinking they would be safe, he summoned his brother back, who was then also put in the back of the pick-up that was going to take them to that safe place.

The real situation was driven home to them when they heard the soldiers ask: 'Where is the rope?' They were tied with what is called the 'death knot'. 'I knew the death knot from the [1945–49] revolution. It was looped around the neck, so if you moved, it would strangle you.' It was then that Pramoedya started wondering to himself: 'Why did I let myself be taken by the military?' He tried to talk to lieutenant in-charge: 'I have manuscripts in the house. I am working on a collection of President Sukarno's short stories. Please safeguard them.' He never saw them again. An attempt to chat with a soldier in the back of the pick-up earned him a rifle butt to the face: 'he aimed for my nose, but I turned and it hit me in the cheek.' They were taken to the Strategic Military Command and then the Jakarta Military Command (KODAM). Pram was already bleeding from the leg, where he was hit by a pelted stone before his detention, and now also from his face. 'The screams and groans of the people being tortured never stopped. Everything was stolen from me. I asked a corporal what his rank was, and he punched me in my bleeding face as his answer. He threatened he would torture me.'

Listening to Pramoedya's retelling of these experiences—and it was the same with Hasjim and Joesoef's stories—this beginning of the counter-revolution reflected the initial confusion among those assigned to carry it out. The next evening, Pramoedya was summoned again by an officer who returned his Rolex watch, saying, 'Give it to your wife, she may need it for shopping now. Do not let anybody see it.' 'Then', said Pram, 'the officer saw that somebody had written on a blackboard "Dissolve the PKI!" He walked up and wiped it off shouting: "Who did that?"'

The tension in political life between the Left and Right, between supporters of Sukarno and those who were opposed to him and the PKI, had sharpened between 1960 and 1965. It was a lopsided polarization, with a clear majority of the population being enthusiastic Sukarnoists. Sukarno's articulation of aspirations of sovereignty and national character and for *revolusi* generated mass *semangat* (spirit) among millions of people. His ideas and charisma had an overwhelming presence. He was also the man who, on 17 August 1945, had proclaimed Indonesia's independence. His nationally broadcast speeches framed political discussion. His slogans were on almost everybody's lips.

From the very beginning of Indonesia's independence, however, there had always been resistance to his vision of mobilization, anti-imperialism and socialism. This resistance was primarily located in the conservative wing of the army, which became dominant in 1952 after most guerrilla fighters were decommissioned, leaving officers from the ex-Dutch colonial army and Japanese militia in control. Conservative religious political groups—Moslem and Catholic, but also Protestant and Hindu—also opposed Sukarno's Left-wing inclinations. Parliamentary social democrats, advocates of gradual and managed social change, mostly organized in the Socialist Party of Indonesia (PSI) were also hostile to Sukarno's politics of semangat and mass mobilization. While the forces opposed to Sukarno were smaller than those of his supporters, organized in the rapidly growing PKI and PNI, they had solid infrastructure—especially the army—and a well-educated leadership. Even so, it was impossible for most of Sukarno's opponents to openly oppose him. He was too popular and omnipresent. It was even impossible for anti-communists to openly oppose the PKI. This was not out of a fear of arrest for doing so, but out of fear of being alone in an ocean of pro-Sukarno and pro-socialist semangat. This was highlighted when a group of prominent journalists opposed to Sukarno's Left-wing trajectory organized themselves in the Body to Support Sukarnoism (BPS) as the vehicle for their criticism. Sukarno banned it for alleged links with foreign intelligence services.

Yes, a military officer could be overseeing the arrest, torture and interrogation of PKI and Sukarno supporters, but could also angrily wipe out the words 'Destroy the PKI' from the blackboard in the very place PKI prisoners were being maltreated. It was almost two years before General Suharto and the army stopped saying they had taken their actions to save the revolusi. Sukarno's vocabulary of revolution had momentum. Only after at least 500,000 people had been killed, could Suharto accelerate the process of switching the vocabulary of national politics away from semangat and revolusi to stabilitas, order and new use of the mantra 'Development' with a capital 'D'. Hasjim and Joesoef, and no doubt many others, experienced these anomalies.

But they were anomalies among the larger systematic murder and detention programme of the military. The propaganda offensive launched by Suharto during the first days after the events of 30 September was particularly aimed at stirring the prejudices of the officer corps. The gruesome stories (all untrue[24]) of the sexualized torture of the murdered generals and the massive military parade for the funeral of the seven-year-old daughter of Army General Nasution at his home portrayed the army itself as the victim of communist horrors. Intense hostility among the army and conservative religious political groups was strengthened. Mercy was the anomaly among the cruelty, persisting despite widespread confusion.

'The interrogation officer put a pencil in between the young man's fingers and pressed down hard to make him scream,' explained Hasjim about his first time in an interrogation room. Like Pramoedya, he told of the ongoing screams and groans that echoed throughout the rooms, this time in Salemba prison. Apart from the hit with the rifle butt and the punch on the first day of his detention, none of the three men, Pramoedya, Hasjim or Joesoef, were tortured.

Interrogation and threat of torture were Pramoedya and Hasjim's first experience of imprisonment. In prison in Jakarta, between October 1965 until 1968, the next issue was survival. Hasjim and Pramoedya were both in the same prison in Jakarta. It is clear from their memories of it that it was quite a shocking experience. It was not the jail conditions—Pramoedya had been in jail without trial for a year in 1960. The bad conditions in the jails were well-known to him. What shocked them was the attitudes of many of their fellow prisoners.

The situation before everybody's arrest was a split reality. There was a massively popular president whose popularity assured his supporters of certain and approaching victory. Sukarno was already president. It was just a matter of retooling the state to bring into the state his supporters: the PKI, the Left wing of the growing PNI, and other smaller Left groups. In many ways, as the primary advocate of Socialism ala Indonesia in its fullest form, Sukarno was in a minority in his own government, even though he had a clear majority of popular support. He had spurned elections after 1957, so retooling the state apparatus from its peak (the presidency) was the only path left to bring change. This was another manifestation of the split reality.

From how Pramoedya and Hasjim related their first experiences of prison in Jakarta, it seems clear that this split reality also helped form a consciousness among the prisoners. Was their arrest an anomaly? A temporary incident? Or did it reflect a more permanent change in the world outside—from which, that time onwards, they were excommunicated? Should they insist that their jailers treat them according to their rights as prisoners and refuse to cooperate unless they did, or was the reality that they were imprisoned by deeply hostile forces and their survival would depend solely on their own resources?

In Salemba prison, Pramoedya told me that Hasjim played a major role in organizing prisoners to make sure they survived, even as others argued that it was not necessary and that it was the regime's responsibility to look after them. 'Hasjim wants to turn the prison into a hotel,' some scorned his efforts.

Hasjim was the publisher of *Bintang Timur*. He was not a writer; he was an organizer—he who got things done. He had enormous energy, which reverberated through his laugh and exploded forth from his smile. He was an irrepressible person, the man whom, before Indonesia had any war planes, headed off to India in 1946 to study to become one of Indonesia's first pilots, until he got waylaid to smuggle guns from

Malaya to Sumatra. In Salemba prison, as Pramoedya also told me, Hasjim played a big role in the organization for survival.

Food was the first issue. 'We could never be sure we would get enough food every day. Once we were given corn, but only sixty to eighty kernels. We had to spread that amount across lunch and dinner. Sixty to eighty kernels! It was like eating watermelon seeds,' said Hasjim in one of our interviews. Hasjim told me how he made a deal with the warden to let the prisoners grow Java spinach in the prison grounds. They also grew morning glories and tomatoes, using human wastewater as fertilizer. Somehow Hasjim got permission to get in a tractor to prepare more ground for planting vegetables. He organized a medicine bank when he moved to the other big jail in Jakarta, Tangerang, smuggling in tablets that were then doled out to those who needed them. He, and many others as well, organized to ration any food that arrived from outside. He organized for the walls in his prison block to be whitewashed, in a war against the bugs and mites. Cigarettes and bottles of 'black and white' delivered from the outside, he said, made the prison authorities amenable. He told me part of this story:

> It wasn't easy, many were against what I was doing. Not just the less educated prisoners, but also the so-called intellectuals. Why would I do such a thing, they said. They didn't want to take any risks; they didn't want the responsibility. "Why do you have to do this, grow food for ourselves, we are political prisoners!" That was what they were saying to me. I was a bit surprised to hear these intellectuals, these so-called progressive revolutionaries, say these things to me. I could not understand. There were 3,000 political prisoners in Salemba, and they all came from different backgrounds . . . The first thing, I thought, was I had to survive physically. I mean, I didn't want to be carried out of the prison, I wanted to walk out of it on my own two feet! So, I grew the morning glories. And the harvest was always good, we could eat all the vegetables we wanted. So much better than our official ration of corn. But still, it wasn't easy. As I said, most people thought, "we are political prisoners, why do we have to do anything ourselves?"

And we had to water the vegetable plants with dirty water from the cesspool, since we didn't have any fertilizer . . . The annoying thing, though, the people who didn't want to raise a hand in planting these vegetables would still ask for their ration once we harvested them. Their argument was always the same: "why do we have to do anything to feed ourselves?" They even accused me once of having been enlisted by one of the "peace corps". Why? Because I was always able to offer them help when they needed it. They thought I was working for the authorities, because somehow, I was able to help them out.

Hasjim was the angriest about those who had been intellectuals and leaders before their arrest, but sought refuge in keeping a low profile once in prison. There were enough of the others—and many of those from worker and farmer backgrounds—to be able to get things done. Pramoedya, Joesoef and Hasjim, all spoke highly of the spirit and helpful attitudes of the grassroots activists who ended up in prison. Even with all these struggles, people still suffered from hunger, weakened by malaria or other illnesses, many dying. The details and numbers of such cases will never be known.

Pramoedya was the writer in the prison cell whose mind never stopped absorbing everything around him; surviving, sharing his food with other prisoners. Hasjim was the larger-than-life Publisher with a capital 'P', afflicted perhaps with a hyperactivity syndrome. I do not draw this conclusion simply from these interviews with him, and how he remembered the experiences in the Jakarta prisons, but from witnessing his role in establishing the Hasta Mitra publishing company in 1980, less than a year after being released from Buru Island prison camp and while still under orders to report to the military weekly. But that story is for later.

It was in 1969, that the final leg of Pramoedya and Hasjim's journey into exile began. Taken first to the prison island of Nusakambangan, a few thousand prisoners were then loaded onto a rundown ship that chugged slowly, when it wasn't stalling, to Buru Island in Eastern Indonesia. As in the prisons, the food got less and less as they days went by. Water was hard to get. Forget being able to wash. Overflow from the toilets washed into the cargo hold where hundreds, if not more, were crammed. All the time, announcements blared from the loudspeakers, proclaiming to them how a new and better future awaited them. 14,000 men—women were imprisoned in a camp on Java and in normal jails—ended up in the Buru island prison camp. It was in this camp, carved out of the Buru bush and scrub, that the embodiment of the original Indonesia in the book *This Earth of Mankind*, was to appear.

Joesoef's Prelude in Limbo

It took almost three years for Joesoef Isak to be properly imprisoned— in 1968. He could not tell me exactly how many times he was detained between October 1965 and his arrest in late 1968. 'I was often taken by one intelligence unit that didn't know that I had already been detained for interrogation. Once, I was kept for a couple of months and the place where I was being kept got overcrowded so they let me out without ever being interrogated,' Joesoef explained, laughing. He added:

> Once they had sent me to a Chinese school that they had converted into a detention centre. We were put into a classroom, maybe forty or fifty people, we were sleeping on the floor. Once, I was arrested not far from there, on this same street, Kramat, in a house. The house was no more than 150 square metres, the land it was on may be 300 square metres. But there were more than 200 of us inside that small house. We were packed like sardines. All the space in the house was crammed with people, we were sleeping in the yard, even on the small terrace in front of the toilet.

It was in these interviews that he told me the story of the spiked eel. It has stayed for me for a long time, and I am rewriting it here as follows:

> The humidity was from sweat and not the air. The sad singing was the whimpers as they dabbed alcohol on the wounds. The music was the brushing of bodies and clothes against each other in the tiny room. The percussion-introduced break was the clang of an opening gate. The crescendo followed the approach of booted footsteps. It ended

as another human being was thrown to the floor. The notes were the
scores left by the spikes of the dried eel across his back. Another was
taken. Do not fear the pain, one said, you do not die, you do come back.
For most, yes, it was true. But not for the other 1 million.

People spent their time chatting. There was nothing else to do.
In that early period, everybody wanted to know the answers about
what had happened. Had there been a real coup? Who was behind it
all? Who else had been arrested? Who had disappeared? There were
also those worried about their family's future: would they be able to
keep their job? What about their pension later on? And then would
they be released, or taken away somewhere unknown?

During one of his periods of detention, his wife, Asni, came under
pressure to sell their home at a greatly undervalued price. This often
happened to people being harassed and those who were threatened
with arrest or worse. They had to take the sum they were offered and
move to a smaller place elsewhere. After Pramoedya was arrested, his
house was confiscated. Almost fifty years later, Pramoedya, as stubborn
as ever, took the owner to court but lost the case.

The government also moved to reconstitute the leadership of the
Indonesian Journalists' Union (PWI). At a meeting which he attended
along with notable anti-communist journalists such as Jakob Oetama
from the main Catholic-owned newspaper, Joesoef was forced to
resign and Oetama and others took over. Oetama later became the
main owner Gramedia Publishing company and the newspaper *Kompas*
that came to dominate the Indonesian press during the Suharto era
and continues to do so until now.

Joesoef's interrogations, unlike many others, were not violent.
The pattern of questioning was also always the same: 'Did you know
in advance about the 30th of September Movement?' Apart from
acknowledging that all kinds of rumours were circulating among
journalists in the months before 30 September, Joesoef could only
explain that he didn't know anything. He was not known as a member
of the PKI, so there were no interrogations to try to squeeze out of
him names of cadres or other information about the internal workings
of the PKI. This was the information sought from other prisoners

through torture. Clearly, the delay and confusion in relation to Joesoef's arrest was partly because, while known as a solid supporter of Sukarno and especially of his international policies of Asia–Africa solidarity, he was not known as a PKI member. For a long time, he had been more associated with the PKI's ideological arch enemy, the Indonesian Socialist Party (PSI), oriented to Western social democracy, and had edited the centrist newspaper *Merdeka*. Joesoef himself explained his analysis this way:

> My experience was a bit different to the other journalists. Most of them were rounded up in October—the incident happened on 30 September—herded into trucks, and sent to the Salemba jail. I managed to escape that; they took their time arresting me. Perhaps the authorities made some political calculation. Because of my international standing. I was a practising journalist, but I was also the president of the Asian-African Journalists' Association. I was also the vice president of the International Organization of Journalists (IOJ), whose headquarters were in Prague. So, they were a bit wary of my international standing.

He was detained in another unidentified safehouse in the Banteng Square area of Jakarta, when he and several others were summonsed and shepherded into a bus, which took them to Salemba prison.

> I can never forget it. That was the first time I saw the inside of a prison. There was nothing romantic about it, no feeling that we were now heroes, jailed for just doing our jobs as journalists. What we saw was a nightmare, there was nothing romantic about it, no. There was a special way of doing things in Salemba. The new prisoners would be put in a special bloc, which they used to call the isolation bloc. There were twenty of these isolation blocs, they had the bigger cells. By big, I mean they were two by two metres, more or less, that was the big cell. Cell number one to number eighteen were in one long row, then there were two bigger cells. The first six cells were reserved for real criminals. Murderers, armed robbers—one of them had killed eight men on his own—they were kept in the first six cells. When we came in, that

is where we were headed, hehehe. Three to four of us were jammed
into each cell. They took all our clothes and our food. And I was a
bit unfortunate as well, usually people were only kept for two or three
months in these isolation cells, then they would be transferred to the
regular bloc with all the other political prisoners. But I was kept in the
isolation bloc for almost a year. It was a year of tragedy for me, to be
imprisoned together with these serious criminals.

Joesoef's journey into exile had thus ended. The exile itself
had started.

Exiled Away from Where?

Survival defined Pramoedya, Hasjim and Joesoef's experience from 1
October 1965 and was, in many ways, to continue to do so from thereon.
Of course, a million did not survive and were slaughtered. Survival
defined life for another 20 million or so people who had campaigned for
Sukarno or the PKI. Most avoided long-term imprisonment, but they
were subjected for three decades, to the oppressive indignity of having
to obtain a 'Letter of Clean Environment' from the authorities if they
wanted to travel, change address or find work. A 'clean environment'
meant that neither yourself, nor anybody in your family or among your
friends were in any way 'connected' to the PKI.

Surviving in Jakarta's prisons meant looking inwards to the
world within the prison walls, isolated from the nation-changing
developments happening outside. Families were sometimes able to
visit and mention what was happening on the outside, although the fate
of family and friends dominated conversation during those short visits,
when they did occur. In this sense, the exile from Indonesia began
immediately because the country was being remade, almost completely.
Its personality was to change from one created by the mass struggle for
political independence, to that of one lying passive under the heels of
philistine military bureaucrats, which of course, meant it would also lead
to the rise of dissident personalities. Old contradictions were buried
and hidden, not resolved and removed. New dissident personalities

would emerge in the 1970s, reflecting the unresolved state of those contradictions.

1965–68 were the years of consolidation of the counter-revolution. This was a pre-emptive counter-revolution. The Indonesian government under President Sukarno during the six years of presidential rule between 1959–65 was not a revolutionary government. It did not begin to seriously implement Sosialisme ala Indonesia or any kind of socialist programme. The largest political party in the country was the PKI, and it supported a socialist programme, but the PKI was only symbolically part of the government, controlling no important ministries, nor any part of the armed forces. The second largest party was the PNI, which was growing rapidly. The PNI's leadership also only had a symbolic presence in the cabinet. Sukarno's allies inside his own cabinet were few and mostly individuals without any significant political organizations behind them. Most of the cabinet were in the 'centre' or opportunists. Sosialisme ala Indonesia was impossible without a new government based on a Sukarno–PKI–PNI (Left) alliance. The counter-revolution led by General Suharto was not overthrowing a socialist government but preventing one from coming to power on the wave of mass popularity for Sukarno. Sukarno, the man who proclaimed independence for the nation, and had been president since 17 August 1945, was, in many ways, alone in government.

Economic conditions under this ambiguous government of the 1960s were also bad. There was no oil income at this point and rubber was the country's most important export. In 1962, the price of rubber collapsed as synthetic rubber came into production. The Indonesian economy was devastated. Earlier, all the Dutch-owned enterprises had been nationalized in the aftermath of an anti-colonial protest wave. These companies constituted virtually 99 per cent of the modern sector of the economy—a legacy of colonialism. These nationalizations happen to take place during a period of martial law and an armed revolt against the government. Most of these companies fell into the hands of army officers who had no experience of managing businesses, especially ones with no capital. Many of these officers used these businesses as cash cows. Production collapsed. The drop in rubber prices and the collapse in production sent the economy into a rapid downward spiral. Inflation exploded. This situation was further worsened by the reality of destabilizing effect of heightening political tensions.

Thus, the Indonesia that Suharto began forging after October 1965 had two weirdly anomalous sides to it. There was the stabilization of the economy, as foreign capital and loans replaced what Dutch nationalization and collapsed rubber prices had taken away. This also soon meant that the army's management of the nationalized businesses had to be accountable to the government to maintain credibility in the eyes of its foreign backers. On the other hand, the prospect of a future with a mobilized and involved population was replaced by one of passive not-quite-citizens, terrorized by the example of mass killings and jailing, and the ever-present demand to see somebody's 'Letter of Clean Environment'. Of course, as the decades passed, the absence of a public with agency meant that the economic benefits of the growth in GDP financed by foreign loans and investment also became increasingly skewed.

In prison, the world was defined by the cell and survival. Outside, the counter-revolution was oppressing into existence a different Indonesia, where its inherent contradictions were buried underground, and its history erased. During those first three years, a lot happened.

University students affiliated with the banned Right-wing Masyumi Party and other students involved in non-political social organizations, were mobilized in Jakarta and other cities against Sukarno and the PKI, and in support of Suharto. They were a small minority among politically active students at the time, but almost immediately the much larger student organizations affiliated to the PKI and PNI were suppressed—their members arrested or worse. The anti-Sukarno students were organized into the Indonesian University Student Action Front (KAMI), which worked hand-in-glove with the military over the next few years. Many KAMI figures later became government officials or MPs in a new, purged, pro-Suharto parliament.

There was another student organization, the High School Students Action Front, KAPPI. Many of these younger anti-Sukarnoists came from longstanding anti-Sukarno families. In the 1970s, many of them emerged as critics and opponents of the Suharto regime. This younger, high school students who protested against Sukarno in the 1960s, while never being able to rid themselves of the anti-Sukarno and anti-PKI sentiments, did take their cries for democracy seriously and found themselves in a contradiction with the Suharto regime later; some of them also ended up in jail in the seventies.

The 1965–66 student demonstrations provided a rather tiny fig leaf to cover up the militarist character of the new Suharto regime, as the arrests and killings occurred throughout the end of 1965, 1966, 1967 and into 1968. In 1968, some PKI members regrouped in a mountainous area of Java and attempted to launch an armed comeback, but were defeated.[25] On 12 March 1967, what was left of the People's Consultative Assembly after the arrests of Sukarnoists and Leftists, appointed Suharto the Acting President and removed Sukarno, who ended up confined to his house. Soon after that, a new law was passed, providing very pleasant conditions for foreign investment in Indonesia.

By 1968, the PKI and all pro-Sukarno forces had been obliterated. Suharto was president. The army, through the Operational Command for the Restoration of Security and Order (KOPKMTIB), established by Suharto in October 1968, became the supreme political authority in Indonesia. All the preconditions for a forced makeover of Indonesia were in place. The makeover would need at least 20,000 activists out of those who had escaped massacre to remain in jail until 1978. They lived in a different world, even if one created by the makeover process. Most of these 20,000 would be shifted to a prison camp on Buru Island.

Chapter 5

Exiled: Buru Island

As I may have mentioned, I met Pramoedya, Joesoef and Hasjim for the first time in 1980. They had been out of prison for about year. At that time, I was the Second Secretary (Development Assistance) at the Australian Embassy in Jakarta. I had come directly to Jakarta from the aid section of the Ministry of Foreign Affairs in Canberra. In Canberra, I had become friends with an Indonesian PhD student, Raharjo Suwandi. Raharjo had studied under Pramoedya at the Res Publika University before 1965. It was Raharjo who brought me for the first time to Pramoedya's home in Jakarta. By that time in 1980, Pramoedya had begun his journey towards international fame. Before the 1980s, he was well-known to students in Indonesia, but otherwise mostly unknown. But Pramoedya had become a key figure in campaigns against political imprisonment in the 1970s and 1980s.

By 1980, my main experience with Indonesian literature, apart from as an undergraduate student, had been in translating the play by W.S. Rendra called *The Struggle of the Naga Tribe*, which was published in Australia and the United States, and performed in English in Australia and several other countries. I had read some of Pramoedya's books as a student, but I didn't know that much about him. I was tantalized, though, by one of Raharjo's stories about his lecturer, Pramoedya Ananta Toer.

Raharjo told me that he had been very seriously reprimanded by Pram once for not following his research guidance. He had been tasked to interview an individual about a prominent political figure, but Raharjo decided to interview somebody else, another politician close to the figure he was researching. Pram, said Raharjo, was angry and told him to go and interview the person he had been instructed to question. 'Pram was right,' said Raharjo, 'I learned so much more.'

'Who was it?' I asked.

'It was the political figure's barber!'

I have never forgotten this story. It immediately told me that Pramoedya was a man who had a true sociological imagination and scoffed at no source of information. I learned later, of course, that while absorbing information and perspectives from every kind of source, he also embraced and loved documentaries. I once witnessed him at home in a state of extreme excitement because somebody had delivered him a diary of a Dutch district officer of the East Indies from the early twentieth century. And he was renowned for having thrown himself into reading the newspapers from the early twentieth century in the national library.

It was in my meetings with Pram and Hasjim and Joesoef during 1980 and 1981, before I was recalled from my position as Second Secretary for being 'undiplomatic', when I first heard all the stories of their experiences in Buru Island prison camp and in Salemba prison.

Pramoedya and Max Lane.

Pramoedya and Max Lane, January 1981.

These experiences were still fresh in their minds, of course. Pramoedya had been repeating many of these stories to the scores and scores of visitors, including foreigners, who came to see him after his release. The same was true for Joesoef and Hasjim, even if they had fewer callers. There were at least 14,000 people detained at the camp on Buru Island and thousands in other jails. As I relate briefly some of these experiences as told to me, the reader should remember that there were thousands of other experiences which may have been different or remembered differently. Other prisoners, especially those with a talent for writing, have written their own memoirs of their experiences.[26] Indeed, Pramoedya himself wrote a substantial collection of essays and reflections about this while he was still on Buru. These were published in Indonesia in the 1980s by Hasta Mitra, under the title *Nyanyi Sunyi Seorang Bisu* (*Silent Song of the Mute*). An abridged version of this was also published in English by Hyperion, and later licensed to Penguin Books under the title, *A Mute's Soliloquy*.

In this chapter, I wish to tell the story, as Pramoedya and Hasjim told it to me, of their time on Buru, as those experiences relate the writing of Pram's books on Buru and their joint commitment to publish them once when (that is, if) they were released. I heard these stories all through 1980–81, and then during later short visits through the 1980s. It was in 1993 that while working with the filmmaker Gil Scrine and his academic friend, Hart Cohen, we recorded the two rounds of interviews with the three men. Although, of course, influence by the hundreds of discussions I had with them in the 1980s, I quote mostly from these recorded interviews.

I will tell Joesoef Isak's story in a separate chapter. His experiences in Salemba prison were very different from those of Pramoedya's and Hasjim's on Buru. Being imprisoned in Jakarta prepared Joesoef for the role he was to play later as Hasta Mitra's editor and politician.

So, August 1969. Buru. Point of arrival was the port town of Namlea. Buru was an undeveloped island almost three times the size of Bali. The indigenous inhabitants of Buru did minimal agriculture, and still engaged in hunting, equipped with spears and machetes. Namlea was a small trading port, whose inhabitants came from many parts of the archipelago. The military units there were from the Pattimura Division, whose soldiers were mainly drawn from Eastern Indonesia, although its officers were of various ethnicities.

As the prisoners were taken ashore in a landing craft, the first to arrive, said both Pram and Hasjim, were subject to beatings by the Pattimura soldiers. The town itself was like a ghost town. Its residents had been told that an army of murderers and rapists would be arriving and that everybody should stay inside: that's what the two of them learned later. They stayed in some barracks in the town for several days before being taken inland to where they would be permanently held. They would be isolated from the world.

Exiled, as the Dutch colonialists had done to all those who had rebelled against them. Suharto was doing it on an even bigger scale. The site where Pramoedya and Hasjim were to stay was only easily accessible by boat. They travelled along the river observing the local boats shipping sago to Namlea. They arrived, walked along rough paths for several kilometres and to their new home—not yet fully built. The half-finished and roughly made barracks said so much about how their time there would unfold and about the character of New Order Indonesia.

Those first days were vivid in Pramoedya's memory, even in 1993:

So we had to finish the barracks ourselves. The roofs were made from leaves, so were the walls. I had seen the work contract for the camps, and according to it, the foundation should've been made from concrete, and the timber from, at least, second-grade wood. But when we got there, there were no concrete foundations, no second-grade wood. They were all softwood and would've collapsed in no time. So we built our own camps. And there were no open lands. According to the contract, we would get a field ready to be planted. But there were no such thing. So we had to clear the land ourselves. The wild grass needed weeding. So everyone worked with no tools. The only tool available was eh . . . what was that . . . machete . . . from metal . . . just metal, no steel in it. If we hit a rattan frond with it, it would break. We couldn't cut anything cleanly.

So we also had to pave roads with no tools. Grass had to be pulled with hands. And there was a type of grass with three sets of leaves. Each leaf had three sharp edges, like knives, they could cut your skin. And if your skin got cut, since you weren't eating well, not eating enough protein, your wound would get infected. According to the rules, we should have been getting 600 grams of rice. After about two weeks, we received only 400 grams. The commander said the rest had been put aside in case of emergencies. But thereafter, it was always 400 grams. And then we no longer had rice, it was replaced with bulgur. The bulgur was mixed up with rice crusts, cardamom and urine. If we ate it, especially myself, we had to go to the toilet immediately to get it all out again. So there it went out again. I became so weak that whenever I had to go to the toilet, and I had to squat . . . then I wouldn't be able to get up again, I had to pull myself up with my hands.

Hasjim detailed how there were three barracks they had to finish building in that first phase, although later there were seven. Each barrack housed 600 people. They had walls and floors of beaten bamboo. The roof was made of palm fronds. Both Hasjim and Pram noted that they later found out that the government in Jakarta had allotted a good budget for the building of the barracks and other camp facilities, but obviously that money had been appropriated by the corrupt officers.

'We were paid with some sugar, coffee and cigarettes for the work we did. That was all,' said Hasjim.

Pramoedya explained how he had caught a glimpse of documents, which set out that the barracks should be made of hardwood and other good materials, but they made it from bamboo and palm fronds. I was told a myriad of stories about the corruption at the camp. Prisoners would wake up to find a sign on banana trees they had planted using wild seedlings: 'This tree belongs to sergeant so and so, or corporal so and so.' The guards would find out who planted the tree and threaten them with beatings if the harvest wasn't delivered to them. Later, when some prisoners had chickens, the eggs would disappear. 'One day, a prisoner spread cow dung all over the ground near where the chickens laid their eggs. That night, we hard angry shouts as the guard got messed with shit. We all laughed. But the offending prisoner was beaten the next day.'

By all accounts, after a first few disastrous years of hunger and illness, the prisoners achieved impressive output from the fields that they had had to clear and plant themselves. 'Even with very poor soil that had to be burned and dried to get rid of the acidity, we eventually had very good rice harvests,' Pramoedya explained. There were chickens and some cattle, too. The prisoners, though, lived off what was left over, with the officers and guards taking most of the output.

If corruption was one fundamental feature of the Buru Camp regime, violence was the other. While many died of starvation and disease in the first years, others were killed, or tortured or beaten. The reality of persistent violence, especially in the first years, provided a part of the context for the creation of the *This Earth of Mankind* stories. I asked Pramoedya about violence in the camp:

> Relatively, not many [murders], compared to the number of people who were there. The ones murdered by the military there . . . eh . . . there were fewer than 100 people, but they were murdered, and the murderers have never had to go to court until now. The murders started in 1971. In 1971, eleven people were murdered in one incident and dozens were severely injured. That happened in 1971. And after that, more murders took place every year.

At one point, things were very bad. In one of the units, five people had been shot dead. And it continued, he related:

> So, the situation was so intense, several people were shot dead, one of them because he was looking for—checking on—his chickens at night. If we had to go to the toilet at night, we had to bring a light, and this man didn't bring a light. Then there was also a friend whose job was to take care of the fish in the pond. Since his fish were always stolen by the military, he wanted to go check on them one night. He was also shot dead.

Beatings were common too in the atmosphere of arbitrary abuse. Once, said Pram, the guards woke them all up after midnight for a special roll call. Hasjim also remembered the incident:

> There was a curfew, we weren't allowed to get out of our barrack at night. A big problem whenever you had to go to the toilet. One day— this was quite funny—the place we were in, our isolation barrack, got a surprise visit from dozens of soldiers and security guards. Each unit used to have a guard. This time, there were thirty to forty of them, and they surrounded us. They were wielding guns with the bayonets at the ready. "Get up! Get out!" they were barking at us. We were all startled, didn't know what was going on. They were trying to scare us, "Hands up! All of you, hands up!" Everyone came out of the barrack and outside, it was pitch dark. We stood in a row, me, Pram, Prapto, Edi and the others.
>
> One of their seniors, a lieutenant named Tris, he was from the National Military Academy in Magelang, we could see that from the ring he used to wear—he told his boys to search our hands. They did their search and then this man Tris asked us, "Do you know what night this is?" We didn't know what he was talking about. "No idea, Sir," we said. "You don't remember? This is the night your friends murdered my generals," he said. We understood what he meant then, he . . . he . . . [went on] "Tonight is the night you murdered those generals. This is how it happened, what's happening to you now," he said. We didn't say anything, what could you say? "You also killed my seniors in the

academy, you killed those generals, that's why you're here now. But, now, let's forget that, now you've got to sing for us." "What do you want us to sing, Sir?" we said.

So this was in the middle of the night, two in the morning, you got woken up in the middle of a jungle, basically, and were being forced to sing. We sang the anthem 'Padamu Negeri'. There we were, just out of bed, still in our underwear, wrapped in our blankets, singing 'Padamu Negeri'. We all sang. "Louder," they said, "Sing it louder! Come on! Stop, now stop, silence! Now take a moment of silence!" They told us to take a moment of silence to remember the dead generals. So we all stood still in the dark, the only light coming from their torchlight. Then one of them with the torchlight went up to Pramoedya, "You, when you were praying just now, who were in your mind?" Pram quickly answered, maybe because he was afraid or nervous, "I was thinking of my wife and kids." Ha ha ha. 'What did you say?' The soldier was angry. And Pram suddenly realized what he was supposed to say. "Oh yes, Sir, the heroes of the revolution," he said. Ha ha ha. He was thinking about his wife and kids, imagine that. We were practically in shock when we heard him say that to the lieutenant, who was trying his hardest to terrorize us. But in the end, he remembered that we should have been praying for the heroes of the revolution. That night was unforgettable. We nearly died of fright when Pram said that to the lieutenant. He was so mad, ha ha . . .

Murder, beatings, theft and corruption naturally corroded morale among the prisoners. Some tried to escape, fleeing into the bush. But neither the bush nor the indigenous inhabitants could help. The bush, a very new jungle, held very little food. And the Buru people kept away.

By the early 1970s, Pramoedya and Hasjim and several other prisoners were separated from the main body of prisoners for a year or more, in a hut they had built themselves. The prison authorities wanted to separate what they called the 'kepala batu'—the stubborn ones. There were a few intellectuals there, including the law professor Suprapto, but according to Pramoedya, also several informants working for the guards. The hut was not like the bungalows that the officers lived in. 'The officers had ones like those you see now in Bali,' Hasjim laughed, 'Romantic, heh.'

It was in this hut that Pramoedya first started to tell the stories that were later woven into the *This Earth of Mankind* novels.

> I started to figure out ways to boost their spirit, because being imprisoned on this island was bad enough, we shouldn't have to deal with low morale on top of it. So, that was when I began telling the *This Earth of Mankind* story, in our isolation hut.
>
> I still remember the first time I started storytelling. It was at night after working; on the veranda, the veranda for the barrack that we built ourselves. I was sitting on a bench that I made myself, the others were standing or sitting down, listening. Among the listeners were Pak Hasjim and a shadow puppet master, a *dalang*.

Already more than five years in the camp, with no materials— reading materials were banned, except for religious books— Pramoedya told the story, with its historical context, out of memory and imagination. Of course, as Pramoedya emphasized to me in the interview, the spoken version would naturally be very different from the written version, which he began in 1975, after he was allowed a typewriter and paper. 'But the spirit was the same,' he emphasized.

It was the story from the first novel, *This Earth of Mankind*, that circulated among the prisoners. It was set at the turn of the twentieth century when the Dutch still ruled supreme in the East Indies. Its central figure, a Javanese village girl sold by her parents as a concubine to a Dutch sugar plantation manager, develops as a person of great strength of character, knowledge and understanding, despite and because of her oppressed circumstances. She resists and teaches others to resist, including a young Javanese high school student, growing alienated from Javanese feudalism—from whence he came—and soon to be forced into questioning European moral superiority. Bravery and strength of character in the face of oppression and in the process of resistance were themes that had the potential to revive morale.

There are, of course, no tape recordings of Pramoedya's storytellings. Pram told me how he remembered the process, as did Hasjim. No doubt there are scores, even hundreds, of other memories of this experience. Pram said the spoken version was in the same spirit as the written, and I suspect the depth of his historical understanding of that very initial awakening of a modern and future-thinking consciousness must have coloured his storytelling. Its depth in the novels is part of its thrilling genius.

Before I continue and describe how Pram and Hasjim remember this process, it will be useful to remind the reader of one of the things that Pramoedya had been up to in the years before his arrest in 1965. As I have mentioned, he edited the cultural pages of the daily *Eastern Star* newspaper, published by Hasjim. Many of his essays in *Eastern Star* discussed characters from Indonesian history, who Pramoedya felt had been forgotten or even denied by existing history, mainly written by the Dutch. He had devoted himself to historical research since the late 1950s, studying the press from the turn of the century, and also the literary output of the period and whatever other document or oral source he had time to get hold of. He had written articles, collated them into a book on Kartini, the first Enlightenment figure to emerge in Indonesia.

He had done the same with the history of the Chinese community in Indonesia, defending their contributions and opposing anti-Chinese policies of the time, using a critical socialist framework. In 1960, he was arrested and detained for a year without trial because of those articles. And in his essays in *Eastern Star*, he had already written about almost all the historical figures that were to appear in or be the sources of inspiration for his *This Earth of Mankind* and its three sequels.

Before 1965, he was seething with anger and curiosity at Indonesia's stagnation, the widespread corruption and intellectual backwardness. He had been to the People's Republic of China in the late 1950s and compared the advances in social welfare and culture there with Indonesia. He became driven to understand the causes of this difference. Eventually, he determined that it was necessary to go to Indonesia's 'creation story' at the turn of the twentieth century. This was the period from the emergence of the first Enlightenment figure, Kartini, to the activities of the first newspaper publisher with a future-looking oppositionist perspective, Tirto Adhi Soerjo. I can only imagine that in the year before his arrest, and no doubt as he sat in a Jakarta cell and then later slaved in the camp to build barracks and open fields, his mind and soul were seething, too, in frustration at not being able to reveal what he had discovered: the contradictions and ambiguities, as well as the adventurous and creative energies of resistance and of discovering the possibility of a future.

This is the reason why I am sure that Pramoedya was correct in telling me that the spirit of the spoken version was the same as that of the written version. It also explains the power of the stories amongst the prisoners and later amongst Indonesian youth when the books were published. A creation story that lived and breathed excitement. Yes, the story was a melodrama of young love, heroism and struggle, but it would have been told, as it was written, as a revelation of the country's real creation story, that had been incubating inside Pramoedya's mind during the years before 1965.

So the storytelling on the veranda of the barracks did not just pop out of nowhere, nor was it only or simply a response to the drop in morale. It spoke to who the prisoners were or should be: proud Indonesians, even if in exile.

Listening to Pramoedya and Hasjim's descriptions of what happened, there seemed to be multiple scenarios of storytelling: on the veranda at night; inside the hut before sleeping; among prisoners while they waited for roll call. Pram explained that he did not tell the stories in dalang mode, adopting different voices for different characters. He was not a dalang—in fact, he was a trenchant critic of the *wayang* culture, although he was in awe of the vocal skills of a good dalang. One of his most powerful essays is 'The Last Time I Watch Wayang'. 'Max,' he repeatedly told me, 'wayang has no place whatsoever for the common people. It portrays only gods and soldiers.' His storytelling was in the same mode as the novels when they appeared: straight Indonesian language narration, the atmosphere created by what people said and what they did, with cause and effect, direct as well as dialectical, portrayed in his wonderful filmic manner.

The story of Nyai Ontosoroh, the concubine who fought and overcame her humiliation, her beautiful but fragile daughter, Annelies, and the politically awakening young man, Minke, certainly enthralled the prisoners who heard the stories. It is impossible to tell from the interviews with Pramoedya and Hasjim, how many of the thousands of prisoners heard the stories. Hasjim tells of how others, including the dalang in their isolation hut, retold the story—but was it scores or hundreds or thousands of people, perhaps we will never know. Perhaps other prisoners have already made notes about this in their memoirs or diaries.

While Pram remembers starting to tell the story of Minke and Nyai after work one evening on the barracks veranda, Hasjim remembered it starting as people gathered to wait for daily roll call. He confirmed, though, that there were many storytelling sessions on the barracks veranda, but also sometimes at night in their hut. With oil lamps lit, they would lay on their beds and listen to Pram tell the stories. 'Occasionally', Hasjim remembered. 'People would ask this or that question about what would happen next, but mostly, we all listened in silence, rapt in the story.'

Hasjim explained that the stories spread widely. 'There was one guy, Muhni was his name, who was a good storyteller and would repeat the stories to other groups of prisoners. And there was a good dalang as well, who did the same. There was also Eko, who went from unit to unit retelling the stories. Later on, when Pram had a typewriter, typescript copies also circulated.'

It appears that the village girl Sanikem, who became the concubine Ontosoroh, was indeed the prisoners' favourite character.

> The name Ontosoroh became very popular on the island, people would quote her dialogues, they gave us a new lease on life. Pramoedya's stories had a very positive impact on us . . . Because, how should I say it, all of us were suffering, so Ontosoroh's words touched us, he he . . . And the stories did raise our spirits—without doubt.

'What about the other characters,' I asked: 'Minke? Annelies?' Some prisoners fell in love with the frail Annelies and Minke was also popular, but Ontosoroh was the character everybody loved. The story of a lowly peasant girl who could evolve with such strength of character and wage an all-out resistance against injustice, despite knowing victory was unlikely, inspired the prisoners, both Hasjim and Pram affirmed. Still, I remember, there was a story of a prisoner who so identified with Minke, he ran off into the jungle apparently thinking he was Minke trying to escape. He was caught and returned.

While it was clear that the key motive was to raise morale in the aftermath of the killings, beatings and harassment, said Hasjim, Pram had another reason to tell these stories:

> I did ask him once, "Why do you tell these stories to us?" He said, "I've been working on these stories for a while. Who knows, I might not survive long in Buru. If I die, at least I've told these stories to you." He thought he was going to die in Buru, he he . . . But if he died, the stories could live on.

From 1973 onwards, as Hasjim noted, Pramoedya was given a typewriter and a space to write, two rooms. It needed repairs and those among the prisoners with the necessary skills fixed it up. Pram had a place to work and a few prisoners helped him find paper and provided other assistance, helping him organize his work. This change came about following a visit to Buru by General Sumitro.

Sumitro was the commander of the Command for the Restoration of Stability and Order (KOPKAMTIB). KOPKAMTIB was a military command structure reaching all the way down to the villages. It was the political security wing of the state, based on military power and coercion. Sumitro, at the time, was considered the second most powerful person in the country after Suharto. During 1973 and into 1974, Sumitro had begun to carve out a public profile for himself independently from and competing with that of President Suharto. He met often with protesting student leaders and artists and talent, about a 'new pattern of leadership', implying a more politically liberal policy.

As part of this, he visited the prisoners on Buru Island and ordered some relaxation for people like Pramoedya. Sumitro was accompanied by both Indonesian and foreign journalists, who could meet briefly with Pramoedya. International campaigners, especially Pramoedya's long-term friend Professor Wim Wertheim in the Netherlands, had been campaigning for the release of the prisoners and had profiled Pramoedya as a special case. Journalists sought him out at the camp and a photo of him behind barbed wire appeared in the international press. Although he had not been widely read in English, his name became more familiar to the international political public.

While the process begun of Pramoedya becoming the key figure for the solidarity campaign attention internationally, he recalls that the Indonesian journalists who talked to him still seemed hostile. Of course, prominent journalists in 1973 were those who had emerged triumphant after the repression of 1965 and could be expected to be hostile. 'Do you believe in God yet?' was the one question that Pramoedya told me on several occasions that he best remembered being asked. He said it was Mochtar Lubis, an anti-communist newspaper publisher, journalist and a successful novelist, who had asked him that question. I don't think Pram ever told me how he answered Lubis.

In any case, now with a typewriter, the words flowed. The first book he finished was *Arus Balik*, a huge historical novel set in the sixteenth century depicting the interaction between Javanese politics and culture and the first contact with Europeans. 'I hadn't written for so long', he said in our interview, 'the words flowed like a storm.' *This Earth of Mankind* was written between 1873 and 1975, in between writing *Arus Balik*. In the early 2000s, Pramoedya gave me a written mandate to translate *Arus Balik* into English, a task I have not been able to carry out to date.

There were several novels finished between 1973 and his release in 1979, that were later published. These were *Arus Balik* (*The Current Reverses*), *Arok Dedes* (a novel set in the eleventh-century Java), *Bumi Manusia*, *Anak Semua Bangsa*, *Jejak Langkah* and *Rumah Kaca*. There was a play, *Mangir*, and another novel whose manuscript was lost. He also wrote many essays later published in Indonesia as *Nyanyi Sunyi Seorang Bisu* (*Silent Song of the Mute*).

According to Hasjim, it was possible to make copies at least of *Bumi Manusia*, which prisoners used to read from in the later years. Some copies were smuggled out of prison, often via church people, for safekeeping in various places. I only ever saw one of the original typescripts. It was in 1980, at the house of Joesoef Isak, which was being used as the office for Hasta Mitra publishing company. It was mindboggling to see. A thick sheaf of pages neatly typed with no top or bottom or side margins—paper was precious in prison. 'Look,' Joesoef said pointing, 'almost no corrections over hundreds of pages.' In fact, later when they were publishing the novels, it was Joesoef who did the editing, picking up the occasional inconsistency or error. Pram himself often told me that he couldn't bear re-reading what he wrote. But he was obviously being accurate when he said that the words just flowed—a complete novel typed with hardly a change.

As the stories had circulated among the prisoners and then the works typed out as novels, a play and essays, Hasjim and Pramoedya discussed what would happen if they were ever released. Hasjim said he wanted to publish them. 'I agreed,' Pram told me, and then it was formalized after they were released and back in Jakarta. 'Pram found a notary,' said Hasjim, 'and the papers were drawn up.' 'I suggested the name Hasta Mitra,' Pram told me, 'It means hands of friendship.'

In November 1979, both Pramoedya and Hasjim were released from the Buru prison camp. Prisoner releases had begun in 1975 at other prisons, and the November 1979 release was the last of the large-scale releases. Pramoedya and Hasjim's group travelled to Surabaya, and then to the Magelang prison briefly, and then by bus to Jakarta, where they were reunited with their families and began living under house arrest as 'ETs—Ex-tapols or ex-political prisoners. The letters ET were printed on all the thousands and thousands of political prisoners' official identity cards, marking them out from all the others.

'At our release ceremony,' explained Pramoedya, 'we were all given letters. They said that legally there was no evidence that we were involved with what happened on the night of the 30 September or that movement.'

Joesoef Isak had been released from jail in Jakarta several months before and was soon to meet up with his old comrade Hasjim, and meet a new comrade-sin-arms, Pramoedya. Joesoef had also been exiled from Indonesia, but in Jakarta.

Chapter 6

Exiled in the Capital: Joesoef Isak

In 2004, Jimmy Carter visited from the United States to talk to the American community in Jakarta. Joesoef Isak figured in this speech:

> I also sent Patricia Derien, my personal envoy, on another trip to Jakarta
> to underscore the United States' commitment to human rights. She met
> directly with President Soeharto, along with Joesoef Isak [correction: not
> along with, but: afterwards also with Joesoef Isak], a respected publisher
> who represented himself and thousands of other political prisoners,
> many of whom had been imprisoned since the mid-1960s, never having
> had a trial. According to Joesoef and other former detainees, because of
> the efforts of our administration and the efforts of groups like Amnesty
> International, over 35,000 political prisoners were freed between 1977
> and 1980 from the penal island of Buru and other prisons throughout
> the archipelago.[27]

The release of the 14,000 prisoners from the Buru Island prison camp in 1979 was partly a result of pressure from the United States' Carter administration. There had been campaigns for the prisoners' release throughout the world for over a decade. The Carter administration reinforced this pressure, raising the question of their release directly with Suharto. It is difficult to know for sure what precisely was in the mind of Suharto and his generals in 1978, but clearly managing 20,000 or more prisoners for decades into the future, was obviously going to be a challenge. Further, by 1978, Suharto had ended the last vestiges of dissent on the campuses and from within the military's own ranks.

No doubt also camp and prison commanders would have been sending assessments of the weakened political morale of the prisoners, while the military's intelligence service throughout the country would have been able to report that there was no serious base remaining for released prisoners to reorganize. Almost a million cadres and members had been killed, a process that acted to terrorize the other 20 million. These killings, alongside the mass jailing, also meant that the Left had lost its experienced cadre as well.

It is clear, whatever the precise balance between all these factors, that the pressure from the Carter administration was very important. This pressure from Washington had many components and one person who played a role in helping this process was Joesoef Isak.

In 1977, Joesoef received a letter from the military telling him that he would be interviewed by American journalists. His curiosity took him to the United States Information Service (USIS) in Jakarta to find out who they were. By accident, while talking to reception staff there, he was noticed by Fred Coffey, the head of USIS, who invited Joesoef into his office, where he quizzed Joesoef about his prison experiences for several hours. Coffey then met the U.S. Ambassador, Edward Masters, and they made sure that Joesoef did meet the visiting American—not a journalist, however, but the special envoy of President Carter, Patricia Derien, being sent to Indonesia to meet President Suharto on the issue of the release of Indonesia's political prisoners.

Joesoef met Derien and Masters on a Saturday at the Embassy. Masters jokingly reminded Joesoef that he had heard him deliver a speech in Jakarta to a mass rally in 1965, calling for the crushing of American imperialism. Derien and Masters quizzed Joesoef again. Joesoef proposed the US government call for a general amnesty for all prisoners. Derien told him that that was the message from Carter to Suharto, although delivered in a roundabout way. She told Joesoef that they had communicated to Suharto that there would be sanctions if the prisoners were not released. Derien offered to smuggle Joesoef on the floor of their car out of the Embassy compound to be dropped somewhere in Jakarta. Joesoef said that it wasn't necessary.[28]

Engaging in this kind of activity was, of course, a violation of the restrictions placed upon Joesoef as a released political prisoner. Yes, Joesoef was released from prison in Jakarta before those from Buru. But how was he released earlier?

As explained before, Joesoef was also detained later than Pramoedya or Hasjim, after experiencing a few years of going in and out of temporary places of detention. Having been the editor of a prominent non-Left nationalist newspaper, while also being an advocate of Sukarno's policies through the journalists' union and international organizations, resulted in him also being treated ambiguously—up to a point. But in the end, his turn came.

Joesoef was being detained in one of those nameless 'safe houses' late in 1968 when he and several other men were summoned to the front of the house and told to board a bus. There was to be no more switching from detention by one group of soldiers to another anymore. They were taken to Salemba Prison in Jakarta. Hasjim and Pramoedya and thousands of others were already being prepared to leave for Buru Island, Joesoef was going to be detained in Jakarta for the next decade. Like the Dutch colonial power before them, Suharto's New Order didn't only exile its opponents to far-off parts of the archipelago, but also to this or that prison on Java. Being in the capital, Joesoef's experience was very different than Pramoedya and Hasjim's and the thousands of others on Buru. Despite the prison walls and cell bars, a process of osmosis with the outside world, with the new 'Indonesia', was possible. Family visits, work outside, rubbish tips, cigarette packet linings and charm, made the prison porous for Joesoef. On Buru, jungle and bush and then the sea and the regimen of a directly military-run concentration camp meant the exile brought a much more severe estrangement from the rest of the country.

The bus delivered him and a few other people to Salemba, Jakarta's main jail. He was placed in an isolation bloc, as related in Chapter 4. The conditions in Salemba were no better than those described by

Hasjim and Pramoedya, when they were there earlier, before being sent to Buru. Prison food wasn't enough to survive on, so everybody depended on what families brought to the prison. 'Food,' Joesoef told me, 'was used by our jailers as a weapon against us. We survived because our families stood by us.'

The guards were cruel also. Joesoef explained how the prisoners learned about the resilience of the human body:

> I also found out that the human body can take a lot of beatings. This is very important to remember. Very important because . . . we had to tell this story to the new people who had just come in. They were afraid to die, they'd get hit once and they were ready to tell everything. We would tell them that yes, when they beat you, you'll come away with your eyes all swollen, you may think that they will torture you until you die; once the torture is over, your body would be black and blue all over, even your genitals, but in a week, you'll recover. But if you spill your secrets to the authorities, you'll regret it for the rest of your life. You will have betrayed your own friends.

Pramoedya and Hasjim and the thousands of others on Buru Island suffered a different kind of torture. They were harassed and beaten and starved while they slaved to survive outdoors—farming and fishing and planting banana trees and raising chickens and, in the first years, clearing land with their bare hands. Their imprisonment made them outdoor heroes, surviving under the tropical sun, feet worn by stone and dirt and worms. Joesoef, and the thousands of others like him scattered throughout the country's prisons, were indoors survivors. And there was one other fundamental difference: the nature of their exiles, their isolation. On Buru, New Order Indonesia was the camp. The actual existing Indonesia that was now evolving under military rule on all of Indonesia's islands with all its new features, could be known only by Pramoedya and Hasjim, as it manifested in the conditions on Buru.

In Jakarta, the prison walls were more porous, the isolation more ambiguous. After all, the prison was in the national capital. The prison commandants went home to a house in Jakarta every day. They were a part of the Jakarta political class, a part of the system keeping the new 'Indonesia' on track. They were privy to the gossip, intrigues, manoeuvres of that class. These commandants were different to those stationed in Buru, who were away from it all and consumed with how they could exploit the productivity of the prisoners for their material benefit. They were in exile too, just not imprisoned.

Joesoef was experienced in diplomatic relations and an excellent networker—he had been able to win support in the polarized Indonesia of the early sixties from both Left and Right. He was a very charming man. It was his relationship with one of the prison officers that highlighted the porousness of the prisoners' exile. I will let Joesoef tell his story of that relationship, but first, the reader must be reminded of what Joesoef encountered when the isolation allowed outside reality to leak into the prison cell.

Between 1967 and 1977, Indonesia changed dramatically. The country was redefined. First, the whole pro-Sukarnoist majority had been massacred or otherwise terrorized. They were either in a prison camp, a gaol cell or lying very low in their homes. Their organizations had been destroyed and their newspapers, magazines and books banned, removed from libraries and schools. The vocabulary of struggle, socialism and sovereignty was replaced with that of law and order, stability, and economic development and growth. The nationalized companies of the Dutch colonialists—Phillips and Unilever among them—were returned to their owners, although not the plantations. The doors to the economy were opened wide to the International Monetary Fund, which had been told to go away in 1962, as well as the World Bank and a host of multinational companies. They had all met with officials of the Suharto government in Switzerland to discuss how wide the door should be opened.[29]

While all the Left-wing political parties disappeared from 1965, after elections in 1972, the remaining Right and Centre parties were forced to 'simplify', leaving just three, all of whom were banned from criticizing each other. Under a policy called 'the floating mass', they were also banned from recruiting members from the small towns and villages of the country, that is, from among most of the population. While Joesoef was in prison in Jakarta, elections took place both in 1971 and 1977.

These changes were huge enough in and of themselves. But the sum was greater than the parts. Between 1945, or even from before the 1920s, both the Indonesia in its inception and well as Indonesia after its independence, was defined by a great struggle over what kind of Indonesia it would be. After 1965, this great struggle was buried and so Indonesia was redefined from above by force, and that redefinition above by force was what defined it. A powerful regime, cooperating with international capital, and a passive population, officially designated the 'floating mass'—whose passivity was ensured by a supervising, coercive apparatus based in the military. While the struggle was buried in a million graves and exiled to prisons and camps and gloomy homes, it did not mean, of course, that contradiction had disappeared from society. The objective conditions remained characterized by contradiction. Militarist power and popular passivity was itself a contradiction full of tension.

Unaccountable power meant corruption. This stood in contradiction to those youth who had been alienated from Sukarnoism because they saw Sukarno's palace as unaccountable and corrupt. Students, especially the youngest, who had opposed Sukarno and the Left, were soon protesting Suharto for his regime's corruption and the huge gap between rich and poor that was developing. There were student protests almost every day during the latter half of 1973, exploding on the streets in January 1974 in mass protests, followed by rioting by the Jakarta proletariat. This was known as the 'January 15 Catastrophe' or MALARI.

Hundreds of students and intellectuals were arrested. Protest leaders were put on trial and handed heavy jail sentences. Newspapers, that had led the anti-Left campaign in the sixties, but which had now become critical of Suharto, were closed down. The dissident poet and playwright, W.S. Rendra, attracted thousands to his plays and poetry readings as he attacked the regime and asked the population: 'Whose side are you on, the armed or the wounded, those who sit or those who are sat upon?' Ironically, Rendra was arrested and imprisoned without trial in 1978 the same year Joesoef was released. The students arrested in 1974 spent their time under incarceration in Cipinang Jail, where they met and mixed with Leftist prisoners from 1965. Many of the students had, as high school students, demonstrated, demanding the arrest of these very same Leftists. In Salemba prison, Joesoef did not come across any of the 1974 prisoners.

Way out east on Buru Island, news of these developments arrived late and without the immediacy of freshly reported details. In Salemba, the walls were porous. Joesoef, while in exile and alienated from the new Indonesia, was also much more a man of this new Indonesia than either Pramoedya or Hasjim. It was, first of all, human interactions that created the porousness. Joesoef tells:

I was given a special role in the prison. I don't know why . . . but one security official in Salemba, he liked talking to me. Maybe he knew that I was an international figure, secretary-general of the PWAA [Asian-African Journalists' Association]. He felt it was some sort of an honour to have me there. I was someone he could spend time talking about politics with. For years, until I was released, I used to talk to him a lot.

This security official was a cruel man, he was brutal. He wasn't the chief warden of the prison; he was the second-in-command. Prison wardens usually last five to six years, at the most. Some were replaced after only one or two years. But he was there from the beginning and never replaced. That should tell you that they needed his strength there; he was the right person for the job because he was brutal. People above him would show a bit of humanity and they would be replaced. But he wasn't going anywhere. He wasn't very well-educated, but he had fought against the Dutch in 1945. Maybe he didn't even finish junior high, but I felt that he had a sort of homespun wisdom. He was very interested in the idea of a republic. He thought that in the prison, he had access to hundreds of thinkers and politicians and that he could learn from them. That was why he liked to talk politics with me.

That was my special role in Salemba. We would chat about politics, about Pancasila but also about Communism and international politics, everything. I knew that he thought he was already a learned man. But I was his match, and I tried to guide him (*membina*)—that's a PKI term, to use their own term; I tried to re-educate him. Maybe not exactly re-educate, but I tried to talk sense into him. I told him what was really happening, in my opinion, what was just and what was unjust. And in the end, it kind of worked, he realized that we weren't supposed to be there, that we should not be kept there any longer, we should be released.

And he took a risk that I thought was far beyond what was expected of him. After the evening prayer, Maghrib, around six or seven, all the prisoners had to go back to their cells, we would be locked there until the next morning. But once everyone was inside, he would invite me to his office, usually at around nine. No one else knew about these night visits, except for another officer, who used to fetch me from the cell. I was allowed to read all the newspapers available in Jakarta in his office. This was extraordinary since one of the rules in Salemba was that not even a small piece of paper could be exchanged with the prisoners. Even the cigarettes we got were stripped of their paper packaging—we just got the cigarettes. They were afraid people would write on the cigarette packaging and circulate it in the prison. And that did indeed happen.

In the beginning, the political prisoners would write poems and political news on cigarette packs and pass them around the prison. They would also use them to communicate with each other. So prison authorities came up with the rule of no paper allowed. No reading materials whatsoever, except the Qur'an and the Bible.

Joesoef also told me of how he himself used to write summaries of important news he gleaned from the newspaper on cigarette packet linings, and they would be passed from cell to cell. His sessions with the prison officer were not the only source of the porousness. He continued later in our discussions:

We also tried to get more information from the outside in other ways. One of them was to smuggle newspaper clippings in our food. Also one of our routine chores was to collect rubbish from outside the prison to be turned into compost for our spinach garden. Someone would almost always manage to smuggle a package neatly wrapped in plastic inside the disgusting, rotten rubbish. The package would contain food, newspapers, and magazines. That was a very reliable source.

And another way was with the help of a group of political prisoners who were allowed to go out of the prison for a limited time. They belonged to a special bloc in the prison, reserved for prisoners who were formally already released. A lot of them were craftsmen, artists and builders. They could build houses, statues, paint pictures, do a lot of things. They were placed in a special bloc and they were allowed to go out. That is, go out to do forced labour. They were ordered to build houses for the prison officers, or to do the interiors. Every time they were allowed out, one or two who were brave enough would sneak out to buy a copy of *Tempo* news magazine or other magazines and newspapers. Then they would smuggle them into the prison.

I would get my hands on these magazines and newspapers, *Tempo* and others, at around ten to eleven at night. Everyone else would be fast asleep by that time, eleven or past that. Lockdown was at seven or eight, and in those crowded cells you could do nothing but sleep. By around ten or eleven, everyone would be asleep already. The magazines would be delivered during the last inspection of the cell. The inspector was also a political prisoner, accompanied by a military officer. The military officers were all sick of doing these inspections, you can imagine, there were dozens of cells in each bloc and he had to inspect each one of them every night. So they usually didn't even get in the bloc, they just stayed outside the door and sent the prisoner-inspector in. These prisoner-inspectors were the ones who would deliver the magazines and newspapers into my cell. My job was to read all of them.

From around eleven o'clock when I got them, I would start reading, finish them, then destroy them. I would bring a pail of water with me when I came back to the cell, then after reading the magazines and papers, I would rip the pages apart into little pieces, put them in the pail of water and mash them together into a paper pulp. Then later, we would use the paper pulp to make papier-maché statues. Yeah, that's just one of the stories of how we used to get news from the outside. Despite the heavy security, news always found its way inside. Then I would retell what I'd been reading to the other prisoners in the bloc before we had to go back into our cells the next day. After the afternoon and the early evening prayers, we were still allowed outside for one, maybe half an hour. That was the time for me to deliver a kind of "briefing" on what was happening outside, in Indonesia and in other parts of the world.

So, we weren't totally isolated from outside news.

Joesoef remained a journalist, writing news reports on the new Indonesia even while in jail-exile. This gave Joesoef a distinctively different political personality than either Hasjim or Pramoedya, but especially Pramoedya. (Hasjim's exuberant personality meant he plunged back into Indonesia with great gusto seemingly quickly dissolving the alienation.) Joesoef described his relationship with the prison security official with whom he had all those discussions as that of 'cultivating' the official. Before 1965, it was a common practice for a party cadre to be assigned to membina (cultivate) somebody outside their immediate sphere of influence. This would involve talking to them regularly and bringing them around to the party position through a process of patient explanation. Sometimes the target person would not be aware that their friend in conversation was a party member until later. Writing news reports like a journalist, on the lining of cigarette paper, or just briefing fellow prisoners orally, or actively trying to convert his prison warden, Joesoef was unknowingly preparing himself for the role of helping Pramoedya and Hasjim politically connect with the new Indonesia once they started publishing Pramoedya's books.

Joesoef was released in 1977. International pressure, including from Carter, was already being exerted on Suharto. Carter's vice president, Walter Mondale, had already visited Jakarta to raise the issue linking it to U.S. airplane sales to Indonesia. Joesoef himself had already had his classification as a political prisoner lowered to a lesser category, partly as a result of the government trying to reduce the number of people it might have to bring to trial or send to Buru. Joesoef describes:

> They also realized that it would take a very long time to process even just the Group A prisoners in Salemba. And consider that there were political prisoners in every major city in Indonesia. According to our own calculation, it would take around three to four months to bring each political prisoner to a full trial. To process all the prisoners in just one Salemba bloc would take at least thirty years! The authorities realized that there were too many people in Group A. So I was demoted to Group B. But then there were too many people in Group B as well, too many of them in Buru. And the international pressure was mounting, from Amnesty International, the Carter government, the Dutch government,

the IGGI countries. They were all demanding that the political prisoners be released.

On his day of release, Joesoef was taken to a military police base, where he was supposed to be met by his wife and three boys. There was an administrative mistake and he was taken back to Salemba for an extra night. He was picked up his wife and boys the next day—he had not seen his now teenage children in ten years—who drove him around Jakarta before heading home. It was a short while after, when he met Patricia Deneria at the US Embassy, that he advocated for all those still in prison.

PART II

Chapter 7

Return from Exile: To Where?

I still find it hard to imagine how the three men must have felt when they returned from exile to the Jakarta of Suharto's New Order. In 1965, before the prison camp, they were active participants in a country where literally 20 million people were striving in the direction of Socialism ala Indonesia. Millions of people were mobilizing in mass rallies and marches in support of President Suharto. Tens of thousands of activists were organizing a myriad of mass organizations—workers, farmers, fishermen, women's rights activists, students, academics and scholars, journalists, artists and writers. There were competing organizations polemicizing against each other. The government had banned some parties whose leaders had supported an armed revolt and established a rival government in the late 1950s, but the mass organizations and newspapers associated with those parties were still free to campaign. Society was alive with political competition and polemics. Newspapers thrived and an enormous number of newsletters, bulletins and magazines of every hue circulated.

But more than that, Indonesia had become a major actor on the world stage. Sukarno had aligned Indonesia with the People's Republic of China and the other anti-US governments in Asia. Indonesia had withdrawn from the UN and was trying to build an alternative alliance of New Emerging Forces, based on all the countries that refused an alliance or subordination to the United States or United Kingdom.

Joesoef Isak, as secretary-general of the Asian–African Journalists' Association, had visited Cuba, North Africa and Eastern Europe. Joesoef had visited Eastern Europe along with Hasjim Rachman. He had also represented Indonesia in negotiations with the Fokker airplane company, while visiting France and the Netherlands.

Hasjim's newspaper, *Eastern Star*, dominated the Jakarta newspaper market and Hasjim had the ear of the president. Pramoedya's columns in *Eastern Star* were at the forefront of the major polemics that divided the artistic and intellectual world. A little earlier, Pramoedya had been able to visit China, where he had toured many cities. He also had the chance to visit Europe, both Western and Eastern. Pramoedya's books from the 1960s: *The Chinese in Indonesia, Just Call me Kartini* and *The Coast Girl*, all had a major profile in the cultural arena. *The Chinese in Indonesia*, which comprised his newspaper columns, was the subject of its own polemic, and Pramoedya spent a year in gaol at the height of anti-Chinese sentiments in 1960.

The excitement of struggle was everywhere. Indonesia was also playing a leadership role among Third World countries—President Kennedy in the US feted Sukarno in Washington in 1962. Soviet leader Khrushchev made sure he visited Indonesia and was feted by Sukarno.

Struggle. Excitement. Pride at being at the forefront of leading the Third World. That was the atmosphere that framed the political world of Pramoedya, Joesoef and Hasjim and 20 million other people. Of course, there was an opposition to all this, especially from significant sections of the army, who by the mid-sixties were also the de facto controllers of most of the modern sector of the economy, made up of all the nationalized Dutch and other foreign companies. Conservative religious organizations also opposed the Leftward direction of the politics of the majority. Those intellectuals, including some students, whose role models were the Western liberal intellectuals, always at arm's length from active political partisanship, also aligned with the army against Sukarnoist politics. Many of these liberal families were also alienated from the personalized palace-based politics that Sukarno came to represent for them, where he was perceived as the single individual lynchpin for the whole system. And, of course, they were all excluded from access to the palace.

When the three men returned to Jakarta almost fifteen years into the Suharto era, what did they find? The paragraphs above already point to the reality of a very deep chasm between Indonesia before and after 1965. This chasm, however, needs to be discussed more fully before we return to the personal stories of Pramoedya, Joesoef and Hasjim.

* * *

Indonesia is the fourth most populous country in the world, holding immense geopolitical strategic importance straddling the sea and air lanes between the Indian and Pacific oceans, and home to substantial mineral resources. Yet today, and for the last fifty years, its international political presence has been almost zero. The primary reason for this is the 1965 counter-revolution in Indonesia and the consequent radical remaking-cum-unmaking of the nation. On the one hand, this counter-revolution produced an Indonesian state and economy that posed no threat to either Western or Japanese imperial economic or geopolitical interests, and on the other, a society whose new post-counter-revolutionary experience would emasculate any progressive politics for decades, and thus, also its intellectual and cultural life.

Some aspects of the counter-revolution have been described in earlier chapters. The reader will be familiar by now with the physical elimination and terror, which were accompanied by formal bans on all the Left organizations, on Left ideologies, including Sukarnoist socialism as well as 'Marxism–Leninism'; bans on the circulation of the writings of all the country's progressive writers and thinkers, and on all mass organization activity, including of some traditional conservative Islamic organizations. There was a massive, and uncontested, tsunami of black propaganda against Sukarno and the Left, especially the Indonesian Communist Party (PKI), depicting them as evil, degenerate and barbarian. There were no shades of grey in this totally black propaganda and absolutely zero voices critiquing this direction, even on the margins.

Within a few years, the new government's official doctrine was that the masses should be a 'floating mass'. They should simply focus on their appropriate functions, that is, working and producing, and stay away from politics. The regime's ideologues took the term 'floating mass' from 1950's American political science, which celebrated public passivity. The passivity which such political science claimed had been achieved in the US in the 1950s through co-option and mechanisms of ideological hegemony, would be achieved by violence in Indonesia.

Even through this brief description, the totalitarian nature of the counter-revolution will be starkly obvious. With such extensive ideological suppression and deep 'de-politicization', almost all aspects of intellectual and political life came under formal state supervision, together with the enforcement, through a massive national propaganda mechanism, of the most banal, anti-critical and obedience-oriented official ideology one can envisage, taught at high school to university and beyond. Indonesian history was rewritten into an official history, which eliminated all political agency by popular forces and all sense of rebellion. Rebellions against Dutch colonial power, when they had been led by communists, were taught as examples of treason against Indonesia. High schools stopped teaching Indonesian literary texts, including and especially those by Pramoedya. With the physical elimination of all left-of-centre forces and the associated terror, as well as the very effective and total suppression of alternatives, tens of millions of Indonesians have grown up knowing only the official history of their country. Until 1998, almost none have had any exposure to the literature of the country, even of the writings of the country's celebrated national heroes, such as the preeminent anti-colonial leaders, Sukarno, Mohammed Hatta and Sutan Sjahrir.[2] At the same time, most of the population have had no serious experience of political activity, except during the sudden burst of resistance against Suharto during the few years between 1996–1998.

The impact of the counter-revolution was, however, even deeper than the sum of these combined policies—from mass murder and terror to totalitarian-imposed ignorance and passivity. The 1965 counter-

---

[2] Max Lane, 'Indonesia 1965 and the Counter Revolution against the Nation', Max Lane Online. Available at: https://maxlaneonline.com/2018/08/08/new-essay-working-draft-indonesia-1965-and-the-counter-revolution-against-the-nation/ - _ftn2.

revolution was a pre-emptive purge aimed at the prevention of the final unfolding and completion of the revolutions that were maturing or brewing: a national revolution as well as a social revolution. The driving momentum of the revolutionary processes was the further unfolding of a gruelling and long drawn-out national revolution, whose first stirrings were in the writings of the young feminist, Kartini, in the 1890s. Kartini, writing and envisaging progress into a new future and not a return to a traditional feudal past, elaborated ideas originating from the Enlightenment and hoped that they would be applied to 'my people'. However precisely she applied that term, 'my people' at the time, it was the beginning of a future-oriented identification of a community that later became the Indonesian nation.

As with all revolutions, the national revolution was doing at least two things. First, it was overturning the pre-existing power structure. A colonial capitalist class and its state, aided by a politically domesticated and nicely salaried local state apparatus, recruited from the aristocracy and allowed to maintain many remnants of despotic culture, had dominated the life of the local inhabitants for 300 years, ruling directly over many areas for up to 100 years. The winning of political independence from the Dutch during 1945–49, and the expulsion of their economic interests in 1956–57 overturned the colonial power structure, including abolishing, in most if not all places, the privileged status of the remnant aristocracies. Indonesia was probably the only large colony that expelled or nationalized all the former colonizer's businesses after independence without a socialist revolution.

At the same time, this revolutionizing process, of everybody involved and of so many things, was an act of creating something that did not exist before. The revolutionizing of themselves and things that was taking place, was indeed creating something totally new: a phenomena that came to be called as 'Indonesia'. It was new generically: the nation was a new post-feudal and post-despotic form of community coming into being only in the capitalist era. And it was new in its specificity: it was Indonesia. Before Indonesia came into existence during the twentieth century, no such thing existed, nor were there any Indonesians. There were Javanese, Batak, Malays, Dayaks, Minangkabaus, Bugis and many more: but not a single Indonesian existed.

The creation of a nation, however, is not instantaneous. It is a long and mostly gruelling process. There is the struggle to defeat the existing power, whether feudal or colonial. This mostly has required wars, death, blood, destruction, turmoil and dislocation. The process has a history.

As a product of the development of capitalism, a shared capitalist economic life within a specific territory develops. In Indonesia's case, it was violently forged within and across the territory of the Netherlands East Indies out of and through externally generated convulsions of many pre-existing productive systems, the most developed of which, such as in Java and some parts of Sumatra, shared the characteristics of what Marx called the 'Asiatic mode of production'. These were highly centralized systems, based on the control of water, with hardened hierarchies of social and productive functions ideologized in a caste system. In the case of the Malay Archipelago, kingdoms mostly produced a limited range of goods and services, and operated over relatively small territories, even when they were rich enough to finance armies that exacted tribute irregularly from other territories.

Then the Portuguese and finally the Dutch arrived. The production of spices for export increased massively. Princes and Sultans became the defeated agents of Dutch mercantilism, which used violence and massacre whenever necessary. Then new export crops were introduced and spread: sugar, tobacco, rubber, indigo, tea, coffee, cacao and more. Mining for tin and other metals and minerals also started. Through the nineteenth century, the whole archipelago underwent economic transformation with modern shipping, rail and the telegraph, giving a start to an integrated territory-wide economic life. Local currency, banking, excise rules and territory-wide taxation helped knit it all together. Dutch capital was investing and expropriating. The archipelago, from the Malay peninsula to the eastern islands of the archipelago, had previously been a singular 'natural' space, where products and ideas were interchanged rapidly, borne over the seas by thousands of locally made ships. Hinduism, Buddhism and then Islam could spread, taking turns, to almost every port across the archipelago, even to the coast of Western Papua. With colonialism, the archipelago was divided up among the Dutch, English, Spanish and Portuguese, forging new separate spaces—colonies mimicking countries.

It was a colony but its economic life mimicked that of a national economy, except that it was deprived of the technological revolution occurring in Europe. Like all capitalist economies (and the economies that existed in most places before nations), it evolved around contradictions, including class contradictions. National bourgeois and national proletariat classes developed, and perhaps even national peasantries. International relations become possible between the ruling classes of nations—oppressor and oppressed nations both—and, potentially, between the oppressed classes also.

The economic transformation created urban centres: Batavia (Jakarta) and Surabaya, on the island of Java, and Medan in Sumatra, were the largest, but there are more spread across the islands. Banks and business offices, ports and workshops proliferated. Of course, these centres were still a tiny portion of the total population. But their population grows enough to support the emergence of a new, cosmopolitan environment. Life changes. Stories change and require a new language with which to relate them. In the East Indies, the first to write these stories—short stories and novelettes—were Chinese and Eurasian town-dwellers. They tell the stories of people no longer bound by strict traditions: of murder and detectives, of Dutch, Chinese, Eurasian and 'native' officials, and dandies and prostitutes. Stories made up of real-life causes and effects, and no longer the whims of gods or fate. These stories inspired, too, I think, the story chosen by Pramoedya for *Bumi Manusia*. And they told these stories in their version of Malay, up until then a language used mainly for local commerce and the colonial administration of the 'natives'. They turn it into a language of a society that was changing, moving, and intense with dynamic cause and effect. They lay the foundation of it being adopted as the language for talking about cause and effect across the territory, that is, for talking about the future.

In 1928, colonial youth around the territory declared they will struggle for a new country, Indonesia, and that its national language will be Indonesian: the Malay that had started to evolve in the hands of the storytellers at the turn of the century. Then it spread as the vernacular, the language of a particular time and place, of the territory's future. Its spread between the 1920s and the 1960s is driven by the ignited fires of political discussion—and struggle—for the future of the new being created: Indonesia. The struggle for the national language, and with it a national literature—poems, songs, stories—recording the experience of this process constitute a central part of the national revolution. Indonesian language and literature were part of that created which never existed before. Pramoedya was an important figure in this process, as were Hasjim and Joesoef, through their journalism. However, in fact, there were tens of thousands writing across the country, and even more reading. Organizations of artists and writers grew rapidly, all of whom, from different ideological currents, took their writings to the people.

Most inspiring of all—though we probably take it for granted now—is that this never-before-existent nation will also develop—did start to develop—its own, distinctive new culture, reflecting a common psychological outlook, including sharing that culture's contradictions. Music and song, poetry and story (novel, short story, film and theatre), paintings and sculpture, are one set of embodiments of such a culture: the arts.

The evolution of a new Indonesian art and literature began at the turn of the century, at first experimenting in Dutch, and then Malay, as it became enlivened as the vernacular of a newly emerging location. Artists came from all classes and across the ideological spectrum. By 1945, when Sukarno and Hatta proclaimed Independence, the voices of a nation's poets, songsters and storytellers could start asserting the reality of the nation's existence: Chairil Anwar, Pramoedya Ananta Toer, Ismail Marzuki and many more. During the following twenty years, the arts flowered even more, freed of colonial suppression and challenged by the need to describe and lead the new experience of living in and through the newly liberated—but not yet completed—nation community. Mass organizations of the arts and culture grew, especially on the Left, among socialists and radical nationalists. This new culture was not Javanese or Acehnese or Bugis or Dayak or Balinese, neither was it some kind of conglomeration of elements from these earlier cultures. It was something newly created on this earth. To the extent it did draw on pre-existing ideas, made it in fact a child of all nations.

Arts and stories were, however, just the tip of the iceberg. The cultural changes that were integrated into the national revolution—

the nation-creation process—went deeper than that. There were many cultural changes but two stand out as pre-eminent. These were the emergence of a culture of conscious, purposeful organization with the goal of changing society, and the mobilization of people on a large scale to achieve it. The breakdown and dissolution of traditional forms of organization, that is from the pre-capitalist social formations, is not unique to Indonesia. 'Traditional' organization that evolved to allow the implementation of the collective duties of different parts of society, especially at the village level, dissolve or retreat into new organizations, established with a conscious goal in mind to replace them. These new organizations have constitutions and members, more or less agreeing upon their methods and aims. This is a revolutionary cultural change: obligation (a duty imposed under a particular class hegemony) is overthrown by its opposite: voluntary action. This came with the shift away from being a *subject* of either feudal despotic or colonial power, accepting a passivity embodied in the Javanese word *nerimo* (to accept)—whose elongated, subdued pronunciation even sounds somehow abject. Popular organization and mobilization overturned and turned upside-down the most fundamental cultural values.

In the case of the East Indies-to-be-Indonesia, this revolutionary organization and mobilization eventually drew in hundreds of thousands, indeed millions of people from across the archipelago. Anti-colonial organizations like the Sarekat Islam, and later the Sarekat Rakyat, the Indonesian Communist Party and the Indonesian National Party (founded by Sukarno) mobilized hundreds of thousands during the 1920s and 1930s. The first of the mass organizations, Sarekat Islam, which campaigned against colonialism and not for religion, is reported to have had between 350,000 to 800,000 members and itself claimed a membership of 2 million, had branches on most islands in the Indies.

Then there were periods of explosions of trade union activity and peasant movements, with contemporary rather than traditional goals. Moreover, the form of mobilizations, such as mass meetings (*vergadesring*), strikes, active boycotts and demonstrations, involved many more people who may not have been formal members. The whole process developed as class contradictions sharpened. The first big split in the mass organizations, within Sarekat Islam, was over the question of opposition to capitalism and the advocacy of socialism as the form independent Indonesia should take. Embryonic as they were, a national bourgeoisie and a national proletariat were thus being formed.

The cultural revolution—whereby what has been called 'modernity', the consciousness produced out of the experiences of capitalist developments—overturns 'tradition'—that is the consciousness that prevailed under European feudal or Asian despotic modes of production—is not unique to Indonesia. What is perhaps unique, or at least very pronounced, was how that revolution was defined by the overturning of a consciousness based on acceptance of obligation and passivity to one based on purpose and the seizing of agency (organization and mobilization), and how that revolutionary overturning was the fundamental creator of an embryonic new national culture. This new culture, given agency, polarized around class perspectives, and was cleaved by contradictions. The clash between contradictory perspectives—capitalism or socialism—was the basis for a deep fragility on the one hand but, while the question was unanswered as to what kind of Indonesia a free Indonesia would be, this unresolved contradiction worked to fuse opposites into a unity. The struggle to resolve the question in real life of what kind of Indonesia would be created, united opposed perspectives, based on more or less opposed class interests, in the one project of a national revolution to create Indonesia.

Stating that there were such class contradictions in the East Indies-to-be-Indonesia may seem nothing special. And just left at that, it isn't. But it can't be left just at that. The creative side of the revolutionary process, the creating of Indonesia and Indonesians, was defined by this process. The culture of organization and mobilization was embodied in central ideas that took hold within the majority of the movement for a nation, in addition to their activities. Central to these were the ideas of the young nationalist Sukarno—motion, movement and popular agency in that motion, the agency of the *rakyat* (common people) imbued with semangat. At the same time, his nemesis, Mohammed Hatta, counterposed Sukarno's motion and popular energy against his concepts of expertise and steadiness.

Sukarno established the mass party, the PNI, in 1927, and constantly debated with Mohammad Hatta on these issues. After the Dutch arrested Sukarno and the PNI dissolved, in 1931, Hatta established the Indonesian National Education Party, also the PNI, a group advocating the spread of education, that is expertise, as the first priority of the moment rather than mass mobilization. After the defeat of Japan, which had occupied the Indies for three years, on 17 August 1945, the two men proclaimed Independence together, after being kidnapped and pressured into doing it by very semangat-filled nationalist youth. They became President and Vice President of Indonesia, until Hatta resigned in 1956—together for eleven years. They were called the 'Dwitunggal'—the two united in one. If there was unity for a while, it was the unity of opposites:

> Sukarno: 'The People's Awareness demands that every unjust situation or relationship be torn down and changed . . . changed fast and in a revolutionary way.'
>
> Hatta: 'A thorough-going social analysis would show that all our rebellions and our splits, our political anarchy and adventurism, and all the steps taken in the economic field which have created chaos, are a result of the fact that our national Revolution was not dammed up at the appropriate time.'

The Sarekat Islam had split to form the Left-wing and secular Sarekat Rakyat, which in turn, gave birth to the Indonesian Communist Party (PKI). After the Dutch smashed the PKI between 1926–27, Sukarno emerged as the voice of revolutionary nationalism, with Hatta as his nemesis. The same contradiction exercised itself all through the war of national liberation between 1945 and 1949, and until 1965. Indonesians' commitment to Indonesia was a passionate commitment to the new nation, as to their hopes for it: that it be Islamic or social democratic, versus socialist or communist; conservative or revolutionary. The contradiction was the energy that pushed along the creation of the nation.

Territory, language and literature, a territory-wide shared economic life and a new Indonesian culture, were forged out of a messy process, in which the struggle against colonial rule was a key part, but only a part of the process. These four aspects each developed unevenly, in fits and starts, in response to a variety of factors, and in most cases, their development and consolidation was still ongoing, up until 1965. The contradictions whose demand to be resolved were driving the process were still yet to find their resolution.

By 1956–7, when all Dutch enterprises were nationalized, after being occupied by their workers and trade unions, the overturning of the colonial power structure was completed. Dutch colonial power had been completely eliminated. The manifestation of Indonesia now asserting its place above and over Dutch colonial power, in an overturned power structure, was the enforced exiting of all Dutch business personnel, the ending of any legitimacy of the Dutch language and the nationalization of all Dutch capital. That aspect of the contradiction was resolved in a very final way. There is less presence of the former colonial power in Indonesia than in any other former colony, anywhere in the world.

However, the deep contradiction in culture—organization and mobilization versus passivity and obedience—which mirrored the contradiction between the desire for socialism or capitalism, remained unresolved. Between 1959 and 1965, the struggle over culture deepened. Levels of mass mobilization and organization deepened spectacularly. The clearest manifestations of this were the spectacular growth of the PKI and its associated organizations and also the impressive growth of the Indonesian National Party (PNI), as its majority moved in a more Left-wing direction. By 1965, their combined membership reached at least 20 million people, almost half of the adult population who would have had the right to vote, if there had ever been elections. Mobilizations in support of socialism and of Sukarno's radical, anti-imperialist policies, grew larger and larger. Mass meetings and marches in support of the nationalization of British, Belgian and British firms, escalated. Rallies and actions demanding land reform were endemic. There were huge rallies in support of the Vietnamese revolution and for solidarity of the Asian, African and Latin American spheres of the world, and the non-capitalist world generally. The growth of this side of the contradiction did not result in its resolution. Instead, two things happened.

First, the original dynamic of the contradiction—agency versus passivity—began to be subverted from within the movement for organization and mobilization. Second, and with considerable finality already lasting more than fifty years, exploiting this subversion of the prior dynamic, forces wanting passivity (and capitalism) suppressed this contradiction. Instead of being resolved, it was buried, left unresolved. Pramoedya explained the writer's block he experienced after finishing the historical novels he wrote, covering the period from the eleventh century until the early twentieth century, by giving the excuse that he couldn't write about the Suharto period of Indonesia's history because the contradictions that existed had not yet been resolved. The thesis and anti-thesis had not yet produced the new synthesis, he said. So he could not write, as there was no way the process could be summed up[3]

He never published anything major after his brilliant six historical novels, which he wrote in prison camp, while he waited for a resolution that would be a long time coming because the very process of resolving had been quashed with such severe violence and comprehensiveness. Quashing that process meant *not finishing* the nation-creation process of Indonesia through the resolution of the contradiction in a certain way, but rather pushing along backwards, into an unmaking process.

* * *

The disappearance of the excitement of struggle and of a world in motion were a part of the counter-revolution against the nation itself. Joesoef was the first to see the new Jakarta out of 'exile':

> I was released at the Guntur military police headquarter. My wife and my children picked me up. My youngest son, who was still in primary school when I was taken into prison, had driven the car. He was already big; he drove the car! And I felt he thought that his dad had spent ten years in isolation and would be surprised by how the city had grown. So, even though our house was further to the south of the city from the military police headquarters, we didn't head home right away. He said, "What do you think, Dad, should we take a look around first, go for a drive on Sudirman St. and Thamrin St.?" The main streets of Jakarta with all the skyscrapers.

---

[3] https://maxlaneonline.com/2018/08/08/new-essay-working-draft-indonesia-1965-and-the-counter-revolution-against-the-nation/ - _ftn10 just yet.

It's true, Max, I have to admit that after ten years in isolation, when I couldn't see anything outside the prison walls, seeing Jakarta for the first time gave me the same feelings as when I used to go overseas before 1965, when I landed in Manila, Singapore or Amsterdam. I saw things that didn't exist before in the old Jakarta—the Jakarta I knew before 1965. There were flashy buildings, many still under construction, very impressive. But I tried to explain to my children that they shouldn't be too easily impressed. They should ask themselves, who owned those buildings? Who's reaping all the profits from this development? As a political person, you can't ignore those questions. I tried to explain that to my kids. How difficult was it really to get all this development done in Jakarta? Where is the art, so to speak? Just invite all the investors you know, give them all the facilities they demand, and voila! Another skyscraper gets built. But at what cost? Who owns the buildings, into whose pockets does the profit go? No one ever discussed that. It was never a problem for anyone. That was my first impression. And you know, they drove me past my house where they arrested me. But I had to head to a different home. I used to live on a major street in Kebayoran Baru. I went home to a small house on the outskirts of Jakarta.

Hasjim said of his reaction:

Some things were different, the roads were better, the cars were nicer, but those things didn't really impress me. A *Tempo* journalist came to my house to interview me, and he asked me, "What did you think of Jakarta with its new, smooth roads?" I answered him spontaneously, "Ah, they didn't mean anything to me. There was capital, you could get loans, buy tractors. No wonder you could build roads and buildings. But what you have to realize is . . .," so I said to this journalist, "in Buru, we built everything with our own hands. We made it fit for human beings to live in." *Tempo* didn't publish the interview. They apologized to me saying that if they published it, I would get into trouble.

Pramoedya experienced it a similar way:

Jakarta had changed incredibly compared to the Jakarta I left. Electricity was everywhere, there were colourful billboards and the traffic was packed. But I wasn't entirely amazed. I wasn't entirely amazed because we understood that all this was a consequence of foreign capital.

Pramoedya, in the same answer to my question about his first impression of the new Jakarta, made the additional point linking the new Jakarta to his and so many others' oppression: 'Truly, our imprisonment was an act of hostage taking, to guarantee the flow of foreign capital. To guarantee that we would not pose any threat to foreign investment.'

Hasjim Rachman, Vice President Malik and Joesoef Isak, after a meeting with Malik, who praised *Bumi Manusia*. Pramoedya Ananta Toer can be seen behind them.

These first impressions reflect how these three men felt the new Jakarta to be alien. Their impressions did not just stay as fleeting emotions. Their response to the new 'Indonesia' through their actions was profound and had—and still is having—profound impacts. They brought the original Indonesia back into view. They formed Hasta Mitra, defied the regime and published *This Earth of Mankind* and its sequels. Within two years of being released, while being under orders to report regularly to the police and under a ban on them working in any vital sector of the economy, including publishing, the original Indonesia was puncturing the ideological hegemony of the New Order.

Yes, Indonesia was back.

Chapter 8

Hasta Mitra: The Exiled Challenge
the New Indonesia

In 1978, one year before Pramoedya and Hasjim and the 14,000 others in Buru Island were released, the poet and dramatist, W.S. Rendra, had spent almost a year in jail without trial. He was arrested after he read anti-government poems at the huge outdoor theatre at the Jakarta Arts Centre compound, called Taman Ismail Marzuki. One of his poems contained the lines:

> There are whispers underground
> There are noisy voices above ground
> There are confused words going from one house to another
> There is indistinct weeping out in the rice fields.
> And look, right behind me,
> There are angry soldiers too.

His poems attacked the government for both its militarist anti-democratic policies as well as its elite-oriented economic policies. In the same year, 1978, scores of students had been arrested after a wave of demonstrations, some sentenced to two or more years in prison. Student Councils were banned from all campuses. This repression in

1978 followed an earlier wave of arrests and newspaper closures in 1974, when several professors and students spent a year in jail. Three of them—Hariman Siregar, Aini Chalid and the economist Sjahrir— were put on trial and sentenced to five or more years. Several major newspapers, including those published or edited by very prominent intellectuals, Mochtar Lubis and Rosihan Anwar, were shut down.

Rendra, the professors and students had all been, and still mostly were, critics and opponents of Sukarnoism and the Indonesian Communist Party (PKI). None of them had ever demanded the release of those detained on Buru Island or in other prisons. Some had been at the forefront of anti-Sukarno campaigns before 1965. Some, like the publisher and writer, Mochtar Lubis, had been arrested by Sukarno and only released after Suharto came to power. Lubis was one among a number of intellectuals who visited Buru Camp in 1974 and met Pramoedya, asking him: 'Do you believe in God yet?' The repression of former allies of Suharto between 1974 and 1978 reflected how the New Order dictatorship was becoming even more authoritarian. Not only having violently smashed the pre-1965 Left, but it was also hitting out at former allies who had become critical on questions of corruption, democratic rights and development strategies.

The thousands of political prisoners were not being released in 1979 because there was a general loosening in authoritarian control. As Joesoef had explained, it was the administrative and political impossibility of putting 20,000 people on trial without evidence, combined with the pressure from the Carter administration, that meant indefinite imprisonment was impossible. So they were all being released just as repression was hardening. In 1980, when Hasjim, Joesoef and Pramoedya sat down together in Joesoef's lounge room and decided to publish *Bumi Manusia*, a work written by a vilified 'communist' to be released by communist ex-political prisoners, they were deciding to defy Suharto just as he was becoming even more repressive. They knew that wherever they were, 'angry soldiers' would be standing behind them. Given what they had been through and the situation they faced in 1980, their decision was a direct and courageous act of defiance. It was an act of defiance thrown in the face of oppression: when *Bumi*

Manusia did appear, it bore across the front cover, the words, 'A Work from Buru Island'.

The first step was for the three men to set up Hasta Mitra as a company. Hasjim and Pramoedya knew each other well, both from the *Eastern Star* period and living together in the same Buru Camp hut for some time. Hasjim and Joesoef knew each other well also, both from being active in the Sukarnoist wing of the journalist associations and working together on the government's plans for getting Fokker aircraft company involved in Indonesia. Pramoedya and Joesoef did not know each other at all. Pramoedya thought he may have seen Joesoef in the Asian–African Journalists' Association office, but they had never met and talked. It was Hasjim who had brought Pramoedya to meet Joesoef at Joesoef's house. This first meeting was not to discuss the book, but to hear Joesoef's views on the political situation and his experiences of life after imprisonment. Joesoef had already been out of jail for more than two years when Hasjim and Pramoedya arrived in Jakarta. Soon after that, Hasjim broached the idea of a project to publish the books Pramoedya had written on Buru Island.

The first thing they had to do was go to a lawyer and set up the company, Hasta Mitra, the name Pramoedya had suggested to Hasjim back on Buru Island. The decision was to publish *Bumi Manusia* first and then its three sequels, so Joesoef, who was appointed editor, had to read the manuscript.

Very soon after I first met Joesoef in 1980, during a visit to his house, he brought out what appeared to be an original typescript of one of the books. It was a thick wad of A4 pages typed without either top or side margins, using up every centimetre of space. 'Look,' he pointed out to me, 'hardly a correction anywhere in the manuscript.' The whole novel must have just flowed without a pause from Pramoedya's brain and heart, through his fingers and via the keyboard onto those sheets of paper. I have heard many versions of how the manuscripts were preserved. Copies were made in the camp by prisoners who helped Pramoedya. They were smuggled out via supportive priests. It seems also that Pramoedya could keep copies. In any case, they were back in the hands of the author and now with Joesoef.

In the interviews, we recorded in 1993, I asked him what his first reaction on reading *Bumi Manusia* was, but I had heard him express the same sentiments back in 1980, when we first met:

> I can't describe it in words. It made me feel alive again. It had been a long time since I read a novel that good, maybe the last time was thirty years before that, when I was still twenty . . . Tolstoy's novels. Journalists don't have that much time to read . . . So, when I read Pramoedya . . . that was amazing.

Hasjim, of course, had become intimately familiar with the plot and sub-plots and characters and Pramoedya's storytelling in the camp on Buru. Like Joesoef, he never stopped being excited by the novels. The story of awakening, of resistance and of fighting back against oppression well and honourably was, for them, the essence of what Indonesia had been and should be. And it stirred many of the same feelings in its tens of thousands of readers later in 1980.

But first things first. Joesoef began his task of editing the manuscript, correcting typos and checking consistency. On Buru, Pramoedya had been able to fact-check many aspects of these historical novels by asking some of the other outstanding intellectuals imprisoned there, but there was still a duty of care that Joesoef needed to carry out. And then there was the physical production of the book. Hasjim had mobilized the funds to print and publish the book, but it was done on a minimum budget. The office was in Joesoef's house, with desks for administrative and clerical operations in the front part of his lounge room. Joesoef himself worked in the back with his assistant, a self-trained computer man and typist, Bowo. The two of them worked in a tiny room, a metre wide and 6 metres long. Perhaps it had been a little storeroom at some stage. They both sat at the same long and narrow bench, their backs to the wall. There was a small window at one end, with a little light getting in but not enough to do away with flicking on the light switch. Joeosef was a chain smoker, so the air was often cloudy.

The narrow bench meant the equipment could only just fit in, with some narrow workspace only alongside the equipment. Although out of prison and returning from exile into a very new environment, the Hasta

Mitra gang didn't hesitate to try what was new. They bought a CRTronic phototypesetting machine. It sat in the semi-dark on Joesoef's and Bowo's bench, where *Bumi Manusia* was laid out for the printer. Later, by the time monies from the book's excellent sales came in, Joesoef was able to keep pace with technological developments and swapped the CRTronic for a new Apple computer and publishing software.

That dingy, usually smoke-filled ex-storeroom, with book cases on the walls lined with dictionaries and encyclopaedias, remained Joesoef's office for the next few decades, right up to the day he passed away in 2009. He edited and typeset all of Pramoedya's books published by Hasta Mitra, and scores of others as well. In between working on Hasta Mitra's books, Joesoef also translated many Dutch scholarly and scientific books into Indonesian as a means of making a living. There was one rattan chair across from where Joesoef would sit behind his computer, where a guest or friend, such as myself, could sit and talk with him.

Hasta Mitra's impact on Indonesian historical processes, as a publisher in the 1980s, was enormous, as we will see later. And for the whole time, it operated out of Joesoef's converted storeroom and half of his family home's front parlour. In those first hectic months in 1980 and 1981, the front parlour saw people—mostly ex-prisoners—coming in and out all the time, picking up materials, checking with Hasjim on this and that. Joesoef's wife, Asni and their three boys, had to make do with a home that was half-office and half-home.

Bumi Manusia was published in August 1980, about nine months after Hasjim and Pramoedya returned from exile to Jakarta. Just nine months! And this was despite having to report to the Army or police regularly, despite Suharto's repression being at its worse and operating in what was an unfamiliar environment returning from exile.

Joesoef remembered the atmosphere when the book was released:

> It was amazing, I will never forget what happened. We were announcing loudly to the public that: yes, we do exist among you. But, Max, if I said I was excited, my heart was racing all the time, it wasn't because I was worried, no, no, we realized we had to wait to see how the authorities would react, what the intelligence agency would do, what the Attorney

General would do—we had to keep those things in mind. But we didn't have to worry about the public, if they would buy the book or not. I was pretty sure; I had no doubt that they would buy the book in droves. And that was indeed what happened. The book was out for two days, not many stores had got it, and we already received a call from the Attorney General telling us not to distribute the book.

The government tried to move against Hasta Mitra and the books before anybody in the government had even read it. Before the contents of the book could make their massive impact, their act of defiance was already a threat. Joesoef continued:

I don't know if you've heard this story, but it's important that you know, at that time, in the early eighties, there was what people used to call "waiting for a call". All the newspapers, the dailies and the magazines, were used to taking calls from the Information Ministry, the Attorney General or the military . . . both from the officers and their underlings. These officials had no problem telling journalists not to print this or that, news that would expose them. "Waiting for a call" meant we couldn't do anything against government censorship. The government was dictating the terms to us. And so they did the same thing to Hasta Mitra.

A direct order came from the Attorney General not to publish Pramoedya Ananta Toer before "we cleared it". That was the term he used, "clear". I happened to be the one to pick up the phone when they called. I listened and told them that I understood what they were asking me. I said I would have to confirm it with my friends if I was going to do all they were telling me to do. But I convinced them that I understood what they asked of me. So, that's what happened. I then spoke to Hasjim and we decided that we were going to go ahead with publishing the book. We knew we could do that since the law didn't say that we must stop publication of a book just because someone made a phone call to us. So that was our official position, we were going ahead with the publication.

It was tense, I think we were gauging each other's strength— ourselves and the regime. They were trying to see how much resolve Hasta Mitra had, were we going to do as we were told? And at the same time, we were also waiting to see if they were going to close us down if we went ahead with the book. And so on the Monday, eh, the Friday . . . you know Max, there was a rule that 48 hours after a book went into print, at least two copies had to be sent to the Attorney General for inspection. So we decided to release the book on Friday, a half-day. Saturday was also a half-day for offices, and on Sunday they were closed. We released the book on a Friday so we had at least three days to distribute it. We sent it to Jogja, Surabaya and to former political prisoners, our own friends, they were selling the book door-to-door.

We were racing against time, for three days. On Monday, we waited for another call from them, and they did call. They told me the same thing, and I told them the same thing, "okay, yes, I heard you". But we didn't do what they asked us to do. This deadlock lasted for ten months, Max, and it was a triumph for us. In those ten months, the first print-run, 10,000 copies, were sold out in two weeks. In ten months, we printed and sold 60,000 copies, unheard of at the time for a serious book like this. It never happened to another book, or another publisher. It was amazing.

Coming out in August, the first review appeared in the prestigious morning newspaper, *Kompas*, and then throughout September and onwards, there were more reviews. The reviews were all written by prominent intellectuals and the overwhelming majority were positive more than positive, almost ecstatic. The long review in *Kompas* newspaper, a newspaper that played a leading role in establishing the New Order and vilifying the PKI back in 1965, was written by well-known writer Parakitri Simbolon. Parakitri was a student in the immediate years after Suharto came to power, who later studied in France, and was a prolific essayist, novelist and critic. He also became a senior journalist at the *Kompas* newspaper, writing with considerable authority and not at all as a marginal intellectual. He included in his review the paragraph:

How wide must Pramoedya's knowledge and understanding be to have written such an extraordinary novel. How deeply has he depicted the essence of the turn of the twentieth century, a period so far untouched by Indonesian literature. How successful has he been in pouring all this on page after page for 328 pages in a lucid and enjoyable language, in a style preferred by the seventies generation, but without losing the Pramoedya Ananta Toer power to grip us.[4]

In the main daily newspaper in the major city of Bandung, Yakob Sumarjo, another prominent intellectual, included these paragraphs in his extensive review, which was entitled 'The Work of Indonesia's Greatest Novelist: Pramoedya's "*Bumi Manusia*":

> We are fortunate to witness the publication of such a great novel in this decade. This is a novel written without any megalomaniac pretensions, but a novel of honest searching, told in a simple and conventional manner. It is a novel that seeks to both ask and answer without relying on this or that philosophy borrowed from the West. Reading the novel we are reminded of Pasternak's *Doctor Zhivago*, which by telling realistically the story of an army doctor, succeeds in capturing and depicting an era. . . . This novel can be a document of its era. We will be enriched over and over each time we re-read it.[5]

These and other similar reviews were amazing to read at the time. Why? Because they were reviews of a writer who, as one of thousands accused of being involved somehow in the so-called 1965 'communist putsch', had been labelled anti-Pancasila, anti-Indonesian, evil, part of a treasonous horde and indeed legitimately imprisoned for fourteen years.

These reviewers, in the major daily newspapers, were defying the regime almost as much as Hasta Mitra. The reviews would have pleased any author and publisher, but they were more than just reviews. They were a rejection of the whole ideological edifice that the New Order had established. Those on Buru Island deserved to be there, they had

---

[4] Parakitri, 'Bumi Manusia Pramoedya: Cambuk Dari Kemaluan Sapi Jantan', *Kompas*, 18 August, 1980. Reprinted in Adhy Asmara dr, *Anlisa Ringan Kemelut Bumi Manusia Pramoedya Ananta Toer* (Nur Cahaya: Yogyakarta, 1981), pp. 43–49.

[5] Yakob Sumarjo, 'Karya Novelis Tersebar Indonesia BUMI MANUSIA Pramoedya', *Pikiran Rakyat*, 10 September, 1980. Reprinted in Adhy Asmara dr, *Anlisa Ringan Kemelut Bumi Manusia Pramoedya Ananta Toer*, pp. 38–42.

proclaimed continuously. But was that true? Had indeed the author and publishers of *Bumi Manusia* ever deserved to have been there?

One often hears the comment, the speculation, that Pramoedya's depiction of colonial oppression was also meant to be a commentary on the New Order. I don't think that is true. Pramoedya's inspiration was to unravel and explain the process by which Indonesians came into existence. Minke, one of the two main protagonists in *Bumi Manusia*, perhaps was many things but, above all, he was an Indonesian-to-be. The social reality of Java and the world at the turn of the twentieth century was what Pramoedya was primarily trying to capture: Indonesia's origin story from before there was even a word for Indonesia. Of course, that does not rule out the reader identifying parallels between aspects of a colony, which was indeed essentially a dictatorship under a governor-general appointed from the Netherlands, and Suharto's Indonesia.

The reactions in the reviews, however, went deeper than simply noting the parallels between two kinds of dictatorship. In fact, it was the recognition of these deeper insights that elevated the book in almost everybody's eyes to a level that above all other existing literature and, most importantly, located its critical function beyond that of simply an attack on the current regime. There were two levels to this.

The first was the novel's character as an attack on colonialism, which is deepened further in its sequels. The exposé of colonialism ranges from the racism of the main character being called a monkey by his Dutch high school teacher, through to very practice of Dutch men taking (more or less by force) of local women as concubines, to the exploitation of the peasant and the dictatorial power wielded arbitrarily by the colonial state. The central plot of the novel evolves out of a series of colonialist interventions even into the private lives of local families, leading to misery and suffering. In this context, the story talks of resistance, the action and the consciousness that is needed for that resistance. There is little doubt that this anti-colonial character of the text struck a chord among a wide readership. This was especially as it showed resistance of intelligent, well-read and thoughtful people—a village girl taken to be a concubine but who developed, including through wide reading in Dutch, to be able to deeply critique

colonial society. This village girl also became the teacher-mentor of
the Western-schooled son of a Javanese feudal official, reversing the
normally depicted teacher–student relationship whereby the upper
class educates the lower.

The fourteen-year-old girl, Sanikem, develops into the awe-
inspiring Nyai Ontosoroh, a concubine to a Dutch businessman, but
greater in understanding or stronger in character than her 'master'.
The quality of the anti-colonial subjectivity was elevated above that
of the angry, unjustly treated but traditional peasant rebel or victim.
Neither Nyai nor Minke (you will have to read the novel, if you haven't
yet) were the innocent Saidjah or Adinda, unable to offer any real
resistance, from Mulatuli's novel *Max Havelaar*.

Suharto's vice president in 1980 was a man named Adam Malik.
In 1945, he had been one of a group of young anti-colonial activists
who had 'kidnapped' the nationalist movement's key figures, Sukarno
and Muhammad Hatta, urging them not to delay any proclamation of
independence, which they had been holding off from doing as they
watched how the transition after the surrender of Japan to the allies
transpired. In August 1945, the Japanese were still in control on the
ground, although they had promised to maintain order until Allied
Forces arrived. Malik was active in the anti-colonial struggle between
1945 and 1949, when the Dutch military and bureaucracy were forced
to leave Indonesia. Between 1950 and 1965, Malik founded and became
the central figure of a political party called the Murba Party. The Murba
Party, sometimes described as a 'national communist' party, initially
had reasonable relations with the PKI. By the 1960s, however, they
had become enemies and the PKI was campaigning demanding that
Sukarno should ban the party, although Malik himself held senior
ministerial positions in Sukarno's cabinet. After Suharto came to
power, Adam Malik served as Foreign Minister, then held positions in
the parliamentary leadership, and became the vice president between
1978 and 1983. Malik had been a campaigner against communism in the
period immediately before 1965 and then a central figure in Suharto's
new regime during its first fifteen years. He eventually left the Murba
Party and joined Suharto's electoral organization, Golkar. At the same
time, he had been a revolutionary anti-colonial activist in the 1940s.

Before *Bumi Manusia* was published, Hasjim, Joesoef and Pramoedya went to see Vice President Malik to tell him of their plans. Malik encouraged them to proceed. Then after the book was published and Hasta Mitra was being pressured to withdraw the book, they went to see him again, by which time he had read the novel. On 16 September, the national press published photos of Hasjim, Pramoedya and Joesoef together with Adam Malik, reporting the Vice President as saying:

> It should be the case that everybody read *Bumi Manusia*, especially our younger generation. *Bumi Manusia* should be read in our schools. I have read the whole book. Its contents are very good and its historical value is very important. Our youth, by reading this, will understand how their fathers confronted colonialism.[6]

Those with the real power did not share Vice President Malik's sentiments and banned the book soon afterwards. Malik's support for the book, and the prominent press reporting of the meeting between Hasta Mitra and the vice president, underlines the contradictions exposed by the publication of the book. For Malik, and for thousands of other readers in 1980, the country's confrontation with colonialism, and the courage, intelligence and persistence associated with that resistance, was inspiring. It had been that resistance that had created Indonesia. It wasn't just Pramoedya, Joesoef and Hasjim—nor even the 20,000 other prisoners who had been released—who were returning from exile but *Indonesia itself.*

Malik, while a part of a regime that had exiled that original Indonesia, was somebody who had been a part of the origin story. He wanted the youth to understand: 'Our youth, by reading this, will understand how their fathers confronted colonialism.' *Bumi Manusia* is not even a novel about the national struggle, but rather predates that and is instead a novel about where Indonesia came from—from fighting back—and the struggle that had originally defined its being. Malik, commenting on the

---

[6] Rendra, 'Si Nyai yang bikin heboh', reprinted in Adhy Asmara dr, *Anlisa Ringan Kemelut Bumi Manusia Pramoedya Ananta Toer* (Nur Cahaya: Yogyakarta, 1981), pp. 28–35.

resistance offered by a woman and her high school protégé, still felt that as a connect with how he and his generation had confronted colonialism.

Pramoedya wrote the novel not only to make the point that the origins of the process that later led to the emergence of a country and the nation of Indonesia evolved out of a resistance to colonialism. It also arose out of the rejection of local despotic tradition. Parakitri began the section of his review in *Kompas* dealing with this aspect with the sentence, 'The novel, with its great depth, delved down into the very roots of our own culture (Java)'.

Parakitri himself chose to focus on how Pramoedya described Minke, the awakening young man of Java, squatted in obeisance to his father, a regent in a town on Java, sitting in his ornate rocking chair, kept tapping him on the head with a whip made from a bull's genitals, reminding Minke of his subordinate position. There were two aspects, at least, to this indignity. The first was the humiliation. Parakitri quotes from this scene in the novel:

> Truly, my friends would ridicule me if they could see this play, where a human being, who normally walks on his two whole legs, on his own feet, now must walk with only half his legs, aided by his two hands, Ya Allah. You, my ancestors, you: What is the reason you created customs that would humiliate your own descendants? You never gave it any thought, you, my ancestors who indulged in these excesses! Your descendants could have been honoured without such humiliation! How could you bring yourself to leave such customs as a legacy?

Having drag-crawled himself along the floor before the rocking chair; he was then reprimanded, with each reprimand being accompanied by that whip's humiliating tap.

It wasn't only the humiliation as such that aggravated Minke but also the context, namely, how it contrasted with the process of achieving the consciousness of a serious agent of change, of the deep social transformation, that had begun. Parakitri wrote of this scene connecting it also with Minke's acute restlessness after being challenged by one of his Dutch teachers, Magda Peters: 'What have the Javanese contributed to the world?' What was the point? Minke tortured himself with the question: What was the point of obtaining all this learning only still to be subject to the humiliation of the whip made from a bull's genitals?

The novel's escape from its exile on Buru and into 'Indonesia' stirred the yearning for that dignified and developed national subjectivity evolving before 1965, through struggle and contestation, in many ways breaking from the past. It was stirring the yearning for a different Indonesia.

Both Joesoef and Hasjim told me many stories during 1980, whenever I visited Hasta Mitra at Joesoef's house, of people's reactions to the book. 'Perhaps you know him, Max, Hariman Siregar?' Hariman had been a high school activist against Sukarno and the PKI in 1965, but then, as a university student, had led the protests against Suharto in 1974, attacking dictatorship, corruption and an unjust development strategy. Along with hundreds of others, he was arrested, but in his case, charged and tried and sentenced to six years in prison, serving two years and seven months. And I did know Hariman, quite well. 'Hariman sent somebody to buy two copies. But then a few days later, he dropped in himself and bought ten copies—for friends, he said.' There were many other such stories but it was the phenomenal sales for a Buru Island book at the height of Suharto's oppressive power, that told the story. Even from within the new Indonesia, created through the burial of the old contestations of visions of the future, the novels answered a yearning—for an Indonesia with a strong sense of subjectivity, without the humiliation of obeisance but indeed the spirit of fight back.

There were though, of course, still ambiguities even to the positive reception of the *Bumi Manusia*—the underlying fundamental contradictions emerged later with the bannings. Rendra, for example, quickly responded to *Bumi Manusia* with a more complicated perspective. Rendra was without doubt the most prominent and popular literary political figure of the 1970s. He had emerged as a critic of the Suharto regime soon after he returned from several years of the study of theatre in the United States. Unlike all of the his fellow artistic critics of Sukarnoism and the PKI, he had been away from Indonesia during the tense years of 1964–65 and the violence of 1965–66. He had been in Greenwich Village, New York City, one of the centres of 1960's US radicalism and counter-culture. Despite this quite different experience, he still identified politically with the pre-'65 critics of Suakrno, the PKI and of Prameodya. Still, he began his review of *Bumi Manusia* with the following paragraph:

> It would be no surprise if readers of *Bumi Manusia*, the first volume in the tetralogy written by Pramoedya Ananta Toer, without being instructed by anybody, immediately encouraged everybody to read the novel with the words: "This is a really good novel. You must read it." And indeed it is a really good novel.

After making some remarks that the novel had a slow first twenty pages, Rendra continued: 'As soon as the story starts properly, it is almost impossible to put the book down. Here is its greatness. Especially when Pram writes about the culture of that earlier period and how it influenced people's behaviour. Aha, here is where this novel excels.'

These sentiments were repeated more than once in Rendra's review, reaffirming the reality of *Bumi Manusia*'s successful penetration into the cultural mindset of the new Indonesia even after sixteen years of exile and the extreme transformation of Indonesia. There were, however, qualifications to Rendra's assessment—not literary, as such, but rather political, which embodied deeper differences in approaching realities.

Rendra explained that he found the character of Nyai Ontosoroh, one of the two central figures in the novel, to be unappealingly formal and bourgeois. It is worth restating two things here: it was the struggle of the young village girl, Sanikem, later to be known as Nyai Ontosorh, against a myriad of oppressions, that raised the morale of the prisoners on Buru Island, during their worst treatment at the hands of the guards. It was the strength of character, critical intellect, and real gumption of Nyai Ontosoroh both in dealing with her degenerate Dutch husband, as well as dictatorial colonial power, that inspired most readers in the 1980s. Indeed, even until today, the figure of Nyai is talked about as another example of the strong, inspiring women characters that Pramoedya consistently portrayed. In 2007, one of Indonesia's leading playwrights, Faiza Mardzoeki,[30] turned Nyai's story into a stage play, performing to packed houses in Jakarta and other cities, and later, in a different adaptation, in Amsterdam and Antwerp.

Rendra viewed this same character, however, as too bourgeois, too formal, too elitist. From informal discussions with Rendra, whom I also knew well at that time, I knew that he viewed Pramoedya himself the same way: bourgeois, formal and elitist. This was partly due to some direct interactions from before 1965 between Rendra, then in his late twenties, and Pramoedya, in his late thirties. There is more to it, than these minor experiences from before 1965. Pramoedya had been driven since the late 1950s to find the source of Indonesia's inability to progress, compared to the progress Pramoedya had witnessed in China in the 1950s.

He found his answer in Indonesia's inability to sweep away the obstacles that its despotic traditions put in the way of the spread of a culture of deep science and learning. Minke cried out in humiliation at the taps on his head while he asked how could ever his people advance without sweeping such legacies from the past away. The three novels that come after *Bumi Manusia* tell the story of the even greater struggles in the embryonic nation to try to awaken a critical, contemporary consciousness. For Pramoedya, it was the objective role of the kind of individuals represented by the Nyai and Minke, that was crucial: what they succeeded and failed in achieving.

For Rendra, the crucial thing was the function of such figures as role models for day-to-day behaviour. A popular and democratic kind of behaviour is inspired from folk perspectives that deride formality and elevate informality as the bridge to egalitarianism. Formality is hierarchical, informality is democratic. Rendra wrote:

> I like the ideal world, the social ideals, the cultural ideals of Nyai Ontosoroh and Minke. But if there were people such as they, they would certainly not be people nice to socialize with. The porotypes of bureaucrats. A picture of bourgeois types. And Pram depicts the egoism and formalism of the bourgeois very convincingly in *Bumi Manusia*. From that we can assume that Pram himself is very at ease with such bourgeois customs.

Rendra goes on to argue that it was this formal, hierarchical approach of Pram's generation that helped foster a culture of 'banning and forbidding' (*larang melarang*) before 1965. Rendra noted earlier in his review how Pramoedya was especially good at depicting 'culture of that earlier period and how it influenced people's behaviour'. For Rendra, it was culture itself—values—that influenced behaviour. Pramoedya focused on uncovering objective dynamics: it was, in his eyes, the early local bourgeoisie that were the first agents of social transformation of change—although in the third and fourth books of the series, he thoroughly depicts their failure as a social layer and hints at the emergence of proletarians as a new key agency.

Rendra's critique came from within the new Indonesia created by 1965, even as he himself, through his own prism, was also by then questioning that new status quo. His questioning of the new Indonesia's status quo included unconditionally opposing the banning of *Bumi Manusia* and ridiculing the various reasons given by the authorities.

Less than a year back from Buru Island (although somewhat longer since Joesoef had been released earlier from jail in Jakarta), Hasta Mitra had broken through onto centre-stage. While still reporting to the police regularly, under city arrest, their identity cards marked to show they had been political prisoners, banned from working in 'vital' sectors of the economy, realizing that they were defying a dictatorship, they had gone on the offensive. Perhaps one of the best manifestations of this defiant offensive strategy was Hasjim Rachman's strategy for promotion of *Bumi Manusia*. He was a businessman himself, a very politically progressive one at that. He had mobilized all the capital he could by selling some of his own goods and chattels to produce the book. He also had the moment to advertise the book in *Kompas*, Jakarta's main morning daily and an early supporter of Suharto's crushing of the PKI. Indeed it had been the publisher of *Kompas*, Jakob Oetama, who, as told by Joesoef and which I recounted in an earlier chapter, had moved into the Indonesian Journalists' Association to oust Joesoef Isak from his position in 1966. Publishers usually just did not spend the large amounts of money required for advertising in *Kompas* for a book title: but Hasjim Rachman did. And so there it was, calling out to the readers: Pramoedya was back and here was his latest book, written on Buru Island and we are advertising it, including with a paid advertisement in the New Order's premier newspaper.

Kompas and other major newspapers; Rendra and several other prominent intellectuals; Vice President Malik and tens of thousands of book buyers, all welcomed Pramoedya, Joesoef and Hasjim, and their vision of being Indonesian, back from exile. All the same, Suharto's regime, ignoring Vice President Adam Malik's statements, banned *Bumi Manusia* on 29 May 1981, nine months after its publication.

Chapter 9

The Books That Killed the New Order

Bumi Manusia was banned in May 1981, nine months after it was published. It had generated so much enthusiasm in the first months that it required an organized campaign by the regime over that extended period, before it could be banned. Besides Vice President Malik's open support for the book, both Chief of the Command for the Restoration of Order and Stability (KOPKAMTIB) Admiral Sudomo and Ali Said, the attorney-general, appeared reluctant to ban the book. They made public statements stating that it should be left up to the readers to determine the content, or otherwise soft-pedalled on issuing a ban. It was while Ali Said was away overseas that the ban occurred.

By May, 1981 Hasta Mitra had also published the first sequel to *Bumi Manusia*, namely *Anak Semua Bangsa* (*Child of All Nations*). Both books were banned together. The reason given was that they depicted 'conflict between classes', although the banning order never cited any instances or presented any argument to support this. The reference to class conflict was meant, of course, to label the books as 'communist', as in the Indonesian context, it was supposed to be only communists who talked about class. Communism was the ultimate evil. In fact, communists were so evil, went the propaganda, as to have warranted political genocide.

Max Lane with Hasjim Rachman, 1981.

Even today, it is still not clear what was going on inside the regime, however an early internal document from the Department of Defence and Security (HANKAM) from September 1980, more fully exposes the thinking of the most repressive part of the state. HANKAM regularly issued political reports, with directions flowing from them to all the Army command posts based throughout the country. Unlike most armies throughout the world, the Indonesian army was structured to have bases in every province, and with command posts in all towns, as well as non-commissioned officers based in every village. Established in the 1950s on the pretext of continuing a synergy with society that had existed, it was argued, during the guerilla warfare against the invading Dutch colonial forces. It in fact, operated as a military shadow government, often more powerful than the civilian apparatus.

To give political direction to this structure, HANKAM issued 'Territorial Assessments'. These were internal documents. The Territorial Assessment sent out just a month after *Bumi Manusia* was published, noted that 5,000 copies had been printed and were already on sale in shops.[31] The first print run was 10,000. The Assessment stated that the book was warmly welcomed by 'certain kinds' of people who appreciated literature. It went on to inform its military readers around the country as to who the author was: 'The author of this book is Pramudya [sic] Ananta Tur a prominent writer and leader of Lekra who was involved in the G-30-S PKI.'

This is stated, even though, as we saw, Pramoedya and all people released from the Buru camp were issued letters stating that there was no evidence of such involvement on their part. The report continued: 'He was classified as a part of the *diehard* B Category of prisoners and so was among the last to be released along with 105 other diehards late in 1979. Throughout his imprisonment and up until his release, he remained hardline as a follower of communist ideology.'

The report also informed its readers that the book was published by Hasta Mitra, led by Hasjim Rachman, who had been released together with Pramoedya. After mentioning the positive reviews of the book by Parakitri, Yakon Sumarjoo and others, it continued: 'Groups of writers of a certain level have given excessive praise to this book to encourage people to read it. It has an attractive title, although not to broader society.'

The promotion of the book and plans for its international publication in translation, was seen as primarily a moneymaking exercise which ignored the needs of 'national security'. This was especially the case, said the report, as the book was explicitly being promoted as 'A work from Buru Island'. However, of greater danger, were its contents:

> If we study the text carefully, we see that there are still depictions of class struggle, a specific characteristic of communist thinking. These are hidden neatly within and so even though they will not be sensed by many readers, yet there remains an attempt to penetrate with the communist ideology. This reflects the diehard commitment of the writer, and also the intention to influence his friends of a similar fate, as is manifested in using the words "A Work from Buru Island".

There was an ironic contradiction in how the Assessment summed the appeal of the book:

> *Bumi Manusia* can only be appreciated by a small number of people, of a certain kind, who appreciate novels/literature but is not suitable for a

wider readership, both because of its contents and what it is as a work
[of literature].

They seemed to be saying it remained dangerous despite it being appreciated by only a small number of people, 'praising it excessively' because of a commercial motivation—although how the reviewers were to make money off of Hasta Mitra's sales was not explained.

In giving directions to the territorial command structure, the report writer summed up, warning everybody: 'The communist threat was a "latent danger" which could still penetrate [society] through various means, including cultural.'

Interestingly, the assessment made no mention of a prospective ban, rather instructing everybody to be ready to explain the dangers that the book represented. Why did it take so long for *Bumi Manusia* to be banned despite this kind of evaluation from the military?

First, the regime was caught totally off-guard. Who would have thought that within only six months of being terrorized in a prison camp for fourteen years or ten years in a jail cell, there would be such defiant, brazen publishing of a novel of resistance to oppression with the words 'A Work From Buru Island' emblazoned across the front cover? And who would have predicted, even after fifteen years of constant black propaganda, all the initial reviews would be 'excessively praising' a novel from an allegedly evil, 'diehard' communist? Who would have predicted that the publisher that most consistently refused to accede to pressure over the phone, would be just-released prisoners?

The terror had not worked and that caught the regime by surprise. There were deeper reasons also.

It may sound cryptic, but banning *Bumi Manusia* was tantamount to banning Indonesia itself.

Vice President Malik's unqualified encouragement of people to read the books, the plethora of reviews appearing in just about every newspaper and magazine published at the time, the popularity of the book, and even the hesitancy of regime figures, such as the security chief Admiral Sudomo and Attorney-General Ali Said, all testified to the reality that the book had struck a chord. The strong Indonesian subjectivity, the novel's powerful characters representing

Indonesia-to-be, in this national origin story, inspired people. Banning the book would mean stopping the circulation within the country, of the most inspiring story of the origins of Indonesia. The country's leading intellectuals, even those who were hostile to the PKI and Sukarno or who had reservations about Pramoedya himself, were not and would not support the banning of the books. Nor would they agree to labelling the book as communist propaganda, something, for example, Rendra had written, was a ridiculous accusation. Most, if not all, of those writers who had been most hostile to the PKI and Pramoedya before 1965, and who did not praise the book, published essays in the press speaking against banning *Bumi Manusia*.

On the back of a truck is painted a picture of Pramoedya and one of the most popular quotes from *Bumi Manusia*, 'Happy are they who eat from the products of their own sweat, obtain pleasure from their own endeavors, and advance because of their own experiences.'

The regime found itself needing to be careful about how to ban this work from Buru Island, even at the height of its power. It went through several stages, the first of which was to apply informal pressure. As related earlier by Joesoef, the first tactic was the telephone call.

As Joesoef explained, they ignored the first call from the prosecutor's office and continued selling the book. Contrary to the practice widespread among journalists and publishers at the time, Hasta Mitra decided that they would not consider phone calls an official communication. They would have been the only ones defying the authorities in this way. After a few more ignored calls, the prosecutor's office switched tactics and telephoned Hasjim summoning him to their office. Hasjim describes:

> Yes, they summonsed me. First, by phone. But I ignored it. I didn't like getting requests on the phone. Journalists, when they get a phone call, especially from the attorney-general, would drop everything to do whatever they were asked to. But I didn't want to do that. That was a bad habit and I didn't want to have anything to do with that. So I never went. Then they sent me a letter. Then I went. They asked me why I didn't come when they called me on the phone. I told them, well, it could've been anyone on the phone. He could've said he was President Suharto. Did I have to believe that was really Suharto on the other side? That's why I never came, I said. But once they summonsed me by letter, I came.

Hasjim related what happened in the first interrogation in mid-September:

> The chief interrogator hated me, because he thought I wasn't cooperative . . . because I didn't want to come to his office when they called me on the phone. He told me I was a typical PKI man, typically stubborn. He thought I was deliberately resisting him. He already had all these prejudices against me. So, I didn't really like this man. Why? None of his arguments made any sense either.

In a resume of all that happened, Hasjim noted that at the end of three days of interrogations, the official interviewing him summed up the four books, only one of which had been published at that time, in the following way:

> *Bumi Manusia* depicts class conflict.
> *Anak Semua Bangsa* depicts internationalism.

Jejak Langkah is the Communist Manifesto.
Rumah Kaca is the communist society.

Hasjim laughed:

How did he come up with all these things, had he read the books? As
it turned out, he had never read those books. He was just looking for
excuses to ban them. His questions weren't hard to answer. Because they
didn't make sense. They weren't difficult questions. He asked, "Who told
you to publish this book?" He thought there must have been someone
who . . . ordered me to publish this book. Then he asked, "What do you
want to achieve by publishing this book?" Answering him was easy. But
he didn't believe any of my answers. He would not even consider that it
would be good for all Indonesians to read the book. He thought it was
only good for the communists . . . He already had the answers himself.
He had them in his head already. That was what he believed.

In October, came another attack from within the regime. The
Ministry of Education issued a circular, banning possession of *Bumi
Manusia* by anybody in any educational institution or venue. The circular
falsely claimed that the Attorney-General Ali Said, had banned the book.
Later, another official of the ministry claimed not to know anything about
the ban. Then on 11 October, Joesoef and Hasjim started to hear that the
newspapers were being telephoned and told not to print any more reviews.
A few days later, they were both were summonsed again and shown a
letter from 1979 by the Chief of Staff of KOPKAMTIB, General Yoga
Sugama, telling the government publisher, Pustaka Jaya, that all writings
of ex-PKI prisoners had been banned. Joesoef and Hasjim rejected the
validity of the letter as applying in 1980. They said they would continue
publishing and selling the book while there was no official banning order.
Meanwhile, on 17 October, the Attorney General's office confirmed it
had not banned *Bumi Manusia*. Still, Hasjim was summonsed again and
again, as was management of the printers handling the book. The printers
were pressured to abandon printing the book.

It was in November, that *Bumi Manusia* had its third reprint, but
with a different printer. It continued to sell and then Hasta Mitra
published its first sequel, *Anak Semua Bangsa*. Again, Hasta Mitra

used the legal loophole: books could only be banned after they were published. Telephone calls and summons continued on a more or less regular basis. There were more summons. At one point, Joesoef was called in three or four days a week for a month. 'It was torture, Max,' he told me, 'but not physical torture.' He explained:

> Okay, I don't feel comfortable telling the story since it involves an Indonesian civil servant, a prosecutor in the Attorney-General's office. But yes, sometimes I had to scratch my head, wondering how someone with a law degree can be so ignorant, and why he was tasked to interrogate me. The interrogator wasn't as well-informed as the person he was interrogating.
>
> They should have selected someone who was at least as smart, as knowledgeable as the person they wanted to interrogate. So the whole time I was thinking: why do I have to deal with this stupid person, yes, that's the most accurate way to describe him: stupid. He asked me: "What does Pramoedya write?" So, I reeled off a list of Pram's writings. The last one was an encyclopaedia he was working on. Then he asked me, "What is an encyclopaedia?" So I explained it to him: "it's a kind of a dictionary, but more extensive". Then he turned over the interrogation note and asked me, "Can you write down 'Encyclopaedia' there, how do you spell it?" Imagine that, being interrogated by an imbecile like that. And he had the gall to quiz me—obviously under instruction—about historical materialism. He asked me all these serious questions as well, and he had to write down everything I said. So, yeah, for a whole month—not every day, sometimes there would be a few days' break, but yes, for the whole month, this interrogator was acting extremely tense.
>
> I had asked him—since one of their accusations was that Hasta Mitra, and the book, were guilty of secretly promoting Marxist propaganda—"If that's your accusation, can you tell me in which sentence, which paragraph, which chapter, did you find Marxist and Communist propaganda?" The only thing he could say was, "Sir, I can't prove it to you, but I can feel it." I mean, you know, a prosecutor must provide proof that the accused was guilty of the crime he is accused of. That was what I expected. He was accusing me that by publishing this book I was guilty of spreading Marxist propaganda. Can you tell me where we did that, where is the evidence. But no, the only thing he

said was no, I can't prove it but I can feel it. I even made a proposal to him: "Let's organize a debate, a small seminar attended by experts." Hasta Mitra was rich then, so I could say to him: "We'll pay for the seminar. You can select the speakers, as long as they are real experts—sociologists, political scientists—you decide. We'll pay for all of them. They can decide if the book really did promote Marxist values." Of course, he refused the offer, as you would expect.

But the end of that interrogation was something else. After a month, remember he was all tense for that whole month, but after the interrogation was over and I had signed all the papers, his whole demeanour changed. He was all smiles then. He wasn't tense anymore and treated me very nicely. And for the first time he told me what he really thought of the book, his personal opinion. He said it was a good book. Great. In a low voice he said, it's a great book. Then he asked me: "Do you still have a copy?" I asked him, "What for? You've got a lot of copies of the book in this building. We gave you thousands of copies." But he said, "All of those have to be burnt. And I can't even ask for one copy to be spared. Do you still have a copy at home?" I said, "Even if I do, I have to hand them in to you, right? I would be breaking the law if I still keep a copy in my house." He said, "Come on, just one for me. For my wife, please." He gave me his address. "Please, send me a copy. My wife still hasn't read it. Everyone has to read it," he said.

That was the last straw for me. He spent a whole month trying to intimidate me, telling me the book was dangerous, fomenting trouble. He criticized the book endlessly. "Now you want to have a copy of the book. Good man. Now you say to me your wife must read it," I told him. He said, "You have to understand. I'm just doing what I was told. We're now on the fourth floor, there are seven floors in this building. The instructions came from above. You must understand these things. He kept saying that. That was the end of my interrogation."

There was worse to come for Joesoef. He may be the only former prisoner from the post-1965 repression to have been detained again—for three months. This time, it was for nothing he did himself but because Pramoedya had spoken at a public forum at the University of Indonesia campus, organized by students, including Joesoef's son, Verdi. However, that was later in the year, six months after the banning of the two books in May.

The formal ban was issued by the Attorney-General's office while the Attorney-General was away overseas. Ali Said later told Hasjim that he didn't know it was going to happen. Hasta Mitra could see it coming. It wasn't only the increased pressure on the printers that signalled what was to come. Suddenly, as the positive reviews stopped following the wave of telephone warnings to the media, negative reviews emerged, all condemning the two books as being communist propaganda. A petition signed by seventeen mostly unknown people, claiming to be writers, was circulated and published in some media. They attracted no support, including not from Pramoedya's opponents from before 1965. It was clear that these were being engineered to provide the cover for the ban that came in May.

The ban did not stop Hasta Mitra from publishing the next two sequels, *Jejak Langkah* and *Rumah Kaca*, nor a collection of prison essays, *Nyanyi Sunyi Serang Bisu*, nor three anthologies of turn-of-the-century literature, edited by Pramoedya. But these titles were each very quickly banned after being published. The May 1981 ban was a blow to Hasta Mitra, but not to their political commitment, which was manifest in the publication of further books. It was a blow financially, which it made it harder and harder for the books to be published using the business's cash flow. Hasta Mitra's sustainability had to have a commercial basis. The enormous success of the first two books had provided a good cash flow, but after May 1981, that was increasingly squeezed. It was clear also that the press was under pressure as there were hardly any reviews at all for *Jejak Langkah* and *Rumah Kaca*.

While the ban was reported widely internationally, the regime was able to keep a lid on protests within Indonesia itself. Hasta Mitra had waged a one-year conventional war with its frontal 'A Work from Buru Island' offensive. From May 1981, they continued a guerilla war. While the huge, exciting and high-profile mainstream reporting of Pramoedya's works may have stopped, the publication of book after book, even if quickly banned thereafter, meant that the return from exile of the original Indonesia continued. Pirated versions of the books and photocopies circulated after each banning. While there were fewer full-page reviews, reports of the books or what Pramoedya or Joesoef or Hasjim had to say kept popping up.

A process had begun which went beyond and deeper than the promotion and sale of Pramoedya's books. As Joesoef said, the daring, frontal launch of the books was an announcement that the ex-prisoners were back; that the original Indonesia was here again. And *Bumi Manusia* had successfully shown that they weren't the evil rapists and murderers of the regime's black propaganda, but the purveyors of works of great humanist values, which brought to a new generation, the country's origin story as one of courageous resistance of an awakening people. A generation of young people, already politicized by people such as the poet Rendra and the student leader, Hariman Siregar, were given a new link to the past and new contacts in the present.

During 1980 and 1981, when I was still in Jakarta, there was already a constant flow of people, especially young people, to Pramoedya's house in Jakarta. As more books were published and circulated in one form or another, he received more and more visits. The books, however, did not only bring more people into contact with Pramoedya, Joesoef and Hasjim. People were now alert to the fact that there were thousands of people back from Buru or out of prison, who may be interesting to meet. Many thousands of those released from Buru or other prisons were peasant farmers or other kinds of proletarians, or perhaps village teachers or clerks, who made their way back to their home villages, where they were mostly received with minimal hostility. Those who had been intellectuals, writers, academics, musicians, film makers, artists or mass organization activists and members of parliament, mostly settled back into the cities. There were hundreds of such people, many in Jakarta.

Students whose curiosity had been aroused by Pramoedya's books or the furore around them in 1980 started to seek them out—a new generation. The 1970's generation of student movement opponents of the dictatorship had found their initial mentors among the intellectuals of the Indonesian Socialist Party (PSI), a Western-oriented social democratic, anti-Sukarno party before 1965, whose central leader, Sutan Sjahrir, had been arrested by Sukarno in 1962. By the early seventies, they had developed an outlook of their own, relating also to Rendra and other government critics. However, they retained a prejudice, received either from parents of PSI intellectuals, against the PKI and Sukarno, if not the Pramoedya of *Bumi Manusia*. The 1980s saw the influence of that generation of pre-'65 intellectuals from the PSI dispersed. While Rendra's poetry and plays retained a huge following, the influence of his ideas on politically active youth weakened.

It was, perhaps, Pramoedya, because of *Bumi Manusia* and his other books, that was the first point of gravitational pull. In November 1981, some students from the University of Indonesia invited Pramoedya to speak at a public forum there. This was Pramoedya's first public appearance and even though on campus and relatively low-profile, the regime obviously thought it was a dangerous precedent. The University of Indonesia had been the epicenter of anti-Suharto protests in 1974. Hariman Siregar had been the chairperson of the student council there. One of the three people eventually tried and sentenced to gaol was a lecturer at the University. Professor Sarbini Sumawinata, a leading academic critic of the government's economic policies, was also from the university, and spent a year in gaol in 1974. In 1978, student councils had been ordered dissolved, but students still met to organize events. According to notes prepared by Hasjim to inform friends, the students at the university had settled on Pramoedya as the invitee after discussion of a few other names as well.

Student leader Hariman Siregar (standing), (sitting, L-R): Joesoef Isak, Rendra, Max Lane at Lane's house for a goodbye party when he was being sent home by the Australian Ambassador, 1981.

Soon after the event, four students were arrested, including Verdi Joesoef. Soon after that, Joesoef himself, who attended with Hasjim, was detained. The students were released but then a few days later, detained again and asked to 'sleep over' at the military command quarters where they were being questioned, but told that they could go home after four days. According to Hasjim's notes, the students were interrogated by a former staff of Karel Supit, a PKI member of parliament before 1965. Former prisoners report that there was more than one PKI official who switched sides and worked as interrogators for the army.

Joesoef's arrest reflected the regime's paranoia that the PKI still existed as an organized force, or rather 'an organization without form'. The students reported that their interrogator and military present did not believe that the invitation to Pramoedya came from the students but that it had to be the result of some nefarious outside influence. It was the possibility of unseen manipulation by 'latent dangers' that was of primary concern to the security people. Pramoedya, who spoke at the forum, was not detained, although some officials did go to see him at his house. Hasjim, who attended the forum, was also not detained.

Joesoef was kept in detention for three months and interrogated almost every day. His wife, Asni, was initially prevented from seeing him, but after lobbying by Asni and also by Hasjim, he was released. Students had also put up posters on campus, and overseas human rights organizations were sending letters of protest to the authorities in Indonesia.

In this case, the superstition fell on Joesoef, Verdi's father. By 1981, the government has also instituted the policy of requiring 'Clean Environment' certificates from citizens. Joesoef later heard a story of how this case was being used for training security personnel:

One day, we heard from an editor-in-chief of a newspaper who was selected to go to a LEMHANAS [National Defence Institution] course. This is a nine-month course designed for military generals, company bosses, or other respected society figures. The major theme for this course is usually "National Vigilance". Apparently, in the curriculum for this course, this incident that involved me and my son was mentioned.

They were using it as a classic case study of an "unclean environment". The University of Indonesia had many faculties, but the Social Science Faculty was seen as the most Leftist. Why? Because Verdi was there. Verdi was my son, he was the son of an ex-political prisoner.

The 1970s had been marked by three waves of activist protests— in 1972, 1973–4 and 1978. In January 1974, the student protests, involving thousands of students, were accompanied in mid-January by tens of thousands of Jakarta proletarians, also demonstrating and rioting on the streets, attack and burning symbols of affluence, such as luxury car dealers. There was another wave of student protests in 1978, at the peak of which Rendra had read his protest poems and was detained the next day. The regime had to formally order the disbandment of all student councils. Now students were inviting Pramoedya, from Buru, to talk on campus.

University students were seen as a kind of wild X-factor in politics by the regime and were watched closely. Interaction between students and what Hasta Mitra represented, was instinctively dangerous for the security apparatus and political elite. Keeping a 'clean environment' was crucial for them. By the time they acted against three activists in the city of Yogyakarta in 1988, it was clear that it was too late to stop that interaction from taking place. Throughout 1988 and 1989, two students, Bambang Subono and Bonar Tigor Naipospos, and one university employee, Bambang Isti Nugroho, were subjected to repeated frightening interrogations and court cases, where they were convicted under an Anti-Subversion Law and sentenced to prison for from seven to eight and a half years. There were two elements to their perceived political criminality. First, they were selling the banned books by Pramoedya published by Hasta Mitra. Second, they were part of a network comprising a discussion group, whose agenda included topics relating to the Left history and ideas, as well as direct links to Hasta Mitra.

The students were pressured into making statements to the effect that they were working with Hasta Mitra and the People's Republic of China to make Indonesia a communist state.[32] The security personnel were horrified to find Indonesian translations of Left-wing books about

Cuba, Marx and other similar topics in the rooms of these students. Both Pramoedya and Joesoef told me in our interviews that they saw these trials as terrorism against the youth and students. According to Pramoedya:

> From a legal point of view, it was a joke, and people will remember it as a joke, a travesty, for centuries. But of course, I understand that all military governments have the need to put fear into the people. If the people are not afraid, military governments cannot work. The incident involving these students in Yogya, it was just an attempt at terror, to scare students and the young people, that's all, nothing more. They just want to be able to control students and young people. This was just a way to scare off the younger generation. But people are laughing at them, people will still laugh at what they did centuries from now.

Joesoef elaborated:

> As you know, Jogja is a student town, a lot of activists live and work there. As many as in Jakarta. The NGOs there are strong, the young activists very militant. Some of them were heavily involved in the fight against the Kedung Ombo dam. The background to the story was that there has been a militant student movement in Jogja. They're been reading Pram's books, distributing them, as well as doing their political activities. Some of them were in contact with us, asking us for spare copies of Pram's books. We gave them the books, but we did warn them that these books had already been banned. If they want the books for research, go ahead. You can still do a research study on banned books. But they were tricked by the authorities. They didn't expect that the government was going to use this as an excuse to silence them . . . to put a stop to their political activities. This is what most people don't see . . . that what the government wanted to destroy was a genuine student movement in Jogja.
>
> We read about the trial. By law, the books were banned so those who were found selling the books could be prosecuted. But as part of Hasta Mitra, as the publisher myself, I was very surprised that the writer of those books was left alone. The distributor of the books was left off the hook as well. Hasjim, the director of the publishing company, was

never summoned. And all of these people were most responsible for the book coming into being! These students got the books from us. The writer obviously was Pram. But the students who sold in total two books, were made a scapegoat. In the trial, Hasjim was finally summoned, as a witness. He told the prosecutor that he gave the okay for the students to sell the books. This should be enough for the prosecutor to charge Hasjim. It was crystal clear that the books came from Hasta Mitra, from Hasjim. But nothing happened to him.

So that's why we think those students were framed. Pram's books became the excuse to destroy their movement in Jogja. But I had a lot of respect for those students, they were never afraid. If you read their defence plea . . . they showed a lot of resolve in that, they were immovable. We are with them and we really wanted to give them something for their trouble, to help them. We managed to do so, though we couldn't do much. But I can tell you that Hasjim and I are with these kids, we felt like we were really involved in their case. Pram himself gave away his meagre royalty to those kids, to pay for the trial and also so they could get better food in prison.

In fact, by 1988, the regime was already too late. Almost immediately after the publication of *Bumi Manusia*, after Hasta Mitra announced: 'We're back', students began to seek out released prisoners to speak to—not just the Hasta Mitra trio. There were many such people. There was Yubar Ayoeb, former secretary-general of LEKRA, the very active cultural organization close to the PKI, with which Pramoedya had also been associated. Hardoyo, Secretary-General of the CGMI, the university student organization affiliated to the PKI. There was Oei Tjoe Tat, a PKI MP, who eventually finished an Indonesian translation of the three volumes of Karl Marx's *Das Capital*, which after the fall of Suharto, was also then published by Joesoef Isak through Hasta Mitra. There were intellectuals and writers such as the prolific (until today) Hersri Setiawan and the poet Putu Oka Sukanto and many others. Buru Island prison camp and Indonesia's prisons had housed a big percentage of Indonesia's intelligentsia from before 1965. A conversation had started with the Indonesia that had returned from exile. The taboo, for a significant even if still small minority of students—the politically active ones—against finding out about Indonesia's Left history was dissolved.

Neither Hasta Mitra nor these intellectuals and former activists were in a position to organize or recruit these students. Indeed, finding an 'Indonesia' and a world completely changed from prior to 1965—includings with China now friendly with the United States, they themselves were still trying to understand their new reality. Pramoedya had very little to say about contemporary Indonesia apart from emphasizing that his generation had failed and that finding a way forward was the business of youth. Apart from that, he would just emphasize that the Suharto regime and all its henchmen were never to be believed. 'If they say Z', Pramoedya would repeat again and again, 'You can be sure they mean Y.' The released intellectuals and activists were not organizers nor recruiters, and not mentors either. However, it was also clear that they were not the devils of the regime's black propaganda and in fact, had many interesting things to tell, and that they wrote good books, essays or poems.

Bumi Manusia was published in August 1980 and banned in May 1981. *Anak Semua Bangsa* was published in December 1980 and banned in May 1981. It took four more years to get *Jejak Langkah* out, given the financial impact on Hasta Mitra of the first bannings and the general worsening level of repression. Jejak Langkah was banned in May 1986. In 1985, Hasta Mitra also published an anthology of the writings of Tirto Adhi Soerjo, the figure who inspired the character Minke, later referred to as T.A.S. in *Jejak Langkah* and *Rumah Kaca*. Pramoedya edited the anthology and wrote an extended biographical essay on Tirto. The book, *Sang Pemula*, was also banned in 1986. Then in March 1988, the most historically and politically intense of the sequels, *Rumah Kaca*, was published. It was banned on 8 June 1988 by Attorney-General Sukarton Marmosujono. The ban specifically cited decrees of the People's Consultative Assembly (MPR) banning the spreading of Marxism–Leninism of which *Rumah Kaca* was being accused.

This banning made it impossible for Hasta Mitra's ambitions to establish themselves as a major publisher, to be realized. They continued to publish more books by Pramoedya, which were all quickly banned, as well as other titles. However, none of these generated the income needed to develop and expand the company, even while continuing to play a major role in expanding critical literature. In 1983, Bumi Manusia appeared in English as *This Earth of Mankind* in Australia, Singapore and the United Kingdom, published by Penguin Books. Other international editions followed bring Pramoedya some modest income from translation rights as well as an enhanced international profile. Pramoedya's international standing was reflected back into Indonesia as word spread of the critical acclaim he was receiving.

Thus, neither the three men nor Pramoedya's books disappeared from circulation. In fact, in the middle of the 1990s, just as the movement to topple Suharto was preparing to escalate, Pramoedya and Hasta Mitra were on centre-stage again. So all the processes that had been set in motion since August 1980 continued, and indeed escalated, but within a new framework. 1989 was the beginning of the last phase for Suharto. In some ways, *Bumi Manusia* and its sequels were the books that killed the New Order.

Chapter 10

The End of the Suharto Dictatorship

Class struggle between capital and labour was not a central theme in *Bumi Manusia*, in fact it hardly arises at all. How social being, how one exists and survives, structured through the kinds of lives lived by different social classes, determines how people think and feel, their consciousness—that is indeed what is central to that book. This includes also how the international processes and machinations of class dynamics integrate and disintegrate individuals and classes. But struggle between classes? Between capital and labour? Or even between serf and lord, or tenant and landlord? Perhaps, yes, between 'natives' of all kinds and colonial capital, but that is rather a struggle between a nation (or nation-in-becoming) and another nation's ruling class.

Pramoedya was not, of course, oblivious to the tensions between the needs and thinking of capitalists and workers. There is a lively hint at this in *Bumi Manusia* and a deeply significant more-than-hint in *Rumah Kaca*. The main protagonist of the novel, the concubine Nyai Ontosoroh, is a successful capitalist. She owns (or she thinks she owns) and manages a dairy farm business. Minke, the teenage boy whom she mentors, is also educating himself to be a businessman. Annelies, Nyia Ontosoroh's daughter by her Dutch master, Herman Mellema, is being trained to be a business manager. There is a scene where Annelies is showing Minke the milking operations when she scolds a worker, asking her how many buckets of milk she had collected, then telling Minke she could always collect more than any worker. The worker, Minem is a cheeky personality, exhibiting subordination to her boss only out of necessity. This is just at the spontaneous, individual level, completely apolitical, but Minem's spontaneity and cheekiness make her a memorable proletarian character, no matter how fleeting her presence may be.

In *Rumah Kaca*, published eight years later (but also written on Buru Island), new characters are introduced as the figures who will carry on Tirto Adhi Soerjo's work of organizing a nation against colonialism. One of them is described as a young worker from a railway yard who sounds strikingly like Semaun, one of the founders of the first Indonesian communist party. But that book came out in 1988. By that time, a generation of young activists had already discovered the concept and reality of class. In the second book, *Anak Semua Bangsa*, Minke does make contact, though in an exploratory way only, with oppressed peasant farmers, although here also, the conflict is not among the Javanese, but against the Dutch. So perhaps also there was a message about exploitation and class that was passed on through that novel, which was published in 1980.

The way *Bumi Manusia* killed the New Order was not through propagandizing for class struggle, but by connecting young, critical-minded students with Indonesian history in general, and with *history*, as such. A part of that history was what had happened and was happening to the thousands of released prisoners, but also included everything that had come before them. Looking at history with a fresh eye liberated them from the hegemony of their immediate seniors and mentors. In *realpolitik* terms, it meant the breaking of the mentorship of all the anti-PKI intellectuals, including the ones fighting against the New Order. There were no new mentors, though: just conversations to be had, books and history to be studied and answers to be found. It was in this process that enough of these new, young activists found 'class', and so began a process of students seeking to organize and work with peasants or workers.

This was already happening by 1988, when the Jogja three were arrested and tried. Students in their protests during the 1970s had asserted their power as a 'moral force', the conscience of the system, a role they had been allowed to play between 1965 and 1978, after first, in 1965, the huge communist student organization had been smashed. In the late 1980s, they began organizing together with peasant farmers in the villagers, forming the first student–peasant alliances.

The most revealing example of the change taking place at the beginning of the 1990s was the emergence of Indonesian Front for the Defense of Human Rights (INFIGHT). INFIGHT, whose activists overlapped with Indonesian Forest Protection Network (SKEHPI), exemplified the change that had taken place. First, INFIGHT took up the cases of some PKI members who were still in prison, awaiting death sentences. They campaigned for their release. The previous generations of student activists had never take up the issue of imprisoned leftists. These same activists were immersed also in organizing with farmers in West Java, campaigning to reclaim land that had been taken for golf courses and other commercial developments. By 1990, there had already been mass occupations of disputed lands by combinations of students and peasants.

I first met these activists when I visited their offices in 1990. As founding editor of *Inside Indonesia*, an Australian magazine that had taken up the cause of solidarity with democratic Indonesia, and also as the translator of Pramoedya's books, I had been invited to chat with the INFIGHT activists. I was driven to their office by Hasjim and Joesoef in Hasjim's car. The activists who came out to meet the car immediately recognized Hasjim and Joesoef and tried to convince them to come in, but they had another agenda to attend to. But the links were all there: Hasta Mitra, Pramoedya, the cause of the jailed PKI members and organization on a class basis with the peasants. To top it off, there were two small children playing in the front yard of the office. They were playing with red balloons with yellow hammer and sickle symbols on it. *What is happening here?* I thought.

There were other examples around the country. By 1991, some of these activists gathered to form new student organizations. By 1994, there were enough people involved for them to launch the People's

Democratic Union (PRD), which transformed in 1996 into the People's Democratic Party. A central figure of this initiative, Danial Indrakusma, had been also active in INFIGHT and SKEHPI. The PRD and other groups as well, were involved in organizing more and more protests, which became referred to as *aksi*. The emphasis shifted from mobilizing peasants to mobilizing factory workers and reflected Indonesia's increased urbanization. While the protests took up issues of wages and conditions, they were also part of the start of an anti-dictatorship movement aimed at toppling Suharto.

In 1995, Pramoedya found himself centre-stage again, in events that further revealed what changes had been unleashed in the 1980s, with the returning from exile of the original Indonesia. In July, the Ramon Magsaysay Award Foundation selected Pramoedya as its 1995 awardee for Journalism, Literature and Creative Communication Arts. The foundation, named after a former president of the Philippines, was based in Manila, the Philippines, and its award was considered as Southeast Asia's Nobel Prize. Among previous Indonesian awardees were Mochtar Lubis, who had been jailed under the Sukarno regime and was a long-term opponent of the PKI and of Pramoedya, as well as in 1993, Abdurrahman Wahid, a progressive Islamic and human rights figure in Indonesia, who would become president of Indonesia for a brief period from October 1999 until July 2001. In 2001, Dita Indah Sari, a labour activist and member of the PRD, who was jailed between 1996 and 1999, was also awarded a Magsaysay Prize.

The award to Pramoedya generated an explosion of polemics that were covered in almost all the media, print and on television. Despite the books still being under a ban, his books, Pramoedya and the history he represented, were just as much in the limelight as when *Bumi Manusia* was first published. These polemics exposed differences over a central question of Indonesia's historical experience. The polemics also revealed the generational change that had taken place.

Mochtar Lubis led an offensive, protesting the award to Pramoedya. Lubis stated that he would return his award and the money that had come with it as a protest. Lubis's antagonism stemmed from the oft-repeated claim that Pramoedya had mobilized harassment and oppression against anti-Left writers before 1965. It was Lubis who challenged

Pramoedya on his visit to Buru, asking, 'Do you believe in god now?' Lubis's campaign gathered support from more than twenty other well-known writers, including Rendra. Rendra wrote that he would support Pramoedya being awarded the Nobel Prize for Literature, but not the Magsaysay Award, which included, he argued, a political element. In the eyes of Lubis, Rendra and others, Pramoedya's association with the PKI and his campaigning against anti-Left writers before 1965 made him guilty of any harassment they may have experienced at that time.

In one interview with the magazine *Forum Keadilan*, Lubis was asked whether Pramoedya's years in prison were sufficient payment for the sins Lubis accused him of committing, Lubis answered: 'That's different. I was jailed for opposing the oppression under Sukarno. Pram was jailed because he wanted to oppress us.' For Lubis, it was simple and he stated it explicitly: Pramoedya was a communist who wanted to oppress others. For Lubis and the other signatories of the letter, 1965 meant they were saved from communism. Lubis was an ideologically committed anti-communist and, according to researchers, was close to the US-based Association for Cultural Freedom, which was funded by the CIA.[33]

For Pramoedya and his fellow prisoners, and for the new generation of his supporters, 1965 meant they were taken hostage, en masse, so that corrupt military officials (*kabir*) and foreign capitalist interests could take over the country, which was what he was warning of, before 1965. In our recorded discussions in 1993, Pramoedya explained why the polemics before 1965 had become so polarized:

> There were a few reasons. The first one was that people were dissatisfied with the results of the revolution. The question was: is the revolution over, or not? Sukarno said the revolution was not over yet, and I agreed, there were revolutionary promises that had not been realized. The second reason, at that time Indonesia was being harassed by the capitalist countries. There were attempts on Bung Karno's life. All this had a direct impact on the literary scene. Literature is about life after all, in the past and the present. That was what happened in the sixties. I wrote a series of articles called "What must be cleared away, and what must be built", which was a rephrasing of Sukarno's speech: "To destroy

and to build". The intent of the article was to draw a line in the sand: those people who wrote just to play around, they should stop what they were doing, the country was in a critical state. We were targeted by capitalist countries who wanted to take over our economy. But they could not get in because Sukarno was against free-for-all, take-whatever-you-want economics. That this political situation had an impact on the literary scene, I think it was just to be expected. When later I was made a scapegoat, well, be my guest. The horse had already bolted. What we worried would happen has already happened. Indonesia has become a playground for capitalists.

Two opposing outlooks on what 1965 was about were starkly exposed.

While Lubis campaigned strongly against the award, other of the PKI's former opponents took a different approach. One of the signatories of Cultural Manifesto (Manikebu), which had opposed the Sukarnoist Left's cultural polemics and was then banned, Goenawan Mohammad, defended Pramoedya's right to receive the award based on his literary contributions. His essay on this still, however, spent considerable space reaffirming the perspective that Pramoedya had acted in an oppressive manner before 1965, and stating only if Pramoedya could bring himself to admit his mistakes.

> I am against everybody attacking Pram. Pram does not have the same freedom as Mochtar Lubis or Taufiq Ismail. Pram is interviewed by the student press and by foreign media, but he will not be interviewed on TV here or be allowed to speak at the Jakarta Arts Centre. I accept Pram with no anger, even though I do not deny the fact that Pram was active in stirring up an intolerant and repressive atmosphere 31 years ago.[34]

Goenawan, also the wealthy publisher for an extended period of the Suharto era's preeminent weekly news magazine, *Tempo*, and a prolific columnist in his publication, has consistently taken positions defending Pramoedya, and other writers, from specific repressive decisions. The real difference between the two perspectives is not whether one or other supports or doesn't support the ban on

Pramoedya's and Hasta Mitra's other books, but whether a political struggle for a different kind of Indonesia is permissible. Even a figure such as Goenawan, or even Rendra, never called for a lifting the ban on the PKI or on 'spreading Marxism–Leninism'. The question here is not whether a specific doctrine or theory can be propagated, but whether the current Indonesia itself can be questioned. Pramoedya argues that the repression of 1965 took place to enable foreign interests to enter and dominate in Indonesia. Prior to 1965, Sukarno and the Left were arguing that that is what corrupt officials, mainly military officers in charge of nationalized enterprises, would allow if they took control.

Pramoedya's article, 'What needs to be cleared away and what needs to be built' was, as some commentators have argued in detail,[35] not calling for the physical elimination or jailing of those who were not concerned with the threat that Sukarno and the Left talked about. But neither was 'clearing away' simply referring to some kind ephemeral literary process. There was a fundamental struggle for power taking place and what was at stake was what perspective would be hegemonic.

Pramoedya, like tens of thousands of others, was 'intolerant'—in the sense that they could not accept the future that they saw as threatening: the loss of the nation's sovereignty, the rule of the 'kabir' and the repression of a popular movement with tens of millions of members, of which they were part.

While these real differences have never openly or properly been discussed, it was becoming clear that the unspoken different orientations about the direction of Indonesia's development were now re-evolving in the country. Out of the interactions with history that was taking place in the 1980s after the publication of *Bumi Manusia*, and via the new political activism manifested in student–worker and student–peasant organizing, there emerged an organized defence of Pramoedya's Magsaysay Award. Of course, Joesoef and Hasjim at Hasta Mitra were prolific in their bombardment of the press with statements and comments as they had been throughout the 1980s. This time, their efforts were complimented by an open letter from 120 writers and activists, enthusiastically welcoming the Magsaysay Award and critiquing Lubis and the others.

Among the signatories were Wiji Thukul, a young working-class poet who was emerging as the poet and dramatist of the aksi movement against Suharto and who was a member of the openly Left-wing PRD. He disappeared, presumed murdered in 1997, during a period when many PRD and other militant opponents of Suharto also disappeared. Another was Hilmar Farid, a young academic who had been bravely defending Marxist analysis of Indonesia and helping document the plight and sufferings of victims of the 1965 repression (but who more recently has become an official of the current government). The open and strong support from 120 of such people would have been unimaginable in the 1980s. It did not only reflect the commitment to the right to produce art and literature 'freely' but also, for some such as the PRD, the right to struggle for a different political vision.

Pramoedya was not allowed to travel to Manila to receive his award, despite a direct request from the head of the Magsaysay Foundation to President Suharto. Pramoedya was not issued with a passport. His speech of acceptance was read by the young intellectual, Marianne Kartoppo. Pramoedya summed up the sentiment that was his motivation as a writer:

> Because of my experience as the child of a family of freedom fighters, I pardon my own self if I do not like this escapist literature . . . Consequent to my personal experience, though at first I was not aware of it, I was drawn directly to a literature that could provide courage, new values, a new worldview, human dignity, and an active role for the individual within society. The aesthetic that emphasizes language and its usage is put to the service of a new orientation of the function of the individual struggling for a better society. It was this type of literature that later became my field of creative activity.[36]

Pramoedya's acceptance speech was delivered in September 1995. It was only a few months later that the events began that saw the end of the Suharto dictatorship in May 1998. During 1995 and into 1996, the daughter of former President Sukarno, Megawati Sukarnoputri began to stake her claim as a potential successor to

President Suharto. For most of the previous ten years, she had been a rather meek member of parliament, representing the Indonesian Democratic Party (PDI). The PDI was one of the only three political parties permitted during the Suharto era. The others were Suharto's own function groups (*Golkar*) and a party based on the fusion of earlier Islamic parties, called the United Development Party (PPP). None of these three had ever questioned—or would ever question, up until today—the basic economic and political strategies of the regime. But mid-1965, Megawati had positioned herself well to become the chairperson of the PDI. Suharto could not have the daughter of the man he had arrested and deposed, emerge as his main challenger, or even as a challenger to whomever he wished to have as his successor. Megawati was twenty-six years younger than Suharto, and could be a challenger to one of Suharto's children or another successor of her generation. Using manipulation, bribery and coercion, Suharto's supporters in the PDI organized a Congress that excluded Megawati and her supporters. There were soon two PDIs: the PDI and the PDI Struggle (PDIP). The government only recognized the PDI.

In June 1996, a demonstration of tens of thousands of people protested against Suharto's moves and clashed with the army and police. The demonstration was led by another daughter of Sukarno, Sukmawati Sukarnoputri, who in 1996, had also signed the letter defending the Magsaysay Award being given to Pramoedya. Pro-democracy activists, with the PRD playing a leading role, turned the Jakarta office of the PDIP into a pro-democracy discussion centre. In July 1998, it was attacked by police and goons. Several people died and many were injured. Protests broke out in Jakarta and soon, there was rioting. The police and army were used to suppress the protests. The government blamed the PRD as the power behind the unrest and accused them of being . . . communists, again. PRD leaders were hunted down and fourteen were arrested. Some were tried and given heavy prison sentences. Later in the year, Dita Sari, Coen Pontoh and other PRD activists, were arrested at a union protest in Surabaya. Pramoedya was interviewed by an Australian documentary film maker, Jill Hickson, and declared that if he was younger, he would join the PRD.

In May 1997, elections were held. Megawati called for her supporters to boycott the elections. The PRD mobilized protests on every third day of the campaign period, a day designated for campaigning for the PPP party. But the PRD initiated protests, though not under their own banner. Rather, they were organized under a banner calling for a united opposition under the slogan 'Mega-Star of the People'. These demonstrations in Jakarta reached massive proportions and were often very militant, clearing away police barricades or burning police stations. They had been, in fact, banned, but the bans were totally ignored by the masses. With Megawati's PDIP masses boycotting the election, Suharto's Golkar easily won and Suharto soon appointed a new cabinet, with his daughter and close cronies dominating the new line-up. This just provoked the masses who had already shown themselves willing to go out on the streets and so, protests escalated. University students from around the country formed campaign committees and the demonstrations snowballed.

Then, in July 1997, just two months after the elections, the Asian Economic Crisis happened, and the Indonesian economy went into a tailspin. Suharto was unable to manage this, while the rupiah collapsed, and millions were thrown out of work or saw their incomes disappear or be slashed. University students from around the country formed campaign committees and the demonstrations snowballed. By February and March 1998, student leaders started to demand that Suharto resign, and threatened larger demonstrations and an occupation of the parliament. Political activists, many from the PRD, and including the poet Wiji Thukul, started to be disappeared or detained. Those detained had been picked up by a special squad and tortured to reveal the location of other key activists, such as Danial Indrakusma, but also Web Warouw, both of whom avoided capture. Others who disappeared have never been found. Twenty years later today, there are still demonstrations every Thursday, led by grieving parents, outside the presidential palace, demanding an investigation into their fate. Nothing has yet been done.

In May 1998, an occupation of the parliament grounds did take place in Jakarta while massive demonstrations took place around the country. Ministers and close supporters of the government started to resign and suggest that Suharto resign before protests grew too big and their political demands too radical. On 22 May, Suharto resigned, and Vice President B.J. Habibie was sworn in as President.

The period between June 1996 and May 1998 had been a time of intensifying struggle. Between May and November 1998, protests and campaigns for the release of political figures, free elections, trade union rights, wage rises and other reforms continued. In November 1998, another escalation threatened another occupation of the parliamentary grounds, demanding the formation of a revolutionary government comprising all the main opposition leaders, both from the mass movement and from among elite politicians, who had begun to be more critical of Suharto since the previous year. This November occupation of parliament was defused when a gathering of all the main elite opposition figures met and announced that they supported President Habibie organizing new elections as the way to stabilize the political situation.

The protest momentum was undone immediately. Specific campaigns around specific issues continued to flare up and the society was alive with discussion of 'reformation' and 'total reformation' to end corruption, collusion and nepotism, and open up democratic space. However, the snowballing protest momentum for an immediate government of the opposition forces was stopped in its tracks. The country shifted to stabilization through elections in a situation where only the various established sections of the political elite, whether pro-Suharto or opposition, had the money, media support or infrastructure to seriously compete.

As President Habibie prepared a new, very liberal election law, other reforms took place. The right to form trade unions was formalized. Political prisoners, including the PRD prisoners, started to be released. A referendum on independence was held in East Timor, where an overwhelming majority supported independence. This was followed by an orgy of repressive violence organized by a recalcitrant military, which Habibie ordered stopped, when agreeing to the presence of an International Peacekeeping Force in Timor. Xanana Gusmao was also released from his Jakarta imprisonment in late 1999.

In these new circumstances, the PRD could organize openly and in March 1999, they held a large public gathering, where Pramoedya Ananta Toer was sworn in as a member and where he made a rousing speech. Joesoef Isak and Hasjim Rachman—who would pass away from an illness in June 1999—also attended. Pramoedya was seventy-four when he gave this speech and was unlikely to become a party cadre, especially as he had always insisted that he was not an 'organization man'. He did, however, want to make where he stood, at the start of the new era. His speech is an appropriate ending to this chapter.

Salam Democracy!

At this moment, in the midst of this spirited and enthusiastic young generation, I truly feel happy. This is the most important event in my life, what I have dreamed of since I was young: to witness for myself the birth of a young generation not burdened by bombasticism, and which is rational, corrective, critical, and all of this bound by firmness of commitment. There are PRD members lost in who knows what jungle: those kidnapped, and those whose jungle we know, those in gaol. They are all victims of the staged trials that are the fashion today. Now I am in the midst of the PRD, among whom are some who escaped from kidnapping. In fact, I was one of the first victims of kidnapping, in 1959, although back then it was not news.

I assess the young generation, I mean the PRD, as being of higher quality than the generations that have gone before. Let's go straight to the core: since you were children, you have been educated with the political lies of the New Order, painting the New Order as angels and depicting all those layers of society who refuse to defend it, as devils. From primary school to university. And all of you have seen through those lies.

You are of the Left, that is, you side with people, the lower levels of society. Exactly, because for so long, the people have just been the playthings of the elite, except during the Old Order, because in that period there were political forces that stood beside the people. The fall of the Old Order meant that the people and the country became booty for multinational capitalism working together with the national elite as their guard dogs.

Let us make a comparison with the young generation of the years before 1920. They, university students who received scholarships from the colonial government in the Netherlands as well as the exiles of the Indische Party, discovered a homeland and nation and they called it Indonesia. This was a glorious and great discovery. It's a pity, but the flaws of this discovery were as great as its glory. There was no socio-political concept and it was imbued with antipathy to history. For example, the name Indonesia means 'Indian islands'. The name itself was invented by an Englishman and then popularized by the German ethnologist, Adolf Bastian (1826–1905). The name 'India' for Indonesia originates from the Western nations' hunt for spices in the Moluccas starting in the early fifteenth century, a hunt that led to the whole of the non-Western world being dominated by the West. These spices came from what is known today as Indonesia, but were always traded as 'made in India'. While under Portuguese domination, it was known as Portuguese India. Under Dutch colonialism, it was called Dutch India. And to disguise this association with India from the native people, this name was written Hindia.

The politics of manipulating words. Some people speculate that the young generation of that period adopted this ethnologist's name to avoid the domination of Java. History had given birth to two names for what is Indonesia now, namely 'Nusantara' during the period of the kingdom of Majapahit, which means 'islands in between (two continents)', and even older is 'Dipantara' from the time of the Singasari kingdom, which means 'fortress between (two continents)'. This older name is pregnant with political meaning because the King of Singasari, Kertanegara, built military alliances with other Southeast Asian coastal kingdoms against the expansion of Kublai Khan from the north. And even till today, there are still no voices, not a single voice, calling for correction of all this.

If we make a comparison with the young generation with their youth pledge, also a genuinely glorious event, the PRD exhibits more ideas with greater depth. We can understand this when we remember that in the twenties, only 3.5 per cent of the population could read and write. The increase in the number of literate people began only with national independence. Taking into account this statistic, we can understand the deficiencies of the young generation of this period.

The 45 Generation was also glorious. With no self-interest, without reserve, they devoted all their body and soul, ready to die in order to defend national independence on every inch of the homeland. Because the main problem they faced were the armed attacks of the colonialists, most of their activities were made up of shooting; the rifle ruled. They did not yet get to developing socio-political and economic concepts, like you are developing now, such as people's democracy, popular democracy. And you must never forget that no matter how glorious was the 45 revolution that succeeded in seizing and defending national independence, it was begun by the gangsters of the Senen Markets in Jakarta.

The 66 Generation? Wow! There is nothing more to evaluate on them. And then came the Malari Generation, who wanted reform under the slogan 'military back to the barracks', in line with the reform outlook of General Sumitro. Both of them, [the students and General Sumitro], were defeated by the New Order, which used tactics which are becoming classic features of our history.

This is why I am proud to be among you all today, you who have prepared your ideas, have started to put them into practice in the field, and smile maturely, ready to accept the consequences, never mind how bitter. There is no cry more appropriate for all this than: Long live the PRD!

I am convinced that you are better prepared than those who have gone before you and will succeed more than those who have gone before you. I know that you will not denigrate the value of the Indonesian human being through the use of massacre, and the theft of their fundamental rights. Because as was taught by Multatuli:[37] the duty of all humans is to become human.

I believe that tomorrow or the next day, you will not speak in the name of the nation in defence of your own interests, or of your group's interests or for the sake of power. It is only ever valid to speak in the name of the nation if there is democracy. It's almost like people have been struck with senility so that they can't remember that the nation comprises three elements: its inhabitants or citizens, the homeland itself or the inhabited territory, and the government. To speak on behalf of the nation requires the representation of all three elements. To denigrate any one element is corruption. And corruption in thinking inevitably spreads into actions.

I say all this not in order to praise you who have not yet had the chance to succeed, but only to locate you in these comparisons. You have what it takes to succeed better in lifting up our homeland and nation to the level which we all dream.

In our modern history, the young generation has always been, except for the 66 Generation, the motor driving things forward. Even though, yes, even though with all its flaws and limitations. And the limitation which sticks out most of all: the lack or absence of courage for correction.

Courage! Again: courage! For the youth in particular, courage is the greatest of all capital. Without courage, as I have often said, you will be treated like cattle: deceived, herded from here to there and back again or even herded ready for massacre. It is only courage that can make a firm character.

Before ending, I would like to appeal to everybody here today at this meeting, here inside or outside this room, wherever you are, to donate money to the PRD for routine as well as non-routine expenses.

Once again: Long live the PRD!

Chapter 11

Unfinished Ferment: 2000–2020

In his speech at the PRD meeting, Pramoedya talked of a new generation, favourably comparing the 1990's generation with others that had gone before them. He clearly envisaged that with this new generation, radical changes would happen. He even raised the issue of the need to give the country a completely new name: Nusantara or Dipantara—not Europe's name for the region: the 'Indies', then later Indonesia. He saw the 1990's generation's achievement of dislodging a military-backed dictatorship without violence as remarkable. And it was indeed a truly remarkable achievement, plus that generation did it in such a short time: easily less than ten years. The student–peasant–worker protests started in 1989 and Suharto was gone by May 1998. A ruling class created by the New Order remained in power, although no longer dominated by one clique and having to allow greatly expanded democratic space for both competition among the factions of the elite as well as from outside the elite, from the broader society.

The fall of Suharto, however, did not bring an abrupt deep rupture between the present and the past. What Indonesia has experienced since 1998 has rather been a period of slow fermentation in creating something new—a process still unfinished. The return from exile of the original Indonesia into the post-'65 Indonesia has been the yeast in that fermentation. There are a few reasons why there has been no abrupt change but rather a process of slow incremental change.

First, we need to absorb how long the New Order was in power. In calendar years, there were thirty-two. As a percentage of the time Indonesia's character was *not* under contestation, it was 100 per cent. In some ways, the New Order has been there for all of (what is now) 'Indonesia's' existence. By exiling the original Indonesia to Buru Island and the chain of prisons and camps around the country, what had happened before 1965 was dissolved away.

Enormous efforts were made to ensure that everything dynamic, reflecting the struggle between visions for the future, from before 1965, right back to the nineteenth century, was obliterated from public consciousness and culture. Second, alongside banning the scores of writers associated with the Left before 1965, literature as a subject taught in high schools was disappeared from the curriculum. A subject 'Language' was retained and was accompanied by a requirement for students to rote learn the names, authors and dates of publication of different authors, although not the scores of banned authors such as Pramoedya. The reading and discussion of even the content of that literature not banned, did not happen. For several generations, young people were not asked to read any of those novels, plays, essays, poems, short stories or speeches which had emerged as Indonesia was being created and which were a fundamental part of that creation process.

All these writings reflected the experiences of the Indonesians-in-the-making that were evolving from the beginning of the twentieth century. The new nation evolving then had emerged out of shared experiences and these could be discovered in what was being written in the Indonesian language. Exposure to literature at school was rare and a fluke dependent on the personalities of different teachers—although some private schools did introduce modern literature to their students, who were a tiny percentage of the population.

Literature disappeared. History became the rote learning of a mostly falsified story. That rote-learned history reflected the ideological priorities of a military regime that needed to justify the physical elimination of both the people as well as all writing which manifested the popular struggle for social justice and progress. With the disappearance of literature and the hollowing out of any historical consciousness amongst its youth, which was all buttressed by constant propaganda from state and media, the Indonesia from before 1965 was disappeared.

Two writers and thinkers of essential importance in the process of creating Indonesia were Kartini and Sukarno.[38] Yet, since 1965 until today, high school students have never been asked to read and discuss in class any of their writings. Both their birthdays are celebrated in Indonesia. Kartini's birthday is a holiday. Sukarno is recognized by most people as the man who formulated the Pancasila, the short five-sentence summary of a national philosophical outlook, but neither his original speech explaining it nor any of his later expositions are studied at school. It is more likely that these speeches are not even mentioned. And, as I said, the stories, poems and essays of that whole period before 1965, and since then also, have not been the subject of study and discussion.

What a massive explosion of light in the midst of such darkness must it have been to read *This Earth of Mankind*, *Child of All Nations*, *Footsteps* and *House of Glass*, which brought history so vividly alive as a creative and rebellious process. As Joesoef wrote in a speech for the 2006 Ubud Writers and Readers Festival held in Bali, about the books:

> They brought Indonesia to life, for those Indonesians able to read the novels, and for foreigners who were introduced to Indonesia via Pramoedya's works. These books gave back to Indonesia their history— their real history, not the falsified history of the History Centre of Armed Forces which was then taught in the schools and universities.
>
> Moreover, our history was revealed as a history of struggle and rebellion, of humanity, of questioning and ideas. What an anti-thesis to the New Order's cultural values: blind obedience, don't question, learn by rote a history made up of lies, and above all else, don't think for yourself.
>
> Into this cultural desert, coming out of the concentration camp on Buru Island, Pramoedya's works appeared as an oasis at which many Indonesians, especially young Indonesians, began to refresh themselves.

Joesoef Isak himself, assisted only by his computer man Bowo, mostly focused on the editing and printing of the sixty-one books published by Hasta Mitra, as well as the translation work he did, to make a living. Joesoef also wrote Introductions and Forewords to many of the books Hasta Mitra published. His contribution to the discussion of issues and history and politics was not unimportant. Of course, he was on a similar wavelength as Pramoedya, defending Sukarno and his ideas, emphasizing the looting of Indonesia by multinational capital after 1965 and the dictatorial character of the Suharto regime. Like Pramoedya, he also emphasized the necessity for the next generation to take up the struggle for change. He said later in his speech in Bali, outlining the challenge the youth faced, even while being deprived of access to literature and history in the schools:

> We need a new cultural movement in our country, a movement to win back our literature and history for our people. Such a resurgence must be based on grappling with the full Indonesian reality. There can be no cultural resurgence based on the 1 per cent of cosmopolitanized Indonesians. . . . There are now many young people writing in magazines around the country, stories and novels, and also on many blogs. I do not know which of them will be the Pramoedya's of the post-Suharto era, but I am sure they will emerge and be a part of a new Cultural Revolution here.

Joesoef also realized that no matter the change in 1998, the process ahead would be grueling: 'But no nation, especially a nation whose revolution is not yet finished, can survive with a single oasis.'

At least 200 million have not yet been able to refresh themselves from this oasis, especially with no literature being taught at schools. Tens of thousands of people, yes! Thousands of students and activists, yes! Enough to kill the dictatorship and seed a process of change, yes! The process of change, though, has had no major force as an agency of change. Hasta Mitra continued to play its crucial part in what was fermenting, creating as many little additional oasis as possible.

The death of Hasjim Rachman in June 1999 had a serious impact on the nature of the Hasta Mitra project. Hasta Mitra had already been hurt financially by the banning of their bestselling books during the previous twenty years and the general harassment they faced. They had published twenty-two titles by Pramoedya. These included seven works written on Buru, three anthologies compiled after his release from Buru and ten books he had published before he was arrested. Before 1998, all these books had been banned after they came out, preventing Hasta Mitra from growing commercially. Between 1983 and 2009, when Joesoef passed away, Hasta Mitra had published thirty-nine other books.

These other titles were often a labour of love or political commitment. For Joesoef himself, the collections of writings on the 100th anniversary of Sukarno's birth in 1901, was one of the most important. An Indonesian translation of Han Suyin's biography of the first foreign minister of the People's Republic of China, Chou En Lai , was another. Joesoef had to find a way to reach out to an aged Han Suyin in her Swiss home to get permission to translate and publish. Joesoef had seen Chou En lai in action at the great 1955 Bandung conference of Third World leaders and always admired his dedication to national sovereignty in the face of imperialism. When all the classified documents on United States' reactions and involvement in the events of 1965 briefly surfaced on the internet after declassification, he ensured they were all downloaded and then translated and published by Hasta Mitra. Another title was the three volumes of *Das Capital* by Marx. As I said, there were thirty-nine books in all, besides the twenty-two books by Pramoedya. Between 1999 and 2009, Hasta Mitra was probably the chief mechanism during the period by which these kinds of books were published. In Indonesia, today there are quite a few publishers of such dissident books and most of them would look back with great admiration and respect for Hasta Mitra.

Despite this wonderful contribution to Indonesia's political and cultural life, the prospects of Hasta Mitra developing as a successful business had shrunk to zero. Hasjim's death in 1999 left Joesoef, the editor and political spokesperson, managing the enterprise by himself, and with no capital. As the businessman of the trio, Hasjim, had raised the initial cash to finance Hasta Mitra, Hasta Mitra had no experienced business manager after Hasjim died, nor any staff that could ensure continuity for the enterprise. Pramoedya himself had always been primarily a writer. This difficult situation, and the stressful experiences that came with it, eventually saw Pramoedya's family, through his daughter, Astuti Toer, establishing a new family-based publishing company, *Lentera Dipantara*, that took over the publishing of Pramoedya's books. Joesoef remained a dedicated publisher of dissident and critical books under the Hasta Mitra label up until his death. As the country's politics stabilized after the fall of Suharto, it has been possible to publish Pramoedya's books free of the fear of being banned. The books were reprinted with new covers, a new look. A new generation could buy them easily and read them. Remember the high school student from the 2019 demonstration, I told you about earlier?

But the new covers no longer carry the reminder that they were works from Buru Island. Since 1998, there has been more open discussion around the books. Public discussions and forums about Pramoedya and his books were frequent and common. Pramoedya himself was often asked to speak where he would repeat his admonition that his generation had failed and that the fate of the country was in the hands of the youth.

Hasjim Rachman had died in 1999, aged seventy-four. He had been suffering from a severe lung illness but, according to his children, he refused to be taken to hospital until he had voted in the 1999 elections—when he voted for the PRD. His early death meant there was not an opportunity for either his smile or his commitment to contribute directly to the new post-Suharto ferment.

But nobody should ever forget that without Hasjim's commitment, energy and tactical business nouse back in 1981, *Bumi Manusia* and all Pramoedya's other Buru works would probably have had to wait for the fall of Suharto to be published properly in Indonesia, as distinct from circulating as photocopies of foreign publications or as clandestine typescripts.

And if they hadn't been published in 1980 with the full fanfare that Hasta Mitra's publicity tactics generated, the process that eventually brought Suharto down may itself been delayed or diverted. Hasjim's contribution was crucial and, like his spirit, enormous.

Pramoedya passed away in 2006, aged eighty-one and Joesoef in 2009, also aged eighty-one. Both Pramoedya and Joesoef never stopped contributing to the creation of the new oases that Joesoef had said were needed. The community of activists and critical intellectuals that recognized these contributions made sure that the two men were properly recognized, organizing major gatherings on their eightieth birthdays at the Jakarta Arts Centre. In 2008, the history journalist, Bonnie Triyana, now editor of *Historia* magazine, and I, edited a collection of Joesoef's writings combined with contributions from both Joesoef's friends from before 1965, as well as younger activists. Pramoedya's words and ideas, of course, lived on through his books and, increasingly, how others interpreted them.

In 2007, just about a year after Pramoedya died, the Indonesian playwright, Faiza Mardzoeki, brought her theatre adaptation of *Bumi Manusia* to the stage. It was performed to packed audiences and standing ovations at Jakarta's biggest theatre, the Graha Budaya, Jakarta Arts Centre. It received wide positive coverage in the media. The Jakarta production lasted three hours and involved a huge cast and team of technicians. At the end of 2007, *Kompas* newspaper named it the iconic theatre production of the year. Her adaptation of *Bumi Manusia* was performed by more than ten other theatre groups, each with their own style, throughout the country in the same year. In 2010, Faiza produced a shorter version, which was performed in the Erasmus House theatre to another standing ovation. She also took the production to the Netherlands, where it was commissioned to perform at the Troppen Theatre in Amsterdam, also to a packed audience, and in Antwerp. The profile of the theatrical productions was another reflection of the impact *Bumi Manusia* had made and was still making.

Nyai Ontosoroh, in both its 2007 and 2010 productions, was not only important as another register of *Bumi Manusia*'s impact, but also as a manifestation of the broadening of the creative interpretations of the novel. In adapting the novel for the stage, Faiza chose to focus on the character of Nyai Ontosoroh, and not the other central character and first-person narrator of the novel's story, Minke.

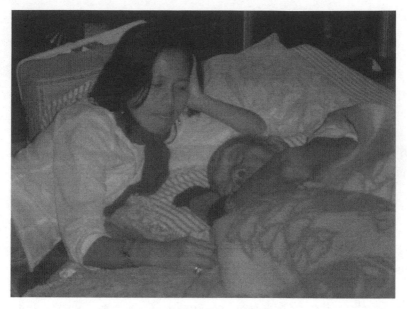

Faiza Mardzoeki with Pramoedya while he was resting when he was ill in 2006.

The play was produced by a coalition of three activist organizations. One was the Institut Ungu, an organization set up to foster feminist ideas through the arts. Faiza was the founding director of Institut Ungu. The second was the Perguruan Rakyat Merdeka (Free People's School), which had been engaged in campaigns around several issues. The third was Perpempuan Mahardika (Free Women), originally started by PRD activists, but then developed independently as a women's rights campaign organization, active among factory workers and students. The fact that the play attracted support from these groups, a broad network of other individual supporters, reflects both the change in thinking occurring and the solidarity with the ideas in Pramoedya's books. The later shorter version of the play that was taken to the Netherlands and Belgium, was produced by Institut Ungu.

Faiza's first experiences of theatre had been in the early 1990s, as an actor in Wiji Thukul's activist theatre group. Pramoedya's depiction of a woman who had overcome her immediate oppression to become an important agent of deep change, mentoring a male formally higher in status than her in the prevailing social hierarchy, was understood as an act of female liberation. The intellectual ferment that Hasta Mitra had strengthened was now spreading beyond both anti-colonial perspectives and generalized struggle ethos, to that of the place and struggle of women. University theses on this aspect and others started to proliferate as the weight of the taboo of talking about Pramoedya decreased.

Faiza's work is a good example of how the fermentation process was working. Faiza's biography took her through labour organizing in Jakarta's factories in the Suharto era, including involvement in Wiji Thukul's August Boal-style theatre for workers. She was involved in various theatre activities, including in the political theatre company led by dramatist Ratna Sarumpaet, who had been gaoled under Suharto. After that, she became involved in organizing women migrant workers in the later Suharto era and participating actively in the mobilizations against the dictatorship. It was in these years, the 1990s, that she read Pramoedya's books given to her by Joesoef himself, when she had cause to meet him. Her first theatre production, produced with another women's movement and anti-dictatorship activist, Yenny Rosa Damayanti, was an adaptation of the great feminist novel, *Women at Point Zero* by Egyptian novelist Nawal El-Sadawi. Thousands of youth flocked to see it in 2002, at Jakarta's largest theatre. Soon after this, Faiza wrote her epic adaptation of *Bumi Manusia*, called *Nyai Ontosoroh* which lasted three hours, and was also performed to packed audiences in the same theatre. This production was organized by the militant women's rights and pro-democracy organization, Solidaritas Perempuan (Women's Solidarity for Human Rights) where both Yenny and Faiza were activists.

The process continued through a series of adaptation of the works of Henrik Ibsen for Indonesia to a new play, *Silent Song of the Genjer Flowers*, a play depicting the trials, emotions and thinking of women who were political prisoners from 1965 until the late 1970s. Detained women activists were not sent to Buru Island but to either a camp in Java, at Plantungan, or to local prisons. Faiza spent years meeting, interviewing and filming these survivors, who had suffered rape, sexual abuse and beatings during their imprisonment.

Pramoedya and Max Lane at the wedding reception for Max Lane and Faiza Mardzoeki (in foreground), 2002.

Aini Chalid (student and political prisoner in the 1970s) and Hariman Siregar (student leader and political prisoner in the 1970s), and Pramoedya and Max Lane at the aforementioned wedding reception, 2002.

The play also performed to packed audiences in the Goethe Institute Playhouse in Jakarta, and received much critical acclaim in the media. Since then, Faiza also translated into Indonesian a Norwegian play, *Time Without Books*, that deals with the memories of political prisoners in Uruguay during its period of dictatorship. Five versions of the play were performed as film theatre productions and streamed to audiences in Indonesia. *Tempo* news magazine selected Faiza and the five women directors that worked with her as the Theatre Artists of the Year for 2021.

Faiza represents one element in the ferment in literature from the 1990s until now. There will be many others. One author who has won recognition is Eka Kurniawan. His style of writing is sometimes compared to Pramoedya's stylistic experimentation in the 1950s. Although not a writer of the encourage-to-struggle genre that Pramoedya classified himself as in his speech for the Magsaysay Award, Kurniawan does talk about social issues in his works. Kurniawan has published at least ten works and has won several awards in Indonesia. Some have been translated and published internationally. His own university thesis, also published as a book, was on the influence of Soviet Union socialist realism on Pramoedya. In 2021, a second edition was published.

Another prolific and well-recognized writer, Linda Christanty, also went through the experience of participating in the struggle against Suharto, and as a member of the PRD. Her works also are deeply responsive to social conditions. It is not possible to survey all the bubbling of ferment in the artistic and literary that can be traced back in one way or the other to the 1980s and 1990s and the return to Indonesia of the pre-65 Indonesia via Hasta Mitra. To be honest, I can't keep up with all the output, let alone research the lines of cause and effect since *Bumi Manusia* came out. I could perhaps add more names, but there is no space to elaborate on them in a meaningful way here. But don't doubt it, the fermentation is strong and still ongoing.

Of course, it is not only in the arts and literature that the fermentation can be seen. When Pramoedya joined the PRD witnessed by Joesoef and Hasjim, and when Hasjim insisted on voting for the PRD before he died, the other message to youth was: organize! Pramoedya was critical of activists who dropped out of building an organization to take up academic studies, saying that building an organization was the best school. Since he made that speech in 1999, political organizing for change has also been in a state of ferment with zigzags, splits, re-groupment and new initiatives. The final products of this fermentation have also not yet arrived.

There are struggle groups based among university students and high school students, among unionized factory workers, women's rights activists, farmer solidarity groups and many others. Some have formed as pre-party formations. Many have regular publications, even if only on the internet, although some do print hard copies. Struggle-oriented trade unions have mushroomed in the hundreds if not thousands, although unions tied to mainstream, elite-owned political parties are also very much present. Students continue to read Pramoedya's books. Union organize reading circles among factory workers to go through books like *Bumi Manusia*, extracting the maximum lessons about strength of character and resistance. Student groups do the same.

Another concrete example can illustrate the politico-chemical processes in the fermentation. Among the central founders of the PRD was Danial Indrakusma. Danial was probably the oldest among the founders in the late 1980s, early 1990s period. He was a central leader throughout the 1990s and found himself, along with another PRD central leader, Web Warouw, on the police's Wanted List after the crackdown in July 1996, when fourteen PRD leaders were caught and arrested, and three were put on trial. Danial was among the activists at INFIGHT before the formal establishment of the PRD, and had met and talked with the Hasta Mitra trio. After the fall of Suharto, he was among those who struggled to keep the PRD going, even as it split and regrouped several times. During this period, alongside trying to build a party group, as well as organize factory workers, Danial was moved, very much in the spirit of Pramoedya, Joesoef and Hasjim, to get history right. To political and labour organizing, he added film making. His film, *Kado Buat Rakyat Indonesia* (*A Gift to the Indonesian People*), which told the story of the events and aftermath of 30 September 1965, is one of the outstanding documentaries on this subject. In 2003, his documentary *Saya Rasa Ini Sulit Untuk Dihilangkan, Sulit Untuk Dihilangkan* (*I think that is difficult to make go away, difficult to make go away*), also about the events of 1965, won a special prize at the 2003 Jakarta International Film Festival. Among those interviewed were Pramoedya, as well as other survivors of political imprisonment, including the moving interview with the seventy-year-old pre-'65 women's movement leader, Sulami. The documentary also featured interviews with those who campaigned for the crushing of the PKI and Sukarnoism. It remains the best film presentation on 1965.

It was Danial also, with another activist, Zely Ariane, who went on to produce *Pikiran Orang Indonesia* (*The Thoughts of an Indonesian*), a documentary about Hasta Mitra, focused on Joesoef Isak. This was screened in Jakarta in the Jakarta Arts Centre in 2008 on the occasion of Joesoef Isak's eightieth birthday.

Meanwhile, as the twists and turns of the survival of Left-wing and progressive activism evolved over the past twenty years, Danial found himself immersed in trade union organizing. He spent some time working inside the Indonesian Metal Workers Federation (FSPMI) but then, after being expelled for being too militant, he went on to help establish, along with his wife Sarinah, the Sedar Union Federation, which is still solidly campaigning today. Following its activities on social media, there regularly appear photos of factory workers—women and men—holding reading group circles. And the book in their hands: *Bumi Manusia.*

Danial is not the only political activist whose outlook connected to the fermentation of the 1980s to the radicalization that followed in the 1990s, and who acknowledges the role and impact of Hasta Mitra and Pramoedya. Pramoedya did not have the chance to consolidate his membership of the PRD as it soon faced various internal debates which led to a series of splits and some re-groupment. Some prominent members dropped out to pursue activities in NGOs, or as academics or writers. Others crossed over and joined or hooked on to mainstream parties. Some continued trying to build a radical political party in the tradition of the PRD, many of whom were also involved in trade union organizing or supporting the student movement. There had been other student activists groups fighting Suharto before 1998, and they have been through similar processes. Women's rights activist groups, such as Solidaritas Perempuan, Suara Ibu Peduli, Kalyanamitra and several others had also played a major role in fighting Suharto. They remained active in 1998, their character and roles evolving, but feminist activism and thinking has continued to strengthen among young women. They are also readers of Pramoedya and Faiza's adaptations of Ibsen, as well as scores of new books on feminism now circulating in Indonesia, both new Indonesian books and translations.

Twenty years after the fall of Suharto, dissident political groups are now more numerous that before 1998, although still small: a part of the early stage of fermentation. Some have a political core with student, worker and farmer groups working in alignment. Some are based around a single trade union. There are now hundreds of new trade unions of all political hues. Some activist dissidents are focused on hosting discussion forums, an activity that has multiplied during the Covid era due to increased familiarity with online meeting techniques. Between 2019 and 2021, their activism was reflected in several ways of protests against new government policies and laws, such as the one described in the first chapter of this book.

Another reflection of this fermentation is the emergence of new independent 'indie' publishers that have taken over the role that Hasta Mitra used to play. There is Marjin Kiri (Left Margins), Komunitas Bambu (Bamboo Community), Ultimus, Djaman Baroe, Mojok, Narasi, and no doubt others, publishing in smaller print runs in this or that province, or publishing on a print-on-demand basis. They publish both Indonesian works and a host of translations of dissident and progressive writings from around the world, including works both about Indonesia as well as other topics. Feminist books in particular are in demand. Independent online booksellers flourish selling these books. In the Indonesian ATM system, it is possible to buy goods online without having a credit card, making this service accessible to students and young workers. There are also now many student resellers who advertise books online by posting pictures of the covers but only obtain the book for dispatch to the buyer after they receive payment. They need no working capital—just a mobile phone. This promotion of dissident books for reselling must be seen as an integral part of the effervescence of the fermentation.

In these last twenty years of open ferment, varieties of interpretation of Pramoedya's books, primarily *Bumi Manusia*, and his statements and interviews, have proliferated. In the first ten years, there developed the phenomena of 'Pramism'. Not being institutionalized, it is perhaps impossible to definitively sum this up, however the Pramists concentrated on Pramoedya's frequent emphasis on how he was not an organization man and how he rejected discipline. 'My ideology is Pramism,' he had once said. Among the Pramists were punk musicians and others intellectuals with a mildly anarchist orientation. Pramoedya had emphasized his own preference for independence from organizational ties, but he had done this always in his specific role as a writer. He did urge others to write, but in being sworn-in publicly as a member of the PRD, he was telling the youth who wanted change that they should be in an organization. The *Bumi Manusia* quartet, as it evolves after the first novel, is fundamentally a novel about the need for and how organization evolves, first trying one approach, which fails, then another, which splits, but makes some progress but then gets complicated and in any case is repressed. The novels also explain the tactics of publishing a campaign newspaper in oppressive circumstances.

The Pramists elevated the individualistic, anarchist side of Pramoedya, that he clung to in defence of his independence as a writer, above that of his orientation to that of struggle and organization. Pramoedya had emphasized that his kind of writing was that which oriented the individual to struggle for change. Pramism was not, however, a monolithic milieu with its myriad of adherents to a certain extent willingly atomized. However, there were forums and meetings and, most significantly, writing and books that kept this approach to Pramoedya, alive and active. It kept Pramoedya's principled stubbornness deeply connected with his name.

Without any doubt, the most present legacy of Pramoedya's novels for the last twenty years is their teachings of character—*kepribadian*—in the sense of strength of character. There are now many, many websites that have published a series of quotes from his works. Let's just look at a few of the kind of quotes chosen:

> An educated person must learn to act justly, beginning, first of all, with his thoughts, then later in his deeds. That is what it means to be educated.
>
> Life can give everything to whoever tries to understand and is willing to receive new knowledge.

'And what can be obtained in this life without payment? Everything must be paid for, or redeemed, even the shortest happiness.'

'I felt that whatever was going to happen, I was dependent on nobody. I felt strong.'

'The resilience and strength—or otherwise—of a person's abilities, and his worth, are directly related to the size and number of the trials he has undergone.'

Apart from being found on numerous websites, many of these quotes, along with a collection of Pramoedya's speeches, were published in a 2014 book, *The Wisdom of Pramoedya Ananta Toer*.[39] Many also appear on T-shirts worn by young students and workers.

In trying to convey this political and cultural fermentation, we must, of course, also be realistic about its spread and depth. It is fundamental to what is happening in Indonesia because of the *potential* for an explosion of radical enlightenment sentiment that it hints at. But the fermentation proceeds incrementally and has not yet reached the stage where a qualitative change takes off across the society. There are 260 million people in Indonesia, with at least a half of the population under the age of thirty. The organized and reading dissident fraction of the population will be a tiny proportion of this. Being organized, active and reading, however, they have the potential to be effective catalysts for speeding up incremental change.

The PRD was a tiny group in the 1990s among Indonesia's 200 million people, but its effectiveness as a catalyst prompted Suharto's regime to wage an all-out war to stop them—banning, gaol, torture and even disappearances (murder). It was only Hasta Mitra's clever political and business tactics, masterminded by Joesoef and Hasjim, and Pramoedya's courage that delayed and weakened the regime's suppression of *Bumi Manusia* and its sequels. The forces that start processes of change don't always need to be big. Small but sharp and well-targeted forces can also put things into motion, if not bring them to a completion.

So in 2022, neither Pramoedya's books, nor any other of Indonesia's literary classics, are taught in schools. No classrooms see debates among students as to whether Nyai Ontosoroh is a realist character.

Nobody discusses how Minke changes under the myriad of interactions he experiences. Why was the beautiful Annelies so fragile? Who was Fatso? What was the value system Pramoedya was promoting? And a myriad of other questions, not least of all: what do these portrayals of the Netherlands East Indies mean for Indonesia today? And are the books really Marxist–Leninist? The classrooms in almost all of Indonesia's public schools are silent on such questions.

Meanwhile, in high schools in Singapore or colleges in the United States, his books are on the curriculum. You can even go online and buy a study guide to *This Earth of Mankind*. More than a million people may have seen the very politically abridged 2019 film version of *Bumi Manusia* in Indonesia, but nobody reads it (or other classics) in the schools. Political groups inspired by the call to organize embedded in the books are still in the embryonic stage. As the fermentation spreads, many elements have also forgotten their origins in the changes that took place in the 1980s, and have taken on their own life and character, whose direction is not yet determined. Yes, Hasta Mitra produced the yeast for the fermentation process—Pramoedya's books—but the process itself requires more than just the yeast. In the 1990s, when thousands struggled against Suharto's dictatorship, that struggle injected the other necessary ingredients for the ferment to accelerate quickly, dislodging Suharto in May 1998. The end of dictatorship opened up more space for struggle but also allowed it to disperse and stagnate, and for new lines of experimentation to emerge.

What might accelerate and crystallize the process again? The process of organizing, reading and mobilizing began back in the seventies, when Rendra challenged the students with the cry: 'On whose side do you stand?' It deepened and radicalized with the return of the original Indonesia from exile and will not stop. How quickly will it grow and strengthen amid an increasingly diverse social and cultural fermentation? We can only observe and document and reflect, as things evolve and encourage the best of the developments. However, I think Pramoedya's books and Hasta Mitra's spirit, have still a role to play. There is still more to be discovered in those books and from what the three men endured. While there are a zillion things yet to be discussed in all this, there is one aspect of *Bumi Manusia* that in particular needs to be a central part of any further discussion.

Joesoef's, Hasjim's and Pramoedya's love for Indonesia was the love of a generation who saw the new national community being created. The secret of *Bumi Manusia* is that Indonesia is not present in/ on this earth of mankind.

Chapter 12

Indonesia is Absent in/on *This Earth of Mankind*

In his 1981 letter, '*Ma'af Atas Nama Pengalaman*', Pramoedya described his This Earth of Mankind series of books, *Bumi Manusia*, *Anak Semua Bangsa*, *Jejak Langkah* and *Rumah Kaca* as books which 'dealt with the currents that ebbed and flowed during the period of the Indonesian National Awakening' (*Kebangkitan Nasional Indonesia*). In the general discourse around Pramoedya's books in Indonesia, and outside Indonesia, this way of conceiving of these books is more-or-less accepted. I also accept Pramoedya's own description of the books as being focused on the 'Indonesian national awakening'. Yet, the word 'Indonesia' does not appear in these four books—in almost 1,500 pages of text.

Indonesia is absent from these works—or is it?

Understanding the presence or absence of Indonesia in these works, which are now the most widely read versions of this period of Indonesian history within Indonesia (although still by far too few people), is crucial for an understanding of the genius of Pramoedya's contributions to literature, history and ideology.

The novels speak to many aspects of the very first creative processes that produced a completely new phenomenon to appear on the face of this earth of mankind: Indonesia. One very central aspect was the dynamic behind the emergence of a language that would become the vernacular later for a whole new national community. What is a vernacular? Its literal meaning is 'the commonly spoken language or dialect of a particular people or place'. In the *Bumi Manusia* books, one strong storyline is around the pressure on Minke to use Malay to 'speak to your people'—and his experiences of doing so. Minke's— Tirto Adhi Soerjo's—experiences in publishing *Medan Priyayi* and other Malay-language publications forms a major part of the novels' story content in *Footsteps* and *House of Glass*. But if the vernacular is a language of a particular people or place, then in the context of the society that these novels describe: what particular people or place?

Absence of Indonesia

It is a part of the genius of these novels that the question of the postcolonial vernacular is put at the centre of its story through the *absence* of an idea, term or concept of 'a particular people or place'. From the very beginning, the spectre that haunts the reality that we are confronted with is the absence of any particular place or people, or people with a place, or a place with a people. Pramoedya, in his 1980's letter, made it clear that he saw the processes he was describing as part of the Indonesian national awakening, yet it is impossible he could write 1,500 pages without mentioning Indonesia, or even hinting at it, except deliberately. The absence is deliberate, it is a *present* absence.

It is true, of course, that at the time in which the novel is set, the idea of Indonesia had not yet emerged. Nobody had thought of such a being, or even used the word 'Indonesia' in society. According to Pramoedya himself, the Dutch adopted the word 'Hindia' (Indies) for the islands as a marketing tactic to compete with the dominant products from the 'East', namely those from British India.[40] 'Hindia' was supposed to blur the difference. With neither the idea of Indonesia nor the word itself circulating in the Indies at the time of Minke's adventures, it would thus be an anachronism to have the word Indonesia appear. Still, Pramoedya could have chosen to have a narrator from a later period when the idea of Indonesia was present, looking back and telling the story. Instead, he chose to tell the story from within the consciousness of the times—a time when Indonesia was absent.

And, in any case, more importantly, the presence of the absence should be meaningful for its present-day Indonesian readers.

In this context, Pramoedya is taking a position in an important historical, political and intellectual debate, namely, on the origins of nations. The present-absence of Indonesia in the *Bumi Manusia* novels positions him in the camp of those who see nations as new creations and not the contemporary manifestations of age-old entities or essences. Pramoedya was very probably aware of the nineteenth-century and early twentieth-century debates on the origins of nations, some of whom were also referenced by Sukarno in his writings in the 1920s and 1930s.

This is a crucial, and, I think, fundamental embedded message from Pramoedya through these novels. Indonesia will be a new being on the face of the earth, and Indonesians will be a new kind of human being. The awakening, which later transforms into a revolution, is a creative process: what is absent becomes present, through struggle.

Of course, if we sieve through the novels, we can identify the seeds of the national process. The liberal Dutch teacher, Magda Peters, is exiled back to the Netherlands by the Netherlands Indies state for advocating 'Indies for the Indies', although it is clear this perspective does not yet assume a dissolution of inequality between races. The dialogues between Minke and the Chinese nationalists, Khouw Ah Soe and Ang Sang Mei, in *Child Of All Nations* startle Minke with the prospect that coloured peoples could survive without foreign rule. There are many little seeds like this strewn about among the reality that the novels describe.

Still, however, I think even by the end of the four novels, after twenty years in the life of Minke, the perception of a particular people and place has not yet become completely clear. Minke's own career is ended by his arrest just as he is about to travel the region, including the Philippines, to start his search for discovering the particular place and people. However, at the same time, it cannot be denied that the process of going from absent to present is felt powerfully in these four novels. It drives the reader onwards through the pages, just as it drives Minke onwards in more and more ambitious projects. The reader ploughs on, despite the history discussions that must be absorbed, just as Minke struggles on, despite his trials and tribulations. All this is driven by the sense that something new is being created, whether the new adult Minke, or a new society, or a new place–people nexus.

A Creative Process

It should be emphasized here, how revolutionary Pramoedya's stand is on this question, in the Indonesian historical context. His perspective stands opposite to that of historians, such as Muhammed Yamin, and even some of the Indonesian Communist Party nationalist 'historiography' that traced 'Indonesia' backed to Sriwijaya and Majapahit. He stands in deeper contradiction to the ideological historiography of the New Order, which combines a sanctification of stereotypes of traditional pre-Indonesian ethnicities (embodied in the temple to premodernity, the Indonesia Indah Miniatur ethnic theme park) with a history comprising the actions of a series of military heroes, and devoid of any serious struggle of ideas.

Indonesia was not present as a continuity with the past. Indonesia would be a rejection of the past, whether recognized as such or not by others. Pramoedya recognized the break and, in his novels, the purist spokesperson for the past, Minke's traditionalist Javanese mother was given the words to pronounce: 'Why do you try so hard to become other than your mother's son?'

'Java' recognized clearly that what was being created was not going to be a child of the past. It was going to be something new. In the Indonesia of the 1980s, when the novels were first published, as well as today, it is not possible to underestimate the challenge that this assertion of newness represented or represents. By positing Indonesia as a self-created, completely new being on the face of this earth of mankind, it challenged all to question the how, the way of this process, rather than to accept the existing pre-packaged, miraculously formed 'Indonesia' that Indonesians were miseducated to accept.

It also cut loose all notions of Indonesian-ness being anchored to the traditional past. It emphasized that the genius of Indonesia was not to be found in its despotic traditional past, not even in the achievements of that despotism, whether in literature or events. Nor was it to be found in its folk traditions. The genius of Indonesia was to be found in its own self-genesis, starting with Kartini and Tirto Adhi Soerjo, but followed by another six decades of creative struggle, using all kinds of elements from many sources, from whatever location or era.

Challenging Hegemonies: An Absence of Response

This challenge to answer the how and why of the creation process is still unmet in Indonesia. There has been a blossoming of interest in history since the fall of Suharto with the publication of thousands of new books on history. The emergence of the popular web magazine, *Majalah Historia*, is another example. It has now attracted commercial interest, although there is the danger that it might lose its subversive power once it is integrated into the mainstream. Some investors clearly see that there is now a market for history.

Still, generally speaking, and even though Pramoedya's historical novels continue to be read, the penny has not yet dropped that there is something drastically missing in the existing historical sense of Indonesia within society. A part of this is simply a result of the fact that Pramoedya's books have a small reach, now published by a family company with no funds for advertising and promotion, and no political strategy to promote his works and ideas. His books are still not introduced to children in school where they should be studied.

However, the problem is deeper than this. For there has been almost no significant discussion or debate amongst the Indonesian intelligentsia specifically about Pramoedya's ideas on Indonesian history. There have been a few books and theses written,[41] but none going into the question of the genesis of Indonesia. There have been none that I know of, which have even begun to respond to some of the analysis embedded in his novels. First, nobody seems to have grasped the significance of the absence of Indonesia, and grasped as a question: if Indonesia was not simply a 'modern' manifestation of an ancient essence, then what exactly was it? Concretely, Batik and Dangdut and Sinetron melodramas are more often perceived as the essence of Indonesian culture than anything that came out of the process of creating Indonesia.

Nor has anybody taken up any of the component parts of Pramoedya's historical analysis. For example, Pramoedya emphasizes on the role of Malay-speaking Chinese and Eurasians as the vanguard of the development of the Malay language in the Indies. They wrote the novels and short stories depicting contemporary urban life at the time. This literary activity, in Pramoedya's picture, provided the basis for the development of a national language. In contrast, most conventional histories emphasize Malay as a lingua franca for trade, and later as colonialism's administrative language, and the basis for Malay as the national language. Pramoedya's depiction of the formation of the Sarekat Dagang Islam (SDI) as partly—indeed primarily—due to Tirto Adhi Soerjo's alienation from the concept of the vanguard role for the *priyayi* (privileged state bureaucrats) and the definition of *dagang* as any activity where one sought a livelihood independently of the colonial state, has also not featured in any serious discussions. The colonial-generated version that the SDI was formed by native traders to defend themselves from the Chinese—a version which Pramoedya ensures is clearly contested in his novels—has also not been discussed. Perhaps, there are articles or books circulating somewhere that discuss these issues, but none have become part of any defining discussions.

The hegemony of the textbooks remains unchallenged, even thirty years after his books have been published. The total *present absence* of Indonesia has been and is also a challenge for foreign scholarship and has too, I think, major ramifications on how critiques of Orientalism need to be applied in relation to postcolonial societies. It is a strange phenomenon, indeed, that thirty years after the publication in Indonesian of *Bumi Manusia* and its sequels, the English-language Indonesian Studies academe has not produced a single major work on these books. Professor Teeuw, in his book on Pramoedya, did cover them. Academics on postcolonial literature, reading the books in translation, have started to write on them.[42] There have been the several highly subjective, art critic-style commentaries on some of

Pramoedya's short stories from the fifties in Cornell's *Indonesia* journal by Anderson, Siegel and others, but very little serious discussion on his historical novels for at least twenty years. Not even one single-authored book in English on Pramoedya in relation to these novels has appeared. Professor Adrian Vickers has used some perspectives from Pramoedya to illustrate his recent textbook on Indonesian history, but that is all that has appeared.

What are the issues here? First, Pramoedya's history challenges the hegemonic perspectives. It challenges the New Order hegemony that Indonesia is essentially a modern manifestation of an ancient essence that is symbolized by tradition. The pre-modern, despotic tradition has been modernized within a framework of modern underdeveloped capitalism: that is Indonesia. Pramoedya's Indonesia is a child of all nations, borrowing inspiration from—in the first instance—the ideas of the anti-feudal revolution of Europe and the Chinese, Filipino and Japanese resistances to Europe, born out of a struggle against injustice and out of a heroic battle in defence of principles, even when defeat in that battle was inevitable. Whether it was Minke and Sanikem's struggle to defend Annelies, or the Acehnese and Balinese struggle to ward off Dutch occupation, the inevitability of defeat was never an argument against action. This is in direct contrast to the opportunist ideology of underdeveloped capitalism, where calculations of profit and loss, and how much toadying would be necessary—an aspect Pramoedya ascribes to the priyayi culture—fuse together. Pramoedya's approach challenges the general cynicism of the intelligentsia towards idealism.

Pramoedya, Joesoef and Hasjim, were all very conscious of the need for idealism and were themselves soaked through with it. In a letter to a friend in the Netherlands, Pramoedya explained the reasons he decided, back before 1965, that he would write a series of novels telling Indonesia's history between 1900 and 1945. He explained that the normal classroom teaching of history was not enough to excite a love for the history of the national movement and the struggle for freedom. Without that real love for history, no manner or number of speeches and proclamations, songs and declamations, would ever be more than empty slogans, or even a form of dishonesty. The enthusiasm of Pramoedya, Joesoef and Hasjim at 'Minke's' graveside was one manifestation of that love, not to mention the foundation of Hasta Mitra itself.

In another letter to the same friend, Pramoedya also reflected on the question of honesty, motivated clearly also by a real love of nation. He commented that perhaps some of his earlier historical work was too much in the tradition of the early Indonesian National Party (PNI) and Partindo (to which *Eastern Star* newspaper had been affiliated). He wrote that kind of approach—meaning an approach somewhat uncritically glorifying the nation—should have been left behind long ago:

> By leaving that way behind, the nation could be educated to see its own weaknesses, mistakes, incapacities, and idiocies. And most importantly to recognize its own gross misbehaviours. Without the courage to look upon its true self, to stand before a mirror and see its whole self, this nation will remain of a weak character.

So yes, Pramoedya's books are written to be tendentious and controversially so.

Indonesia: Auto-didact

They challenge another hegemony that is strong both within and outside Indonesia: namely, that Indonesia is fundamentally a creation—albeit as a by-product—of the Dutch. This is an all-pervasive perspective. It can also take the form of an assertion, stated explicitly or implicitly, that Indonesia is an artificial creation, with an artificial unity. Sometimes, this comes with hints, or even arguments, that the true 'nations' are to be found in the ethnic identities of the archipelago. The total absence of Indonesia within the four novels is a kind of huge exclamation mark emphasizing that Indonesia was to be a completely new thing: it would not be the child of any existing entity, but a child of *all* nations. In this way, Indonesia is, in the literal sense, artificial: 'produced by humans (as opposed to "natural")'. The point is, of course, so are all nations.

Furthermore, in Pramoedya's history, Dutch power does everything it can to either destroy or pluck out the seeds of any newly forming entity within the historical processes. The reason there is the need for struggle, even in the face of an inevitable loss of many battles at great cost, is precisely the determination of Dutch power to stop any creative processes from unfolding.

What about the role of the Dutch as teachers? There are so many Dutch teachers in these novels. There is the de le Croix family, Magda Peters and the journalist Ter Haar, for example. But they are all exposed in the end as being failed teachers with inadequate ideas. They offer Minke inspiration and make him think, but so does Trunodongso and Surati and Darsam, as well as, of course, Sanikem. Minke learns much more from Khouw Ah Soe and Ang Sang Mei, and from reading about Japan and the Philippines, than he does from his Dutch teachers. Most of these Dutch teachers are much like some more books, like those he read about the French Revolution in the Dutch-language high school. The Dutch teachers are sources of information and ideas, not examples or models: and in the end, all their teachings are found wanting.

Pramoedya does not ignore the 'physical' contribution of Dutch power in forming the borders of Indonesia. The final surge—to use the contemporary terminology of colonial occupation—instituted by Governor-General Van Heutz to occupy Bali and other independent pockets of sovereignty, is well-covered by Pramoedya. There was an official map of the colony, which came later, to define its borders. In these books, however, these maps are also initially negated in the final pages of *Jejak Langkah* (*Footsteps*). Minke convinces the SDI to carry out long-range propaganda work. The SDI conference that mandates Minke agrees that he visit 'Singapore, Siam, Malaya and the Philippines'—all of which were outside the map of the Netherlands Indies. In fact, Minke's conception by the time wished to embark on this was that of the 'Greater Malay Nation', which included all Malay-speaking peoples (even in Sri Lanka).

> So, my brothers, our nation is not just that of the Javanese, but includes many other peoples as well, bound together by the things I have explained to you. It is much greater than that which has been described as the Indisch nation or the Indies nation. As for its name, I do not have one yet. Perhaps we will need a new name for it.

The dynamic Pramoedya describes as driving forward the nation-creation process is a *fusion of experience*: use of a common language, in particular, to discuss the future; a common psychological outlook formed out of the experience of struggle, which Minke called 'independent endeavour', that is survival independent of any sinecure or largesse from the colonial state. As there were embryonic centres of Malay-language usage in Malaya, Singapore, the Philippines and Siam, the Netherlands Indies map was, in the end, irrelevant in the self-genesis process of this 'nation'. Its relevance was in the ability to constrain that process—reflected in the failure of the nation-creation process to burst beyond the Netherlands Indies borders. And represented in the novel in the arrest and exile of Minke before he can begin in his travels, and, in fact, manifested in the successful destruction of Minke, in Pramoedya's version—his murder. It is not the map as a constructive instrument of nation creation that is important here, but the power behind the map as a destructive power over the process.

For Pramoedya and the *Bumi Manusia* novels, Indonesia is in *no way* the product or by-product of Dutch colonialism. This is not to say that none of the raw materials for the nation-production process had been sourced from the Dutch. Minke describes himself as a child of *all* nations, not all except the Dutch. The point is that the whole nation-creation process is a self-genesis. To use a much-liked Indonesian term at the moment, this process was that of an auto-didact, like Pramoedya himself. The process that the four novels describe is one of self-genesis using all suitable available materials. In the end, Minke adopts Malay rather than Dutch.

Pramoedya's framework poses questions that require a richer understanding of the nation-creation process than that embedded in the simple binary opposition of nationalist movement versus colonial power. A nationalist movement (that is, a movement to establish an independent nation-state) usually can only grow strong on the basis of the creation of a 'particular place and people' having come into existence. It is the conception itself and the early embryonic development of 'particular place and people' that the novels deal with as a starting point.

Experience and Consciousness

Pramoedya peppers his depiction of the historical processes with mentions and descriptions of myriad of texts: novels, short stories, articles, reports. However, ultimately, the processes that Pramoedya identifies that will eventually lead to the formation of the material basis for a national community pose the community as the product of a shared experience.

The novels depict the beginning of the process from absence of particularity of process and place to its later presence (later beyond the time period of the novels), inclusion of such shared experiences and inclusion of the contradictions within them, create both a national consciousness, and a variety of new individual consciousnesses.

The question of the experience of reality seems to me to have a very weighty, or deep, place in Pramoedya's perspective on Indonesia. Of course, all depictions of reality will include descriptions of people's experience in their surrounding, their relationships with other humans, and the material world. However, reality can be romanticized, ignored, misunderstood and underrated and so on. Minke's life is like a yo-yo bouncing between what he reads and hears about reality, and what he experiences. And he and his friends experience everything deeply, through loss—losses that have brought many readers to tears in whatever language they read it—or through exhilaration. And observed in detail; uninformed by prejudice. In *Anak Semua Bangsa*, especially, but not only there, the reality of the peasantry is highlighted. In the portrait of pockmarked Surati and her experiences, as well as the more marginal portraits; or of peasant farmer Trunodongso and his family, Pramoedya is even rejecting the concept of 'kerakyatan', a concept that romanticizes the style of life of the 'little people' setting it up as something to mimic, as a form of being progressive. What was important for Pramoedya was the actual, real experience of the peasants.

In the novel, Minke experienced it directly, meeting Surati, staying with Trunodongso; he didn't read about it and then conjure it up in his imaginings. He not only heard and read about the struggles of the Chinese young reformers, but experienced them, suffered because of them. They were also not simply imaginings. But it is true, he never went to Bali or met any Balinese. Yet, after receiving a letter from

Ter Haar admonishing him not to be indifferent to the suffering and struggle of the Balinese—who ate the same rice and drank the same water as Minke, wrote Ter Haar—as they waged a war of defence against the Dutch colonial army, Minke narrates: 'He was right. The Balinese were my fellow countrymen.'

This was a powerful statement of understanding by Minke, by now referred to as T.A.S., still early in his development. He was still a medical student, writing only in his spare time. The other students were not focussed on this, despite the newspaper reports; 'Newspapers were more expensive than cigarettes', Minke muses. And it is Ter Haar's letters that really tell him what is happening, not the newspapers. It is the experience of interaction that gives the Balinese experience reality. But it is more than that. Minke's own ability to respond to the Balinese 'fighting back as well and as honourably as they can' is also forged out of his own experience of fighting back and his interaction with others doing the same. And by this time, the list is long, very long, only halfway through the second novel.

Minke is living in and travelling through a community forged out of the interaction between people involved in some form of fight for their rights and dignity. It is a real, experienced community, not simply imagined. The ability to identify with others he had not met; to imagine their plight and see them as being part of the same community, was a result of the fact that they were indeed part of that emerging single community entity. And there was another layer that Pramoedya also did not forget. The common experience and the spreading interaction between those who shared that experience, was also a function of material reality. The colonial system had to expand. 'Expand, don't you mean', the radical Dutch journalist challenged General van Heutz when he said that the Indies would have to be unified by force. The experience of exploitation and oppression would inevitably spread, not as a separate process, but as part of the same process. On other fronts, sugar capital or tobacco capital, Pram shows, spread the same experiences to more and more people, who interacted more and more.

The embryo's development starts to accelerate once the interaction starts to take on the form of organization—the subject matter of much of *Footsteps*.

Orientalism/Postcolonialism

I have stated above that Pramoedya's historical novels also have major ramifications for how critiques of orientalism—and indeed postcolonialism—need to be applied. Probably one of the most oft-quoted relevant definitions relating to this is given by Edward Said:

> To the extent that Western scholars were aware of contemporary Orientals or Oriental movements of thought and culture, these were perceived either as silent shadows to be animated by the Orientalist, brought into reality by them, or as a kind of cultural and international proletariat useful for the Orientalist's grander interpretive activity.

In Pramoedya's novels, he has done both the proletarian work of research (though as a writer, not an historian) as well as the fundamental interpretation—an interpretation, I have argued above, which challenged all the major existing hegemonics. Furthermore, the 'contemporary oriental movement of culture and thought' that began at the turn of the twentieth century and was the genesis of Indonesian national culture in Pramoedya's works, was brought out of the shadows and allowed to animate itself. Indeed, Dutch scholarship had written Tirto Adhi Soerjo out of history just as Dutch power, alleges Pramoedya, murdered him. In these terms, Pramoedya, primarily through his historical novels, is the archetypical negation of Orientalism.

There is a way in which these works also stand as a challenge not only to orientalism, but also to 'postcolonialism'. There is no doubt whatsoever that it is the colonial experience that constitutes the terrain on which the self-genesis of Indonesia took place. There is a truth, a deep truth, to an approach that acknowledges this and also seeks to identify the way this terrain can frame or impact on what happens after independence is won. There is a truth, too, to the effort to seek the similarities in the way this happens across societies that have experienced colonialism. I think there is indeed the basis for postcolonial studies and postcolonial literary studies. By now in 2022, the body of postcolonial studies in literature is huge. So is the variety of material available. Much of what is written today—overcome by postmodernism and deep textual analysis—would be alien to Fanon, Said and others, who first attracted attention in writing about the postcolonial experience; even much of subaltern studies, which seem to revel in the permanence of oppressed class's resistance that is, the permanence of their subordination.

What appears to haunt postcolonial studies is the issue of identity. Of course, this was also at the heart of Fanon's seminal works: how people of former colonies had absorbed identity or psychology from the colonizers, as well as out of their experience as the colonized. There is no issue of identity in the *Bumi Manusia* novels. That is to say, the 'auto-didact self-genesis' dynamic neither produces nor is confused over issues of identity. Of course, the young Minke has some related issues, but the auto-didact process clarifies these. Minke knows who he is, just as does Pramoedya. And who he is, in any case, is not a postcolonial issue. At the end of *Jejak Langkah*, when Minke has grown determined to set off to travel around the Indies, as well as outside the Indies, he knows clearly who he is, even though as he tells his SDI comrades, he does not know even the name of the embryonic national community he belongs to.

Minke's journey is not a journey of discovery vis-à-vis national identity, but of what he believes in and how he sees the world. In reality, Pramoedya turns the postcolonial concern with identity on its head. If anything, what we can learn from these novels is that if there is a basis for postcolonial studies, there certainly is also for 'imperial society studies', and it is in fact in imperial culture that the question of confused and contradictory identities and psychology, is the more apt focus for study and analysis. Contradiction—almost irresolvable contradiction—is the characteristic of almost all of the colonial European characters in the novels. The more 'moral' or well-intentioned the personality, the deeper and seemingly more hopeless their contradictions appear. Oppressor or educator? Democrat or racist? The imperial relationship, also given its skin colour and racial legitimization, imposes a contradiction on all people from an imperial country, which is very difficult to rise above.

The Question of Other Absences

The present absence of Indonesia in these novels of the 'Indonesian National Awakening' is a not only an historical accuracy, but the novels' genius. It is amazing how many people, including Indonesians, never realize its absence, unless brought to their attention. It confronts its Indonesian readers, unknowingly, with the truth that Indonesia is not a given—nor ever was—nor is it governed by some divine or other unchangeable evidence: it is a self-made entity.

But there remain very important unresolved questions—all marked by absences rather than presences.

The epic tale of Minke and Nyai is a story of the conception and the development of the embryo—but we *do not get to see the birth in any of his historical novels*. In fact, the question arises if what we have seen is a miscarriage. Minke dies. His mass organization, the SDI, falls into the hands of others. Nyai Ontosoroh, unable to save Annelies, witnesses the murder and destruction of Minke. Nyai is in exile, in fact, in France, and ends up absent from the Indies, in a different place–people context. A miscarriage? Well, no—we know and Pramoedya knew, and his readers sort of know that the 1920s was the 'age of motion' and that indeed the new people–place entity did obtain its new name, Indonesia, legitimized in the 1928 Sumpah Pemuda. Is there any significance of the absence of a witness to the birth of Indonesia, even if just the idea of Indonesia with its new name, in Pramoedya's historical novels?

Pramoedya's achievement, while imprisoned on Buru Island prison camp, was truly amazing. He wrote *Arok Dedes*, *Arus Balik*, *Mangir* and the four Bumi Manusia novels, as well as the lost *Mata Pusaran*. These manuscripts present a picture of the dynamics of Indonesian history from the eleventh century, through to around 1920. They are Pramoedya's attempt to explain 'why are we like this today?' But why stop at the death of Tirto Adhi Soerjo or Minke? Had he just not got around to it, not having the time to have done any research before 1965? Of course, he had written a great deal of spontaneous, immediate experiential-based short stories and novels on the revolutionary period and then the early and mid-1950s. Why nothing on the post-Minke period then? Why is that absent?

Pramoedya complained in his 'Ma'af Atas Nama Pengalaman' that he was often asked a clichéd question: when will he write about the present? 'Will you write about the present? Haven't you already written a lot about past times that are already history? What is more, the present is also history, contemporary history, right?' His explanation for not writing anything on the Sukarno period was:

> The era of Sukarno and the Trisakti doctrine was nothing but a sort of thesis. The New Order, an antithesis. Therefore, for me, it is something that in fact cannot be written about yet, a process that cannot yet be written as literature, that does not yet constitute a national process in its totality, because it is in fact still heading for its synthesis. While I was still at Buru, an Indonesian.

Later, he confirmed in the same letter: 'All that has passed, but not yet become history, because as a process it has yet to reach a resolution in synthesis.'

It is an interesting way of looking at history, but it still reads as an excuse. It is also not clear when the 'era of Sukarno' starts. Is it with Sukarno's emergence in the 1920s? Or is Pramoedya referring to the period of Guided Democracy, 1959–65? He calls it also the 'Trisakti' period, so perhaps he is referring to 1959–65, when Sukarno popularized the Trisakti: the struggle for independence and sovereignty in politics, economics and culture. In that case, how would he have described the 1920–59 period: a part of what thesis-antithesis-synthesis process? Or perhaps he sees the Trisakti campaigns of the early 1960s as the more final manifestation of a process that started in the 1020s, or even with Kartini or Tirto Adhi Soerjo?

It is not clear what exactly he thought because this whole period after the 1920s is absent from his in-depth analysis, either via literature or non-fiction analysis.

In fact, Pramoedya offered nothing major for publication after his release from Buru Island in 1978. Perhaps there are hidden, undiscovered or unfinished manuscripts or notes. But he himself did often complain of having 'writer's block'.

The post-1920 period is absent from Pramoedya's historical survey and Pramoedya himself—in terms of new works—was absent from Indonesia, after 1978. There is another twist to this: not only were these novels created in exile from Indonesia, in the separate universe of Buru Island, but the Bumi Manusia novels were also conceived before 1965, in the period of the 'thesis', to use Pramoedya's terminology. In some respects, both in terms of content of the Bumi Manusia novels, and the conditions of their production, researched before 1965 and produced in exile in Buru Island, their presence in Indonesia, via publication in the 1980s, becomes a dramatic presence because it is the presence of something otherwise *totally absent* in Indonesia since 1965: namely, the Indonesia from before 1965. True history was erased from the collective consciousness of the country as a result of the militarization, falsification and rote-ification of false history after 1965, as described in the chapter 'Memory' in my book, *Unfinished Nation* (2008).

Pramoedya's novels negate the absence of history in the present while, at the same time, Pramoedya is absent from the present, as is his history, or more precisely, the history of his generation—at least through his works. Pramoedya's thirty years' writer's block is symbolic of a much bigger, major problem. The intellectuals of the antithesis (the New Order 66 Generation and their descendants) have their version of history. However, the intellectuals of the thesis generation (Pramoedya and the rest of the Left from before 1965) have not produced a history of their own, neither have their intellectual descendants, the Left-leaning young intellectuals of the 1990s or today.

Pramoedya himself did reflect on the 1960s in his 'Ma'af Atas Nama Pengalaman' letter, defending himself from the attacks that he was part of an oppressive power system persecuting non-Left writers during the 1960s. These reflections were very brief, but also very defensive and lacked any element of critique of the praxis of the Left before 1965. Pramoedya is, in my opinion, fundamentally correct in his reflections. The PKI was not in power. On the contrary, as a party with no significant ministers in the cabinet and operating most of the time under conditions of Martial Law, the PKI—and even Sukarno himself—in some respects, was part of the opposition to the state, not a part of the state power.

However, there can be no escaping the fact that nothing that Pramoedya (and Sukarno) fought for until 1965 was achieved, apart from the formal existence of Indonesia. The Indonesia created by the New Order was the opposite of everything which they fought for and which was embodied in the life and political values embedded in the characterizations of Minke and Sanikem and all the positive characters in the Bumi Manusia novels. What is absent, and the absence that Pramoedya's writer's block symbolizes, is the historical explanation of this failure. Thanks to Pramoedya, Indonesia has had a good start in bringing to life the history of the conception and early development of the particular people-place-being that became Indonesia. But the revolutionaries, such as Pramoedya and his intellectual descendants, have never written their own history examining the causes of their failure, giving rise to the 'antithesis' of the New Order. At the most, his generation, and even his intellectual descendants, have confined their intellectual activity to documenting their situation as 'victims' of the New Order and Suharto and the 'tragedy' of 1965, but never assessing their situation as victims of their own failure. Pramoedya wrote in his 'Ma'af' letter, explaining his motivation for writing *Bumi Manusia*: '*Why does all this happen and continue to happen*? But I am a writer with minimal education, so it is not the materials of history that I examine, but its spirit. This I began with the tetralogy Bumi Manusia.'

There is a writer's block representing the failure of the emergence of a re-evaluation of the revolutionary tradition, from within that tradition, asking that question of its own failure: 'why does all this happen and continue to happen?' This was also the origin of Pramoedya's writer's block. Such a failure is a double failure: because Indonesia as we know it today was, in many ways, a product of the failures of the Left. Without understanding that history, contemporary Indonesia will remain mostly a mystery, beyond anybody's efforts to change it.

A Present Absence

The absence of any self-critique in the revolutionary tradition, manifested in, among other things, Pramoedya's writers' block, was and is a failure. Still, Pramoedya was honest on this issue. Time and again, he repeated in a message to the younger generation that they should write their elders off as unable to make any new contributions. Pramoedya held tight to what he saw as his major contribution to the future: the analytical depiction of the origins of the 'particular people–place being' that was to become Indonesia and its dependence on resistance against oppression in defence of dignity as the engine of its birth. Most importantly, standing against Orientalist theories of confused identity or colonial origins, Pramoedya revealed Indonesia as the product of self-genesis, self-agency. It is a wonderful and dynamic picture he painted. But it is also a good place to start for any history of the Indonesian revolution after 1920: both successes and failures are self-created.

Chapter 13

This Earth of Mankind, Indonesia, and the World

The first English language edition of *This Earth of Mankind* was published by Penguin Books Australia and released in Australia, the United Kingdom and Singapore in 1982. Australia and Singapore were its primary initial places of circulation. It was listed among the 'Top Ten Bestsellers' in the *Sydney Morning Herald* for several weeks. In Singapore, an additional special print run was found to be necessary to meet the demand. Reviews were positive and enthusiastic in both Australia and Singapore. My early recall from my position as Second Secretary (Development Assistance) at the Australian Embassy in Jakarta, back to Canberra in 1981, for carrying out the 'undiplomatic' activity of translating a banned book, attracted attention and increased the profile of the publication.

An Australian postgraduate student, then in Indonesia, researching Mochtar Lubis, David Hill (now Professor David Hill A.O.), wrote an anonymous article on my recall, which was published in the *National Times* weekly newspaper.[43] When Penguin published the book, more press, radio and television interviews followed. The Australian Ambassador who recommended that I be recalled, Fred R. Dalrymple, did us a great favour.

Prior to Penguin's publication of *This Earth of Mankind*, Pramoedya's works were little-known in the English-speaking world. University of

Queensland Press in Australia had published a collection of short stories, *A Heap of Ashes*, produced by the prolific Australian translator, Harry Aveling.[44] No work by Pramoedya had been published by a mainstream American or British publisher. The decision by Penguin Australia was made by its Publisher Brian Johns, who later went on to head the Special Broadcasting Service (SBS) as well as the Australian Broadcasting Commission (ABC), Australia's two major public broadcasting institutions.[45] It was a courageous decision to take on a book set at the beginning of the twentieth century in the Dutch East Indies, by an unknown Indonesian writer, which was also just the first volume of four. When Joesoef Isak visited Australia in 2005 to receive the inaugural PEN Keneally Award[46] for publishing, Johns, who attended, stated that publishing these books was the best decision he had ever made.

Joesoef Isak (centre) with Brian Johns (left), former CEO of Penguin Australia, who took the decision to publish *This Earth Of Mankind*, and Australian novelist Thomas Kennealley, while being awarded the PEN Sydney Freedom Publishing Award, 1981.

I had translated *This Earth of Mankind* in the evenings and weekends while I was working at the Australian Embassy. Friends and acquaintances, including the Australian poet R.S. Brissenden, read and provided comments on the manuscript. Once in Penguin's hands, it went through more editing with inputs from the Australian novelist, Blanche d'Alpuget, who had written novels set in Asia and had lived in Indonesia; and it was also scrutinized and edited by Bruce Simms, a chief editor at Penguin. It remained in print with Penguin Australia but then in 1991, was published in hardback by William Morrow.

This began its journey from being an Australia-based to a US-based publication. Its successful launch in the United States was due to the personal enthusiasm of the William Morrow Publisher Will Schwalbe.[47] Schwalbe, who later went to write a bestselling book of his own in the United States, on the topic of reading and books,[48] first read a translation of one of Pramoedya's earlier novels, *The Fugitive*, at Yale, guided by his professor, James Rush. Schwalbe first published *The Fugitive* by Willem Samuels (a pseudonym). This was the first publication of Indonesian fiction in English in America, outside one book published at a university press. He then shepherded the publication of the whole *Buru Quartet*, in a translation which was further revised, with William Morrow.[49]

Morrow bought the rights and later sold the paperback rights to Penguin USA. Schwalbe then moved to Hyperion Books, where he published more Pramoedya titles, including some of Pramoedya's prison essays, in *A Mute's Soliloquy*. It was only after Schwalbe's crusade to publish these works in hardback through William Morrow and then Hyperion, that Penguin USA bought the paperback rights from Penguin Australia. Pramoedya had won some profile in the US as an imprisoned writer. He won the Barbara Goldsmith/PEN Freedom to Write Award in 1988 and the Hellman/Hammett award, which recognizes writers from around the world for their commitment to free expression and courage in the face of political persecution. The German novelist Gunter Grant, had played a role in promoting Pramoedya with PEN Networks.[50]

This Earth of Mankind and its sequels were well-received in the United States, with the author of the review in *The Washington Post* calling it the 'Indonesian *Iliad*'. The response was similar in all the major publications with book reviews (See Epilogue for more on this and other US reviews). Today, thirty years later, the four novels are still in print, being promoted as the *Buru Quartet*, with enthusiastic comments from readers on a number of bookseller and other websites. The books are on the reading lists of college and university courses, especially comparative literature, and postcolonial studies. There are even now teachers' and student's reading guides for *This Earth of Mankind*.[51]

In 1998, Schwalbe and others organized a speaking tour across the United States for Pramoedya to launch *A Mute's Soliloquy*. This was Pramoedya's first trip outside the United States since his release from Buru Island. Pramoedya received several university awards and honorary degrees during the tour. Joesoef Isak also was part of the tour and often spoke at the forums with Pramoedya. After the United States, they went on to Europe, visiting the United Kingdom, France and the Netherlands, among other places. By the 2000s, the *Buru Quartet* had been translated into many European and Asian languages, sometimes directly from the Indonesian, sometimes from the English. William Morrow, through Schwalbe, began to operate as the global representative for translations, bringing the international translation work under systematic and proper supervision. Later, Schwalbe helped Pramoedya find an international literary agent.

I argued in the last chapter that an essential part of the picture that Pramoedya painted of turn of the twentieth-century Indonesia-to-be was that Indonesia was still not yet there—it was still indeed 'to-be'. People who have read *This Earth of Mankind*, or even more so all four books, and have also spent time in contemporary Indonesia will say to me: 'Max, it was only after I read these books that I understood what was going on around me here.' The books are dense with insights into how caste and class, tradition and contemporary dynamics, authority and rebellion, foreign domination and new national creativity flow and interact. What they show helps explain life in Indonesia today, especially for the foreigner experiencing Indonesia for the first time. This is the case even though the novels are about life before Indonesia.

Outside of Indonesia, while still being enjoyed by so many who like a rich, inspiring, and well-told story, the novels have been intellectually located in the realm of postcolonial studies and discussion, especially in the United States and Europe. Of course, they are novels written by an author of independent Indonesia about a period of colonial history, so this is not surprising. More Indonesian literature is being published by mainstream international publishers—such as the novels of Eka Kurniawan and Intan Paramaditha—as international publishers seek more varied content.[52] However, Indonesia as the fourth largest country in the world is still not present in global intellectual and cultural discussions, either in the literary or political realms. In the period from 1945 until 1965, this was not the case.

Sukarno hosted the 1955 Asia Africa Conference in Bandung, which brought national leaders such as Jawarhal Nehru, Chou En Lai, Gabdel Nasser and others to Indonesia.[53] Representatives from twenty-nine countries representing more than half the world's population attended. It was a forum where differently aligned nations robustly debated international issues and where Indonesia, through Sukarno in particular, looked outwards, speaking to the Third World. During the 1960–65 period, Indonesia's activities speaking to the world—the Third World in particular—also intensified.

In the wake of the 1955 Bandung Conference, Indonesians took on important roles in a variety of Asia–Africa solidarity organizations. One of these was Joesoef Isak, who was Secretary-General for the Asia Africa Journalists' Association, until he was arrested. Indonesians were active in the Asia Africa Solidarity headquarters in Cairo, the Asia Africa Women's Congress and the Afro-Asian Writers' Bureau based in Sri Lanka. Sukarno became a critic of the United Nations as an institution dominated by the great Western powers and advocated forming an organization of what he called the 'New Emerging Forces' (NEFO) which he saw as confronting the 'Old Established Forces' (OLDEFO). The OLDEFO comprised all the former colonial, now imperialist, states and all other governments and social forces that supported them. The NEFO comprised all the states who had won political independence and were now resisting imperialism as well as the socialist countries who were in contradiction with US power. Furthermore, he included in NEFO, non-state forces such as the civil rights movement in the US and national liberation movements.

In 1965, the new government reversed the flow and opened the door wide for the outside—the West—to come into Indonesia. The outward flow of ideas and spirit from Indonesia stopped. The nation ended its activist alignment with the Third World and aligned itself with the West—an alignment that has continued today. In 2022, Indonesia will formally preside over the G20, which sees itself as a grouping of the 'most developed as well as emerging economies'. As the idea of 'emerging economies' has won hegemony in the discussion of the relationship between the rich and the poor countries of the world, it has been easier to co-opt weaker, underdeveloped countries with political elites formed out of the suppression of national liberation or anti-neocolonial political movements. From speaking outwards to the world, often in defiance of the 'West', today what is hegemonic in the West also frames intellectual discourse within Indonesia.

The original outward-looking Indonesia was exiled. With Hasta Mitra's books, and all the other writings from Buru exiles that followed, and the actions of the protest generation inspired by the Hasta Mitra books, the original Indonesia returned from exile in the 1980s to meet the new inward-looking Indonesia created out of 1965. The struggle to displace the 'new' with a renewed twenty-first-century version of the original Indonesia is still at an early stage. Indonesia's deepest literary works—Pramoedya's *Buru Quartet*—are focussed on the country's origins and *not* on either its current state of economic and social development/underdevelopment and the reasons for that situation, nor on its place in a still fundamentally divided world. In this sense, Indonesia has a very small presence in the world compared to its size, as well as compared to the period before 1965.

The question of looking outwards and engaging with the world intellectually and politically in an earlier period of the archipelago's history was depicted by Pramoedya in one of his other major historical novels written on Buru Island, *Arus Balik* (*The Flow Reverses*). This novel deals with the early sixteenth century when the rulers of Java were faced with a struggle to establish an archipelago-wide polity to counter the encroaching European, mainly Portuguese, cannon-bearing ships. This 750-page novel—almost as epic as the whole *Buru Quartet*—tells the story, among many, of how the key rulers of the day decided to turn inwards and concentrate on trying to protect their individual little kingdoms. During the previous period, that of the kingdom of Majapahit, its ships had been able to explore far and wide and bring back both goods and ideas from the places they reached. This then changed as fewer and fewer ships travelled north to mainland Southeast Asia and China: ships from Arabia, China, India and then Europe travelled to the archipelago instead: the flow reversed. Resiling from any serious confrontation with the newly arrived Europeans, the decision to turn inwards resulted in a reversal of the flow of energy from Java outwards to the involuted stagnation of the small inward-looking kingdoms.[54] They were not then in a position but to do anything else but surrender to pressure from the European colonizers or when eventually they were forced to resist, they were weak and easily defeated. This was, according to Pramoedya in *Arus Balik*, a consequence of both the inward-looking self-interest based motivations of the numerous small kingdoms of that time as well as a similar inward-looking passivity among the population.

The Flow Reverses depicts a crucial period of history, interpreted through the insertion of the fictional narratives of imagined characters alongside real historical figures, and is both a mammoth and engrossing read. Except for one chapter, *Arus Balik* has not been translated into English.[55] After translating *Arok Dedes* for a Singapore publisher who serviced the Southeast Asian market, in 2004, Pramoedya authorized me to translate *Arus Balik*.[56] It is a debt I still owe him. Whatever debates may be provoked about the precise historical analysis[57] in *Arus Balik's* stories of kingdoms and merchants and soldiers, the message is clear: the societies of the archipelago stagnated once they gave up on resisting the cannon-bearing merchants of the West and flowing outwards themselves. Remember the words that Pramoedya put into the mouth of the Dutch high school teacher and which Minke found so confronting: 'What have the Javanese contributed to the world?'

If referring to the period of Indonesia's history before 1965—then Indonesia, no longer Java—Pramoedya, Joesoef and Hasjim would provide a positive and enthusiastic answer, pointing to the country's role in the Third World, starting with the Bandung Conference. The forty-year-long circulation of Pramoedya's origin story novels in numerous languages, apart from English, is itself a major contribution to the understanding of how nations emerge and how colonialism works. Joesoef Isak himself was able to attend as a speaker at the 2005 Asia Pacific Solidarity Conference in Sydney, Australia, where activists from around Asia spoke.

Meanwhile, the world waits for a fuller turning outwards of the minds and energies of the world's fourth most populous nation, when the flow will reverse again, but this time, outwards. Like all Third World countries, even those with the largest of economies, such as China or India, Indonesia is still burdened by the underdevelopment that colonialism left behind—not a single modern factory was operating in the Netherlands Indies, even in 1940. When in 1965, Suharto turned the country inwards, letting the West come inside the country almost without conditions, it meant that Indonesia's economic dependence further worsened.

Joesoef Isak in Sydney at 2005 Asia Pacific Global Justice Conference. (Photo by Sarah Stephen)

It is, however, not material poverty that holds back Indonesia from engaging outwards again. The journey back from exile and the winning of a new hegemony by the original Indonesia over Suharto's Indonesia, in whatever precise form the new generation determines, has not yet finished. It is in the pre take-off stage. Sparks will fly soon. Indonesia wasn't there yet back at the turn of the twentieth century and when it did appear, finally, after a short burst of creativity energy, it was exiled again. The creation of the Indonesian nation was self-generated and so will be its reincarnation. Whatever form this reincarnation takes, we can be sure that *This Earth of Mankind* and its sequels will be among the prescribed texts in all schools, as Vice President Adam Malik said back in 1981 after he had met Hasjim Rachman, Joesoef Isak and Pramoedya Ananta Toer.

I hope you have enjoyed reading this story about their story and the stories they wrote and published, and the story they restarted. Meanwhile, I hope the cover of this book is soon on the T-shirts of young people in Indonesia.

Epilogue

Why You Should Read *This Earth of Mankind*[58]

In January 2014 Joshua Oppenheimer's film on Indonesia, *The Act of Killing*, was nominated for an Academy Award, reflecting its penetration into mainstream film-watching. Many people will be introduced to Indonesia by this vivid study of the country's ruling lumpen elite. Another, very different, introduction to Indonesia might be reading Pramoedya Ananta Toer's historical novel *Bumi Manusia* (*This Earth of Mankind*).

The English-language edition of *This Earth of Mankind* was published by Penguin in 1983. The sequels to this novel, *Child of All Nations*, *Footsteps* and *House of Glass*, were published over the following several years by Penguin in Australia and the United Kingdom. They were launched into the United States by William Morrow, Hyperion and Penguin in the 1990s. As their translator, I am very pleased to see that they are still in print thirty years later, having undergone many reprints. The four novels are likely to appear soon as ebooks with Penguin USA having bought the eBook rights. They appear already to be advertised as eBooks for Kindle on Amazon.com.

The first English Edition of *This Earth of Mankind* by Penguin Australia.

The current Penguin *Buru Quartet* editions.

Pramoedya's work has, on the whole, met with critical acclaim in the West, in particular, the United States. The publication of other translations followed, such as *Silent Songs of a Mute, The Fugitive, Girl from the Coast* and collections of short stories. In 1992, a *New York Times* reviewer wrote:

> Now comes a book of far greater scope and depth from independent Indonesia's greatest but still most controversial fiction writer, whose career spans more than 40 years. *This Earth of Mankind*, the first in a cycle of four novels, is the tale of a bittersweet coming of age in Java, Indonesia's dominant island, almost a century ago. Through it, we are taken back to the days of nascent Indonesian nationalism. But the author is a humanist, not a propagandist, and so his novel is also a wonderful example of the best storytelling tradition of his country.[7]

In 1996, after *House of Glass* appeared, the *Washington Post* reviewer wrote:

> The Buru Tetralogy is one of the 20th century's great artistic creations, a work of the richest variety, color, size and import, founded on a profound belief in mankind's potential for greatness and shaped by a huge compassion for mankind's weakness.[8]

Jamie James, in his article 'The Indonesiad' in *The New Yorker* (27 May 1996) wrote:

> The series follows the life of a revolutionary journalist named Minke. The first native Javanese boy to attend the elite Dutch colonial high school, Minke is full of idealistic notions about European progress. The process of his disillusionment and forging of his Indonesian identity—a new element in the periodic table of history—[forms] the novels' core. The *Buru Quartet* is saturated with the gothic gloom and steamy atmosphere of the rain forest.

---

[7] Barbara Crosette, Book review: 'Banned in Jakarta', *The New York Times*, 19 January 1992. Available at: https://www.nytimes.com/1992/01/19/books/banned-in-jakarta.html?pagewanted=1.

[8] Alan Ryan, 'Jakarta Quartet', *The Washington Post*, 11 August 1996. Available at: https://www.washingtonpost.com/archive/entertainment/books/1996/08/11/jakarta-quartet/c4b08980-adea-434f-b6dd-0f0387ad3a59/.

James' description of some of Pramoedya's style—'the *Buru Quartet* is saturated with the gothic gloom and steamy atmosphere of the rain forest'—speaks as to how the novels reach across cultures. The reception in the US is a particularly convincing tribute to Pramoedya's storytelling and writing, remembering that Indonesia is almost invisible and unknown in the United States, unlike the situation in Australia.

Pramoedya's books besides *This Earth of Mankind* and its sequels, such as *A Mute's Soliloquy*, *Fugitive* and *Girl from the Coast* (translated by Willem Samuel), were also received with acclaim. Schwalbe also published a collection of short stories, *All this is Gone* and Penguin USA published another collection, *It's Not an All Night Fair* Most of the reviews in the mainstream media in the West have been kind also to the English translations.

A google search for 'Howard Fasr *This Earth of Mankind*' will bring up thousands of references. It is clear that this book, and to some extent its sequels, have entered into a certain realm of canon for those interested in world literature, comparative literature, postcolonial literature and just a good read. When a high school or university student can now find a wide selection of possible essay answers to a wide selection of topics on a novel, it is a sign that the book has entered a sustainable cycle of reading and is well-loved and appreciated, even in English translation. Teaching guides and lesson plans for teachers are now also available.

Among Indonesianists (Indonesia specialists and fellow translators), as one might expect, there are more criticisms and different evaluations. Different approaches to understanding Indonesia—from Orientalist, disguised and open, to historical materialist—and different levels, depths and character of experience with Indonesia and its language and its discourses, produce different tastes and evaluations.

When I translated *This Earth of Mankind*, I was thirty years old and had ten years of experience with Indonesia. I was working as staff at the Australian Embassy there. Now, thirty years later, with a new variety of engagement with the country, more familiarity with the language and a longer period to get to know Pramoedya, perhaps I would have translated differently. But then again, perhaps not; perhaps there is continuity in the nature of the engagement with a society, even as time unfolds.

My engagement with the beauty of Indonesia has always been in the form of friendship and collaboration with those struggling for, or who stood for, radical political change, including Pramoedya, his editor Joesoef Isak and publisher Hasjim Rachman, as well as the poet and dramatist Rendra, but mostly those much younger. Their language, expression and communication, amongst themselves and with their society, produce a 'text' of their own. In Indonesia, where modern literature is only now beginning to assert itself as a separate existential realm, the 'text' of radical political interaction has determined a lot of how literary communication takes place. Political Indonesian youth who have read *This Earth of Mankind* love it, as do many who have lived through the politicizing period of the rise of the opposition to Suharto. I have met many fanatical lovers of these books. For them, the mode of communication used in big sections of the novels, described below by the pioneering US anthropologist of Indonesia, Clifford Geertz (not a sympathetic reader of Pramoedya), is beautiful.

> Western critics have been generally at a loss to convey the peculiarly didactic and reiterative quality of Pramoedya's writing in general, and of the tetralogy in particular—its relentless succession of desperately earnest conversations between typified characters in schematized scenes. . . . For the reader used to crises and conclusions, to peripeties of character, and to the seaward flow of cause and consequence, it may seem hardly to move at all.[9]

Judging from the reactions of the scores of readers who have written to me as translator of Pramoedya's books or searched me out to talk to me, and who also have expressed their views on websites like Amazon.com, there are also Western readers for whom the 'desperately earnest conversations' meld into a gripping and beautiful storytelling. Apart from the resilience of the books remaining in print, it is to these

---

[9] Clifford Geertz, *Java Jive*, New Republic, 22 April 1996, p. 31.

readers of the English editions that I turn for the occasional counter-balance to the less happy evaluations of the expert colleagues.

James in *The New Yorker* feels what Geertz called 'desperate earnestness' differently:

> [T]he scale of the Buru cycle . . . sprawls across twenty years and more than fifteen hundred pages in the English translation, by Max Lane. The first volume of the series, *This Earth of Mankind*, is one of those books that, like *The Catcher in the Rye*, inspire such devotion that an admirer instinctively mistrusts anyone who scoffs at them. As I read it, I kept regretting that I had not been able to do so at fifteen, when, with the fanaticism of adolescence, I could have appropriated Minke's passionate idealism as my own.

Although James, too, feels the earnestness in his own way:

> The earlier novels are the better ones: tightly written and swift-paced, they strike a careful balance between narrative and ideas. In the third and fourth volumes, there are some fairly rough patches that approach nonfiction, with characters setting forth Pramoedya's version of Indonesian history to one another in 'he said/she said' form. Hugo and Dostoyevsky are the writers Pramoedya resembles at his best. Somehow the roughness is part of the greatness: it conveys a sense of abundance—of ideas, history, plot—pressing against and sometimes overflowing the capacities of literary assimilation.

However, in Indonesia itself, the most dynamic aspect of contemporary culture has been precisely the hundreds of thousands of desperately earnest conversations that drove the emergence of a mass protest movement and a thousand other little but very earnest subversions that were central to the ending of a dictatorship and the *creative work* of bringing into existence the Indonesia as the work in progress that exists today. Desperately earnest conversations are taking place in even greater numbers and intensity today, and they will still comprise the textual context and the most beautiful aesthetic for the coming period. To what extent a still embryonic literary arena—represented by writers like Eka Kurniawan, Linda Christanty, Faiza

Mardzoeki and others—will overlap and interact with this context and aesthetic is yet to be seen. It is in the earnestness that the most beauty is to be found, not, for now, in the nuances of 'style'.

Another US academic, Benedict Anderson, wrote of Pramoedya: 'Only after his death did he become accepted as his country's grandest modern writer.' Unfortunately, this is a completely wrong conclusion. I wish it were true, but it isn't. There has been no public announcement that his writings are no longer banned—they may very well still be formally banned. His works are not introduced, or even mentioned, in the high school curriculum for Indonesian language or literature in state schools. (Is this like US schools ignoring Steinbeck or Howard Fast?)

In fact, there is no separate subject 'Indonesian literature' in the state school system. The novels are barely studied at university level, depending on the youthful rebelliousness of staff and students. He has won no awards or prizes in Indonesia. Those who still wield power in the institutions of the literary establishment still minimize reference to him. Over the last ten years, in a country of 230 million, no more than 30,000 copies of any one title have been printed annually—although there is also a small thriving market for pirated copies. In fact, public recognition and publicly expressed praise for Pramoedya's novels were much higher in the early 1980s, in the brief period before *This Earth of Mankind* was banned. Caught off-guard, Indonesia's conglomerate-owned media published excellent and positive reviews. Indonesia's Vice President Adam Malik, a revolutionary in his youth, invited Pramoedya and his publisher comrades, Joesoef Isak and Hasjim Rachman, to his office for a meeting. Their photograph appeared in the major daily newspapers. Despite Malik stating publicly that the novel should be read by all students in the schools, today, more than thirty years later, that is still not the case. This is a direct reflection of the repression, control and hegemony of the still-ruling lumpen elite and its hangers-on in the media and schools.

Of course, since the books were published more than thirty years ago, there has been a steady accumulation of devoted, even fanatical, readers. But the very limited circulation of the books means that this readership remains a tiny percentage of the population. This lack of

society-wide recognition is in turn a product of the refusal of the
Indonesian elite to recognize the novels properly—for example, by
announcing loudly the lifting of the ban (if indeed it has been lifted)
and by teaching them in the schools. Understanding this reality is
fundamental to contemporary Indonesian political and cultural reality.

What began in the 1980s, after Pramoedya's books were published
and as new small revolutionary groups were formed, was a new process
of preparing the ground for the relaunching of the national revolution
whose origins are the subject of Pramoedya's novels, and the social
revolution for which he declares between the lines, in the resolutions
of the novels. The absence of full and official recognition of his works,
their still marginal position, is a manifestation of the unfinished nature
of this revolutionary process. The analytical task is to understand the
dynamics of this process, the dynamics and aesthetics of its earnest
conversations and the political and cultural outcomes it produces. One
fascinating part of this, although by no means the most important, is
the emergence here and there of reading groups around *Bumi Manusia*
and its sequels, including among young factory worker members of
trade unions as well as students. Among the many new unions is one
that has called itself the Bumi Manusia Trade Union.

Another reflection of the still marginal (but subversive) status of
Pramoedya's works is the almost total absence of an impact of his
radical contribution to understanding Indonesian history in public and
academic discussion. He depicted the formation of Indonesia's first
truly mass organization, Sarekat Islam (first as Sarekat Dagang Islam,
SDI), as driven by its founder, Tirto Adhi Soerjo, understanding that
a movement resisting the excesses of colonialism needed to be based
on those earning their living separately from the colonizers. His first
attempt was to organize the civil servants in the Sarekat Priyayi, who
were dependent on a Dutch salary and whose consciousness was formed
partly by their identification with the colonial state and its regulations.
This failed, and he turned to the free people, the burghers, the *pedagang*,
those who traded or otherwise earned their living by working for it.
I regularly teach classes of candidate teachers in Indonesia, and their
textbooks still say that the SDI was set up purely to counter Chinese
Batik traders, and that another very feudal Javanese organization, Budi

Utomo, was the first modern organization in Indonesia, not Sarekat Priyayi, as Pramoedya showed clearly was the case.

Real recognition of Pramoedya as the country's greatest writer, by the majority of society, will be won as part of the unfolding of a relaunched national and social revolution. The ground for this was partly prepared by the movement against the Suharto dictatorship and is being further prepared now by both natural sociological processes connected to labour organizing as well as to radical artistic, intellectual and cultural ferment, alongside more conscious efforts to lead conditions towards such a relaunch. One of the important claims to greatness that Pramoedya's novels have, and will continue to have, is that the appreciation of them has been and still is an integral part of that preparation of the ground. They will be one of the cultural weapons of these revolutions: in any case, these revolutions will also entail a cultural revolution.

Pramoedya, until his dying day, was a supporter of Sukarno, who argued right up to the moment he was overthrown in 1965, that neither nation-building nor character-building for Indonesia was completed. *This Earth of Mankind* and its sequels are not only rich in their exposition of the experiences of political struggle and organizing and how this is linked to class and socio-economic processes, but are also very much about *character*, that is, strength of character. This orientation to issues of character is also the origin of its powerful statements, through its characters and stories, against sexism. Human beings are valued based on their character. Gender becomes irrelevant and some of Pramoedya's most inspiring characters are women whose character has been forged out of their resistance to their oppression as women.

For those seeking to be active in the unfinished process of preparing the ground, the books provide guidance on struggling for all these. Factory workers post quotes from the novels on the question of strength of character on their Facebook walls. Activists and organizers draw on the books' treasury of statements on the principles of organizing. Collations of quotes from the novels abound.

Geertz, as quoted above, claims that Western critics have sought comparisons with 'Solzhenitsyn, Steinbeck, James Baldwin, Dashiell Hammett, Dickens, Conrad, Nadine Gordimer, Camus, and Dostoyevsky' as well as, he adds, a television mini-series. (It would be

great to see a well-made Indonesian mini-series based on the novels).
As for me, I see the clearest international comparison with the great
US novelist Howard Fast, particularly the historical novels of his early
writing, exemplified by *Last Frontier*, *Freedom Road* and especially *Citizen
Tom Paine*, but also slightly later works such as *April Morning*. Both are
great storytellers of their revolutions. Fast's novels depicted the first US
revolution against British colonial rule and the second against slavery.
(He also wrote eloquently on the US counter-revolution embodied in
the occupation of the 'West' and the extermination of the Indians, and
the great novel of rebellion, *Spartacus*). Pramoedya's historical novels
depict the pre-Indonesian origins of what he called the 'Indonesian
national awakening', the gestation of the Indonesian national revolution.
Both were associated with the far Left of their respective countries,
although Fast later dissociated himself from it. Fast's books are now
off school curriculum's and disgracefully forgotten.

In any case, as great revolutionary storytellers, they were both
harassed and suppressed, because neither the values and content nor the
aesthetics of revolutionary narrative coincide with either the political
or literary elite's own ideology or aesthetics. Pramoedya's historical
novels are in some ways safer in terms of the West's dominant political
tastes, dealing as they do with a time and place far away and a form
of oppression—colonialism—which everybody now claims to oppose.

Even so, Geertz's comments being just one example, not everybody
relates to the aesthetics of earnestness. Some fans of Pramoedya,
especially in the West, prefer his very vivid but less didactically earnest
short stories from the period before his revolutionary storytelling.
Recognition for Fast has still not been properly re-won in the United
States. While Indonesia has still not completed its national revolution,
whose origins and gestation Pramoedya so brilliantly relates, and is in
that sense an unfinished nation, perhaps in the United States, where the
nation creation process has finished, it is not a matter of completing
the national revolution, but re-winning its ideals, probably requiring
an even more radical social revolution. Re-winning Fast for the US
population and extending recognition and appreciation of Pramoedya's
novels to the whole of Indonesian society are both connected to a
necessity to relaunch revolutionary processes.

Pramoedya never published extensively, either in fiction or non-fiction, on the history of his own generation (1930s to 1965), nor on Suharto-era Indonesia, nor on the contemporary world. His greatest contribution to understanding Indonesia was his works dealing with the pre-colonial and colonial periods. However, *This Earth of Mankind* and its sequels did make a statement about the dynamic behind the historical processes that were driven forward by the vanguard of his own generation and, I think, the necessary trajectory of the process ahead for Indonesia now. The heroic protagonists of the four books were Minke, inspired by the historical figure of Tirto Adhi Soerjo, and Nyai Ontosoroh, the concubine taken by a Dutch colonial businessman. Nyai Ontosoroh becomes the spiritual guide for Minke in *This Earth of Mankind*. Nyai essentially educates Minke in the ideas and values of the European Enlightenment, some of which he has already inculcated, as well as Europe's black hypocrisy in how it deals with its colony. Later, in *Footsteps* and *House of Glass*, Minke—reflecting Pramoedya's assessment of the real Adhi Soerjo—becomes a more and more committed democrat and partisan for social justice. He is also a newspaper proprietor and entrepreneur, owning a printing press, stationery business and a hotel. Both he and Nyai are figures of the bourgeoisie: perhaps, if we applied an orthodox Marxist categorization, they are representative of a revolutionary bourgeois democratic outlook.

A crucial point—and I don't want to act as too much of a spoiler for those who haven't yet read the novels—is that the characters fail totally in all their *immediate* efforts to resist and change. Of course, Adhi Soerjo and his associates and their social layer left an important legacy. But they were crushed. Indeed, until Pramoedya wrote these novels, Adhi Soerjo had pretty much disappeared from Indonesians' historical radar. And their fate in the novels was no less final. Towards the end of Pramoedya's depiction of this process of their failure, as he explains it throughout all four books directly and indirectly, he points to where he thinks the real energy and intellect for change will come from. New characters are introduced, more or less as cameos. They are not playing the main roles in the epic Pramoedya has written, but will do so in the epic to come. They are figures from the revolutionary working class movement that will shake up the Dutch East Indies during the decade or more that followed Adhi Soerjo. Of course, we know, and Indonesians know, that that generation, too, was crushed by colonial power and had to await colonialism's next weak moment in the aftermath of World War II.

That Pramoedya saw the future as a revival of that revolutionary working-class political tradition is not only to be deduced from his introduction of these characters into the final parts of his storytelling of the origins of the Indonesian revolution. His statements after his release from prison—especially in the 1990s, when the protest movement was emerging, as well as after the fall of Suharto—again and again emphasized that the future needed a revolution that wiped away all that Suharto's New Order had created, and that the agency of change must be the youth. Furthermore, he underlined that he did not mean just any youth, but youth building an organized revolutionary Left. In 1999, he took the step of being sworn in at a big public event as a member of the People's Democratic Party or PRD, which at the time represented that trajectory. It was a symbolic act, but one that emphasized his perspective.

In March in Jakarta, after speaking to a crowded-out public forum on the Indonesian poet Rendra, I was introduced to a worker from a factory belt area outside the city. We sat on the steps chatting with a couple of other activists. He explained that he was organizing a reading group among the workers in his area, based on the This Earth of Mankind series. You could see he did not just respect and admire the books; he loved them. To him, they were beautiful. And yes, he was a very earnest young man. Even though it is still early in the process of preparing the ground for the relaunching of the country's social and national revolution, I know that the number of this kind of reading group is growing. I am very sure that Pramoedya Ananta Toer will be recognized as Indonesia's greatest modern writer or—when others emerge to rival him in the future—the country's first great modern writer. This recognition will be won as part of either the process of preparing the ground for the relaunch of the revolutions or of the relaunch itself. And I am sure, too, that winning such recognition will be part of a flowering of revolutionary literature in general. It will necessarily mean an end to the situation in which the appreciation and study of literature are not taught at all in Indonesian schools, and the beginning of literary communication becoming part of the revolutionary process.

Internationally, I am hopeful that *This Earth of Mankind*, its sequels and his other novels will remain in print in English. I am sure more people will read and love them, despite the fact that the translator is certainly not a literary figure of Pramoedya's own stature. But will there ever be a real internationalization of Indonesia's *This Earth of Mankind* and will Indonesia's Pramoedya become household words? This I am sure will also happen. When it does, it will be primarily because Indonesia as a country, a nation, a people, will also have burst upon the world scene. And when the revolution in the fourth most populous country in the world is relaunched—and all the ingredients are steadily maturing—the revolution's intellectual and cultural output will be of interest to many.

Why am I so convinced that this will happen, and not so far in the distant future? There are many reasons, which will have to be set out elsewhere. But one thing that gives me confidence is that all the young men and women committed to this course remain today excited and inspired by the power and beauty of Pramoedya's fictional painting of their country's origins. A very good start. And prizes? I think this will be part of winning a prize indeed: as the song says, there is a 'world to win'.

Meanwhile, you don't have to wait; if you haven't read *This Earth of Mankind* and its sequels, you should do so now.

* * *

Notes

1. This is the Sumpah Pemuda (Youth Pledge), see the entry under 'Youth Pledge' in Audrey Kahin, *Historical Dictionary of Indonesia*, Third Edition, 2015, p. 735. Most of the figures and incidents referred to in the coming ages have entries in this historical dictionary. Readers interested in further information can refer to this dictionary—and, of course, today there is also the internet.

2. Three major English language scholarly works documenting the political killings and suppression after 30 September, 1965 are Robert Cribb (ed.), *The Indonesian killings of 1965–1966: Studies from Java and Bali*, Centre of Southeast Asian Studies, (Monash University, 1990); Jess Melvin, *The army and the Indonesian genocide: Mechanics of mass murder* (New York, NY: Routledge, 2018); Geoffrey Robinson, *The killing season: a history of the Indonesian massacres, 1965–66* (Princeton: Princeton University Press, 2018). For a journalist's reportage of events at the time see John Hughes, *The end of Sukarno : a coup that misfired : a purge that ran wild*, Fourth edition (Didier Millet, Csi, 2002).

3. See under entry 'Generations' in *HDI*.

4. See Max Lane, 'Pramoedya Ananta Toer' in David Smythe (Ed.), *Southeast Asian Writers (Dictionary of Literary Biography)* (Gale Research,

2009) For a range of materials easily accessible on Pramoedya in English see: https://sites.google.com/site/pramoedyasite/.

5   Max Lane, 'Protests Against the Omnibus Law and the Evolution of Indonesia's Social Opposition', *ISEAS Perspective*. Available at: https://www.iseas.edu.sg/articles-commentaries/iseas-perspective/2020-128-protests-against-the-omnibus-law-and-the-evolution-of-indonesias-social-opposition-by-max-lane/. Accessed June 2022.

6   Max Lane, 'The KPK Controversy Keeps Corruption a Central Issue in Public Consciousness', *ISEAS Perspective*. Available at: https://www.iseas.edu.sg/articles-commentaries/iseas-perspective/2021-110-the-kpk-controversy-keeps-corruption-a-central-issue-in-public-consciousness-by-max-lane/. Accessed June 2022.

7   'Sang Pemula' or 'the pioneer', he who began things, is also the title of a book that Pramoedya edited that comprises a selection of the writings of Tirto Adhi Soerjo as well as an introductory essay by Pramoedya. It was this book that popularized the picture of Tirto that was now emblazoned on this student's T-shirt.

8   *Progres* was a political magazine printed between 1991 and 1992 by progressive, pro-democracy activists and circulated within the protest movement, even after it was banned. It stopped publication due to financial constraints. The original article on the visit to Tirto's grave was in Volume 2, No. 2, 1992.

9   For a history of how Suharto was forced from power, see Max Lane, *Unfinished Nation: Indonesia Before and After Suharto* (Verso, 2008). See also Stefan Eklof, *Indonesian Politics in Crisis, The Long Fall of Suharto, 1996-98*, Nordic Institute of Asian Studies, 1999.

10 See entry 'KOSTRAD' in *HDI*.

11 See Soewarsono, *Historiografi 1965/66 Menimbang Lagi Sejumlah Pandangan* (Gading Publishers, 2019).

12 This brief account is primarily based on Roosa's work (see note above).

13 From Karl Marx, *The Eighteenth Brumaire of Louis Bonaparte, 1852*. Available at: https://www.marxists.org/archive/marx/works/1852/18th-brumaire/ch01.htm. Accessed June 2022.

14 See the entry 'Sarekat Islam' in *HDI*.

15 The most recent survey of international involvement in the events of 1965 is Vincent Bevins, *The Jakarta Method: Washington's Anticommunist Crusade and the Mass Murder Program That Shaped Our World*, (Public Affairs, 2021).

16 Pramoedya Ananta Toer, *Sang Pemula*, (Jakarta: Hasta Mitra,1985). This book also contains original writings of R.M. Tirto Adhi Soerjo.

17 Quoted in Herb Feith, *The Decline of Constitutional Democracy in Indonesia*, (Ithaca, NY: Cornell University Press,1962), pp. 607–608.

18 For interesting commentary on Pramoedya's writing in this period see Keith Foulcher, 'In search of the post-colonial in Indonesian literature', *Sojourn*, Vol. 10, No. 2, 1996.

19 Pramoedya Ananta Toer, *Panggil Aku Kartini Saja*, (Jakarta Hasta Mitra, 2000).

20 See entry JAPAN, in HD, p. 311.

21 Many of these speeches are collated in Budi Setiyono, Bonnie Triyana (eds.), *Revolusi belum selesai : kumpulan pidato Presiden Sukarno, 30 September 1965, pelengkap Nawaksara*, (Jakarta: Scrambi Ilmu Semesta, 2014).

22 The most informative analysis of the Army's entry into organizing among society is David Reeve, *Golkar of Indonesia: an alternative to the party system*, (Singapore: Oxford University Press, 1985).

23 For a study of the autopsy on the murdered generals see Ben Anderson, 'How Did the Generals Die?', in *Indonesia*, (Ithaca, NY: Cornell University, 1987).

24 See Vannessa Hearman, *Unmarked graves: death and survival in the anti-Communist violence in East Java, Indonesia*, (Copenhagen: NIAS Press, 2018).

25 For an excellent example of such a memoir in English, see Hersri Setiawan, *Buru Island: A Prison Memoir*, (Clayton, Victoria: Monash University Publishing, 2020).

26 Quoted in *Mantan Presiden Jimmy Carter tentang Joesoef Isak*. Available at: https://www.hastamitra.org/2011/09/presiden-jimmy-carter-tentang-joesoef.html. Accessed June 2022.

27 Some of this story is also related in a report by Jane Perlez, 'A Former Indonesian Dissident Makes His Peace With America', *New York Times*, 13 February 2003.

28 For a detailed look at this meeting, see Jeffrey Winters, *Power in motion: Capital mobility and the Indonesian state*, (Ithaca, NY: Cornell University Press, 1996).

29 Disclosure: I am married to Faiza Mardzoeki.

30 This material was located among archival collections in the International Institute of Social History in Amsterdam.

31 Ariel Heryanto, *State terrorism and political identity in Indonesia: Fatally belonging*, (New York, NY: Routledge, 2006).

32 See David Hill, *Journalism and politics in Indonesia : a critical biography of Mochtar Lubis (1922-2004)*, (New York, NY: Routledge, 2010).

33 Oleh Muhidin M. Dahlan, 'Gemuruh Kontroversi Hadiah Magsaysay', Edisi Khusus. Available at: http://suplemenibuku. blogspot.com/2009/04/gemuruh-kontroversi-hadiah-magsaysay. html. Accessed June 2022.

34 Ben Abel, 'Beholding a Landmark of Guilt: Pramoedya in the Early 1960s and the Current Regime', *Indonesia*, Vol. 64, 1997, pp. 21–28.

35 Pramoedya Ananta Toer, 'SASTRA, SENSOR, DAN NEGARA: Seberapa Jauh Bahaya Bacaan?', Web Archive. Available at: https://web.archive.org/web/20080220022719/http://www. library.ohiou.edu/indopubs/1995/10/11/0024.html.   Accessed June 2022.

36 Multatuli was the pen name of Edward Douwes Dekker, who wrote the classic nineteenth-century liberal critique of some Dutch colonial policies at the time in the Netherlands Indies, the Dutch language novel *Max Havelaar of de koffiveilingen der Nederlandsche handelmaatschappij* (*Max Havelaar* or *The coffee sales of the Netherlands Trading Company*).

37 See their respective entries in *HDI* for basic biographical information.

38 Pramoedya Ananta Toer, *The wisdom of Pramoedya Ananta Toer* (Bandung: Mizan Media Utama, 2014).

39 He explained this history in his speech on the occasion of his swearing-in as a member of the PRD.

40 One thesis by an Indonesian is that by Hilmar Farid, *Rewriting The Nation: Pramoedya And The Politics Of Decolonization*, (National University of Singapore, 2014).

41 See for example Christopher Gogwilt, *The Passage of Literature: Genealogies of Modernism in Conrad, Rhys, and Pramoedya*, (USA: Oxford University Press, 2011); Peter Hitchcock, *The Long Space— Transnationalism and Postcolonial Form*, (USA: Stanford University Press, 2009).

42 Namely, *National Times*, 11 October 1981.

43 Pramoedya Ananta Toer, *A Heap of Ashes*, edited and translated from Indonesian by Harry Aveling, (St. Lucia, Australia: University of Queensland Press, 1975).

44 These are the two major public broadcasting institutions in Australia, covering both radio and television.

45 For a slide presentation on this award and Joesoef Isak's winning of the Jeri Laber Freedom to Publish Award from New York PEN, see YouTube, available at: https://www.youtube.com/watch?v=bBKR1OyIVHE [video].

46 There are two published interviews with Will Schwalbe, where he explains his attachment to Pramoedya's works. Harold Augenbraum, 'Fear of the Word: A Conversation with Will Schwalbe on Publishing Pramoedya Ananta Toer', *Manoa*, Volume 12, Number 1, 2000, pp. 183–192 and also 'NPR interview—Book Club of the Month featuring *This Earth of Mankind* by Pramoedya Ananta Toer'. Available at: https://sites.google.com/site/pramoedyasite/home/concerning-pram/schwalbe-npr-interview. Accessed June 2022.

47 Schwalbe's *The End Of Your Life Book Club*, (USA: Knopf, 2012), was on *The New York Times* bestselling list for four months.

48 This information is based on correspondence with Will Schwalbe.

49 Thanks to Will Schwalbe for this information.

50 *Lesson Plans: This Earth of Mankind*, (BookRags, 2012).

51 For a discussion of some of the works now being published in English outside Indonesia by an new Indonesian novelist herself,

see Intan Paramaditha, *Five Indonesian Authors You Should Read* at LitHub. Available at: https://lithub.com/five-indonesian-authors-you-should-read/. Accessed June 2022.

52 See Jamie Mackie, *Bandung 1955: Non-alignment and Afro-Asian solidarity*, (Singapore: Editions Didier Millet, 2005).

53 The Canadian historian of Indonesia, John Roosa, has written on the novel *Arus Balik* and its theme of Java turning inwards.

54 Pramoedya Ananta Toer, 'The Port of Tuban', in *Emergences: Journal for the Study of Media & Composite Cultures*, Volume 10, No. 2, 2000, pp. 277–300.

55 Letter signed by Pramoedya dated 14 January 2004.

56 For one view of Pramoedya's historical interpretations, see Savitri Scherer, 'Globalization in Java in the 16th Century: A Review of Pramoedya's *Arus Balik*', in *Archipel*, Volume 55, 1998, pp. 43–60.

57 This article has been published on maxlaneonline.com and in other publications.

Acknowledgements

The writing of this book would have been much more difficult without material support from several sources over a long period. These include the New York Foundation of the Arts and, a long time ago, Asialink in Melbourne, Australia. Several individuals have also supported me in Indonesia, Australia, the Netherlands, and the United States, who have asked to remain anonymous. Thank you all.

Much of the material quoted in this book has been taken from the hours of interviews with Jocsoef Isak, Pramoedya Ananta Toer and Hasjim Rachman in 1992 and 1993. These interviews were videoed by the Australian filmmaker, Gil Scrine. Also part of the team at the time was Dr Hart Cohen from the University of Western Sydney in Australia. The quotes from these interviews are based on translations into English by Mikael Johani from transcriptions from the video recordings by Danial Indrakusma. Thank you both.

Many people have supported me with encouragement over the years also, none more than my wife Faiza Mardzoeki. Thank you so much.

I have had the opportunity to speak about the struggles and ideas of Pramoedya Ananta Toer, Joesoef Isak and Hasjim Rachman to many students and activists in Indonesia. Dialogue with them has also kept me inspired. Terima Kasih.